W9-ATO-238

London's Number One Dog-Walking Agency

LONDON'S NUMBER ONE DOG-WALKING AGENCY

A Memoir

KATE MACDOUGALL

THORNDIKE PRESS
A part of Gale, a Cengage Company

LIBRARY OF CONGRESS CIP DATA ON FILE.
CATALOGUING IN PUBLICATION FOR THIS BOOK
IS AVAILABLE FROM THE LIBRARY OF CONGRESS.

ISBN-13: 978-1-4328-9351-4 (hardcover alk. paper)

Published in 2021 by arrangement with William Morrow, an imprint of HarperCollins Publishers

Printed in Mexico
Print Number : 3   Print Year : 2022

To Finlay
(he'll get around to reading it one day)

FRANK

JACK RUSSELL, FIVE, GREENWICH
OCTOBER 2006
NUMBER OF DOGS WALKED BY LONDON'S
NUMBER ONE DOG-WALKING AGENCY: 1

It was pigeons that started it all, not dogs. Pigeons were the catalyst to the whole thing. A brace of them, garish and cheap, perched on my desk while they waited for an expert valuation. They were porcelain, mid-nineteenth-century, and exceptionally ugly. One looked pained, in anguish, as if it might be watching a lover depart for war, while the other was fat and mean with angry beady eyes and looked as if it wanted to settle a score with another pigeon. They wore pink bonnets and carried wicker baskets as though they were just popping out to the shops, an activity that seemed incongruous for a pigeon. Ducks or geese do shops and bonnets, while pigeons are more suited to flat caps and park benches. They were badly miscast, in appearance and execution, an unfortunate waste of time, clay, and paint.

The pigeons had been in the owner's family for generations, passed down from mother to mother like an unfortunate genetic disease, and carried with them the heavy weight of sentimental value. Their monetary valuation would have been a disappointment to their current custodian, a sprightly retiree from Acton with a Saga brochure under her arm and a winter cruise in her sights. With no offspring to bestow them upon and a penchant for *Cash in the Attic,* she had decided that they must be worth at least a lower-deck cabin to the Canaries and had dropped them off at the front desk of Sotheby's to see how they might fare.

There was of course a slim chance that somebody might have parted with their hard-earned cash for them. A camp pigeon fancier perhaps or an eccentric ornithologist. But that was before I smashed both their heads off. The first was whisked clean off the desk by my elbow as I leaned over to pick up the phone, the second joining shortly after with a nudge from a binder — both siblings not only decapitated but irreparably fractured on the purple carpet in a splatter of ceramic dust and shards of beak and claw.

It was, of course, an accident and, certainly to my Sotheby's colleagues, nothing out of the ordinary. I was "clumsy" Kate. Tall, gangly, butterfingered. There had been one or two porcelain mishaps in the past, a few broken bits of furniture here and there, and of course the time I spilled an entire chicken Cuppa Soup on a very rare Persian rug. My clumsiness extended to more than just the objects themselves: I had failed to master the telephone bidding system and frequently cut important people off, usually just as they were about to bid on something expensive, and I often forgot to press mute when needing to describe someone on the other end of the line as an asshole. I was congenitally uncoordinated, committedly scruffy, and not at all suited to the old-school poshness of the place, despite having the "right kind of background," the right school, the right pronunciation of "escritoire," and the prerequisite qualification in art history from a prestigious university. The demise of the pigeons was in fact just one more calamity of many in the four ineffectual and stagnant years I had spent at the auction house.

Simply put, I was bored. Stupidly so. As a back-office helper in the antiques department, most of my days were spent answering inquiries, filing reports, or sitting in pointless meetings. We supported the experts in their cataloging and selling but we weren't allowed to learn about the objects, to appraise and critique them, despite the fact that these were skills the job description had demanded when I applied. We ensured it all ran smoothly, that all the boxes were ticked and the forms filled in, with absolutely no room to use our ripe and expensively cultivated minds, no space to expand, to inquire, to advance.

Working life seemed to be one enormous con to me, a deception so brilliant that it had reeled in entire generations of wide-eyed graduates bursting with ideas and energy and youthful enthusiasm, only to station them in front of photocopiers or laminators or shredders. It didn't really matter what your job title was or which company you worked for, most jobs seemed to boil down to moving bits of paper from A to B, appeasing unnecessarily awful people over the phone or email, and staring incomprehensibly at spreadsheets. Even friends in sophisticated-sounding jobs like television or finance or the ones who did important things with computers would attest to a preponderance of repetitive software-based activities, interspersed with filing and highlighting and stapling things together. Our education, the years and years of hard study, the accumulation of endless facts and skills, the achievements, the goals, the quiet hopes and guarded dreams, all were seemingly pointless and redundant. The world appeared to be put together by nothing more than stationery and data.

Stumbling blindly into the wide, murky pool of "administration" was an easy mistake to make as a graduate of the early aughts. It started with temping, the arts graduate's first stop on the very bumpy road to forging some sort of career. A receptionist. Data entry. PA to a PA. Making tea, photocopying. I filed papers into a cabinet for one whole week and then shredded paper for another week in an office one street away. I hid the holes in my tights. I was "chair number four" in a bank of ten receptionists, headsets on, nails to be painted ruby red, directing calls to brokers for eight hours a day, and once made 147 cups of Nescafé before 9 a.m. at an insurance company that needed an emergency "refreshment assistant."

When you couldn't stomach the temping anymore, you waded into even deeper administration, full-time positions, your own desk. You attended meetings, put things in your drawer, and, before you knew it, you'd White-Outed your name onto a stapler and knew the names of everyone in IT. This was when it became harder to clamber out of the administration pool. Once you were in, nobody ever wanted you to get out again, as they didn't want to do the admin either, so you were stuck, wallowing in the mire, praying that some of your brain would cling on and not be completely eroded by the sheer tedium. Unless of course you wanted to submerge yourself to an even deeper level, to the admin apex: executive assistants, office managers, coordinators. And this is where I ended up. A fully immersed dunking into the role of "Furniture Administrator."

"Is this *it*?" I would occasionally say to my mother on the phone. "*This* is adulthood?" Despite her enthusiastic embrace of large swaths of twenty-first-century living, my mother had never fully shaken off her old-fashioned upbringing — the office was just a holding pen until a husband and children came along. Hers had been the interior of a British Airways cabin. It paid the rent and introduced you to eligible men. It didn't have to be *interesting*. "Yes darling," she would reply. "Parts of it are very dull indeed."

Most people settled for it. Of course they did. A job is just one step on a career path, and perhaps they could all see that path more clearly and optimistically than I could. Plus, most people don't particularly want to leap into deep, dark vats of the unknown. But I was restless. I was discontent. And, as a result, I was clumsy, just one too many times.

Just over a week before the pigeon incident, I met a man with a dog at a barbecue. The dog was a beautiful stracciatella-colored cocker spaniel with long black eyelashes and low-hanging tummy fur that made him look like he was wearing a valance. The dog was called Crumpet. The man, Dan.

"What a beautiful dog," I said, as you do.

"It's not mine," Dan replied, blandly. He was concentrating on his burger, while Crumpet ate a tub of taramasalata at his feet. "I'm walking it. For a close friend."

The friend was a famous actress whose name he dropped like breadcrumbs onto the grass beneath him. She was currently onstage, a lengthy weekend matinee, and he was a minor theater acquaintance now elevated to "close friend" status simply by doing a freebie.

"This isn't what I normally do, of course," he continued. "The dog-walking thing. I don't *walk* dogs. It's a favor really. She's a close friend and she couldn't find anyone else to do it."

"Dog walking? Wow, lucky you. What an amazing job!" I said, giving the spaniel a scratch on the ears. And with that one sentence, a small idea started to form.

"It's not a *job*," he retorted, spitting burger fragments into the air. "Well, she offered to pay but I said no, of course. I mean, you don't take money from your *very* close friends, do you?"

I stared at those pigeon pieces on the carpet for a very long time, the claws and the beaks and the awful beady eyes shattered into debris below me, and a calm and pleasant realization came to sit down among my thoughts: not only was the pigeons' demise the best thing that could have happened to them, but how remarkable it was that two mundane and irritating life occurrences could smash into each other and be the start of a new beginning. For the first time in years, there was clarity about what I needed to do.

"*Dogs?* Crikey. Right. Well! Good luck with that," said my manager when I handed in my notice soon after. He was signing off on the large check the lady from Acton had managed to extract from the insurance department and his gray, lipless face barely managed a smile. "Might be easier than some of our clients, I suppose."

"Well, let's hope so!"

"Righty ho! Well, do let us know how you get on with all of that."

His response was fairly typical; over the next few weeks, while I worked out my notice period, I spent a lot of time repeating the word "dog" to confused and concerned-looking people.

"Dogs! Yes, dogs. Real dogs. Yes, I know, it is a bit of a surprise isn't it? Yes, walking them. Walking the dogs, to the park. For money. Yes, dogs. Yes, we walk them back again. Actual, *real* dogs. Other people's dogs, yes. The world *is* a very funny place, I agree!"

Dogs. Saying it over and over and then over again. Dogs, dogs, dogs. The more I said it, the more I explained it, the more I keyworded it in the text for my new website, the more I began to believe in it all — this little idea germinating and blossoming and pushing its way toward the light. It had become something to get excited about. It felt like exactly the right thing to be doing.

But spontaneous and unpredictable career shifts don't tend to go down too well, particularly with mothers. People like to digest things gradually in small, bite-size chunks and as far as my mother was concerned, anything that could not be explained cheerfully and succinctly over soup and bridge was an automatic nonstarter. She wrote me a letter on blue Basildon Bond, her concerns laid out in numerical order. Number one said, "This is a GHASTLY mistake."

Despite having a boy's name, Frank was a girl. She was small in stature, even for a Jack Russell, but very solidly built, with a thick, strong back, smooth black-and-white fur, and dark silken eyes. Always on high alert, her muscles were taut, head cocked slightly to one side as terriers like to do, and she vibrated ever so slightly with excitement.

"She's a live wire, Kate," said Lauren, looking exasperated. "I don't think we have ever been able to tire her out, not even after a ten-mile hike up the Cairngorms, but I am sure you know *a lot* of dogs like that."

"Right!" I chuckled, nervously. "So, do you, um, think an hour's walk a day is going to be enough?" I asked, hoping I didn't sound too concerned. Frank had already been on a five-mile run that day with Lauren's boyfriend, Mark, but seemed barely able to contain a monstrous mass of energy.

"Well, we will just have to see how it goes.

If you throw the ball for her, you should be able to tire her out a little bit, at least till we get back from work, anyway."

At the foot of Frank's bed was a yellow ball, about the same size as the tennis variety but made of hard plastic rubber and punctured with a myriad of small teeth marks. She guarded it with the dedication and ferocity of a lioness with her cubs, unless of course you were the Thrower, in which case it was regularly deposited at your feet with the urgent instruction to throw it again. And again. And again and again.

I was to be the New Thrower. The dog walker. Frank was my first customer, signed up before I had even left the world of auctions behind, one foot still wedged into furniture and the other eagerly stretching toward a new life. I had met Lauren and Mark after work one evening just before I left Sotheby's — office attire, deceptively professional. As far as they were concerned, I was a dog-walking expert.

"She just loves that ball. Takes it everywhere with her. She even sleeps with the damn thing. Not interested in teddies whatsoever. Or other balls for that matter. Believe me, we've tried."

"Oh, right. Well that makes it easier I guess? She knows what she likes!"

"Just try not to lose it, Kate. We don't have another one."

"Oh."

"They don't make that one anymore."

Frank's first walk was on a Saturday in early October 2006, the day after I left my office job. Lauren was going to a wedding, an all-day church-and-marquee affair that the bride had outrageously decided was a "no-dog sort of event."

"Are you sure you don't mind? It's ridiculous that we can't take her, really. She's no bother. I hate to impose on your Saturday but I know she will go nuts if she doesn't get some exercise."

"It's absolutely fine. My boyfriend, Finlay, can come with me." Finlay. My lovely, kind, funny boyfriend. The one who doesn't like dogs. At all.

"I know I said weekday walks only but this is an emergency."

"It's no problem, really. We'll make a day of it. Walk and then pub. It'll be great."

Saturday was cold and damp and London was gray. It wasn't a great day for a wedding, or for a dog walk for that matter, especially as I was painfully hungover and had left my only sensible coat in a pub in Soho the evening before. Leaving drinks. A big night out.

We caught the train at Vauxhall around midday and thankfully found a seat. Finlay sank into the upholstery and closed his eyes, his hangover reaching its peak. He had needed some persuasion to get out the door.

"Why am I here again?" he groaned.

"It's an adventure. The first walk! You'll love Frank. She's full of beans."

"But I don't like Frank. I don't like dogs."

"Don't be silly."

"It's true. I don't like them."

"You don't like your hangover. *Everyone* likes dogs."

"I don't."

"What, all dogs? You hate *all* dogs? You don't *know* any dogs."

"I hate. All. Dogs."

He put his head in his hands as the train rocked from side to side and screeched on its tracks on the approach to Waterloo. We changed trains and headed southeast to Blackheath, arriving just as the rain started to fall in thick, cold drops. It was a short walk to Lauren's flat but our progress was slow, stopping for emergency bacon sand-wiches and coffee on the way.

Frank was waiting for us to arrive, sitting behind the door with the ball at her paws and her patience wearing thin. Lauren and Mark's flat was on the third floor of a beige-bricked Victorian house, once a large family home but now sliced into smaller homes for tighter budgets. It was a compact, one-bed — two if you counted Frank's — with a clothes rail in the bathroom and shoes stacked up behind the door. Newspapers and mugs were piled high on the coffee table and last night's washing up was balanced precariously in the sink. I'd been there only days before but it seemed so different now. Private. It was someone else's home and I felt like an intruder.

Frank looked Finlay up and down as he loitered by the door. She was ascertaining his throwing potential and, seeing something she thought she could work with, she trotted over and dropped the ball at his feet with a portentous thud. Finlay is tall and strong, Celtic, the sort of man you might expect to be throwing a ball for a Jack Russell, if only he liked dogs. They eyed each other up for a moment, both feeling unsure, before I quickly grabbed the lead and ushered everyone out.

"Come on," I said, "a bit of park air will do us good."

They were both happy to be led, Frank straining ahead with the ball in her mouth and Finlay limping behind looking unwell. The clouds started to lift and tiny splinters of sunshine broke through to the pavement as we made our way, lighting up the route across the heath to the top of Greenwich Park and the view down to Queen's House, the Thames, and the shimmering city beyond.

When we finally got there, the throwing began. We threw and we threw and we threw until our arms ached and Finlay started to moan about getting a repetitive strain injury. Frank's inexhaustible joy and excitement at repeating the same action again and again and again was completely mesmerizing. Humans would never be able to achieve this extended level of ecstasy, not unless something medicinal was involved. We would get bored or distracted or start worrying about what we were having for dinner. But Frank's endless reserves of energy, her focus and concentration, the delight she took in running and catching and running and catching were so wonderfully simple, so perfectly uncomplicated. It seemed to be the very purest form of joy.

"Can we go home now?" asked Finlay, like a small, cold child who has fallen in a puddle. He had given up throwing and was curled up in a sort of half-fetal position on the grass while Frank sniffed his hair. We had done an hour and the time was up. We would have to take Frank home.

She sensed that the fun was over and her tail dropped, the muscles relaxing as she prepared for the walk home and confinement once more. The autumn sun was now blazing in the sky and it had turned into a beautiful afternoon. A beautiful afternoon for a wedding. A beautiful afternoon for a dog walk.

"I think I feel a bit better," said Finlay as we headed back to the tube.

"There you go, you just needed a bit of fresh air. A bit of dog. Everyone needs a little bit of dog."

After that first Saturday outing, my old life now tucked in just behind me, Frank and I walked together every weekday and it wasn't long before we became good friends. She was in many ways the perfect first customer: delighted to see you, even more delighted to be going to the park, and wanting nothing more than a ball to be thrown for her and a farewell tummy rub.

Her owners, too, were what I might have planned for had I taken a moment to sit down and visualize my archetypal client: hardworking, busy young professionals, met through mutual friends, similar interests, similar goals, similar jobs. Working in PR, in finance, in property, they're out three times a week, after-work drinks, takeaway on a Friday, sex on a Sunday, and all the enjoyment of having a dog, but only really at the weekends and only after 11 a.m. Life is hectic, life is fast, but that doesn't mean they were willing to compromise. If they want a terrier or a holiday to Morocco or an enormous flat-screen telly, they will squeeze it into their life somehow and somewhere.

London was filling up with women and men like Lauren and Mark, forging ahead with careers, climbing up corporate ladders, and putting future children firmly on hold. They had disposable income in a buoyant housing market and had started to set up home. Having a dog *and* a full-time job was no longer seen as complete lunacy or the preserve of farmers, shepherds, and the blind. In fact, it was often now seen as a sensible, logical first step in creating a family unit. A dry-run child who could help rein in the all-night benders and introduce you to morning get-up-and-go starts, to *Saturday Kitchen* and *Steve Wright's Sunday Love Songs,* to the way the sun climbs slowly over red London brick and the eerie quietness of early-morning parks. Dogs show you fresh air, exercise, and open spaces but also bring the sense that there is someone other than yourself to think about.

I only met Lauren and Mark once on the day they introduced me to Frank but before very long I knew everything about them. It was all there, laid out in front of you, a book just waiting to be read. It was in the new gym shoes and the Tupperware and the stack of unread issues of the *Spectator.* In the dying fern and the half-eaten croissant and the piles of neatly ordered receipts. It was in the Post-it notes scribbled in ballpoint saying "Sorry" and "I love you" and "Frank needs more Chum." They were us, Finlay and I, reaching the cusp of full-fledged adulthood, sifting through all the many thoughts about who you want to be and what is really important in life. Only Lauren and Mark seemed far more evolved than us, the various minutiae of their lives slowly stitching together over the days and weeks to create a far more sophisticated picture of living than the one we had created. They had both cheese *and* ironing boards and they had real, proper jobs. And the dog, of course. They had something to look after. They had responsibilities.

But sadly I didn't get to know them for very long. It was only a snippet of their lives after all. Just as I was starting to get the hang of it all and to feel as if I might not only know my customer but that I might actually be able to do the job, it all ended, abruptly, three weeks in, when an enormous Rottweiler ate the yellow ball. It was my fault of course, a momentary lull in concentration and a very bad throw that saw the ball land directly in the Rottweiler's mouth, an opportunity he was far too pugnacious to squander. Frank and I looked on aghast as he ripped large chunks from it, ingesting the ball almost entirely before I even had a chance to protest.

"Sorry about that," chuckled the dog's owner as he ambled over. "It's not a favorite, is it?"

"No, no, not at all," I replied cheerfully. He seemed like a man that you might not want to quarrel with.

Frank was fine at first, coolly shrugging the whole thing off by nonchalantly trotting back toward the park gates. But as we got home she started to look a little restless. "I will get you another ball, Frank, I promise," I said as I shut the flat door behind me. The full gravity of the situation must have only sunk in later when she consoled herself by eating five pairs of Lauren's shoes.

"She's eaten five pairs of shoes," read the email. "Bits of heel everywhere. Bite marks on strappy sandals. Sole ripped off trainers. Mark's untouched, annoyingly. What happened to the ball????"

I wondered just how many pairs of shoes you needed as an adult and how many you might have to spare if your dog ate five of them? Based on Lauren's moderate to mordant reaction, I surmised she'd had around eight or nine pairs in total as she was fairly cross about the whole thing, describing it rather damningly as a "disappointment," even after my detailed and somewhat dramatic description of the Rottweiler and his enormous, savage jaws. These things could happen to anyone, although somehow they always seemed to happen to me. I had only three pairs of shoes after all, not nearly enough for serious adulthood.

I never saw Frank again. Lauren's job was changing and she had more time to walk her she said, although I am fairly sure the diminished shoe collection might also have had something to do with it. It wasn't the greatest of starts. After all, there is nothing quite as bad as being a disappointment. It implies a level of expectation — the expectation of others and also the one you should have of yourself.

If Blackheath hadn't been quite so far away, if it wasn't all so new and different, and if I hadn't already acquired one or two new clients much closer to home, my upset about Frank might have lasted a little longer. I may have started to wonder if I had made an enormous mistake. That would all come later, once the reality of just how bonkers and difficult what I was attempting really was. In those first couple of weeks, when I had just recently been released from the confines of the office, it all felt manageable. It felt exciting and freeing and full of possibility. I hadn't gotten around to thinking about word of mouth or client retention or the consequences of a dog eating too much pleather. I hadn't gotten around to considering whether I needed a cheese board or a mortgage or maybe even my own dog.

But you can't avoid being a grown-up forever. You can't hold back life, not when it hurtles along at such a dizzying pace. I had been allowed a trial run. Now I had to do it all for real.

WINSTON, PART ONE

Winston was a beautiful, deep-chocolate Labrador with a dusky pink nose, bright chestnut eyes, and enough energy to power half of south London. His daddies, Joe and Carl, lived on the top two floors of a pretty terraced house in the smarter end of Vauxhall. The house had shiny black railings, hand-painted window boxes, and a bondage shop around the corner.

This was also the corner where we lived, Finlay and I, tucked into the basement of a large Victorian house, once proud, clean brick but now creeping with grit and fumes and with windows that everyone had long given up cleaning. Next to the bondage shop was a café that made great peanut-butter toast and over the road was the all-night chicken shop where, to this day, angry teenagers gather in the glow of the red neon hen, gnawing on bones and yanking their Staffies' leads.

Our flat was narrow and damp and very small with ceilings that skimmed our heads, stubborn black mold in the bathroom, and easy burglar access at the back. We had been broken into twice in the space of a couple of months despite there being nothing to steal and a kid with a rusty bread knife had threatened to kill me on the front doorstep of our building when I asked him not to kick his dog. The windows shook with every passing bus and the floor rumbled with tube trains below but the rent was cheap and central London only minutes away by train, and when you live month to month, ready meal to ready meal, that's all that really matters.

Even before my career shift, we were already broke most of the time, living off tiny salaries that barely sustained us to the next paycheck as we eked out the last dregs of our twenties before all the grown-up decisions had to be made. Finlay had recently chucked in a career-for-life type job in the City, mainly due to his colleagues being awful and the work utterly soul destroying, but also because the hours trespassed a little too far into time at the pub. He moved to a cozy 9:15–4:45 research role for a friend's dad at St. Bart's Hospital and was enjoying a period of procrastination. Out most nights, beers in the pub, in to eat, sleep, and wash. We were hovering in that middle bit between the spinning giddiness of first falling in love, needing to be with each other every second of every day, and the slower calm of commitment and domesticity. It was a seesaw, back and forth, exciting and impetuous, then still and ordinary. The wall we kissed against on the way home, the weekends in bed, then the weekly shops, the routine, bills we struggled to pay, laundry. At times it tipped too far one way, with shouting and fights and half-day breakups, followed by periods of comfortable quiet with long hugs and times when we didn't need to say a word.

Joe and Carl, deep into their thirties, were fully established in adulthood, their seesaw tilted to homely. They had careers, not jobs, and gym memberships and money in the bank. They had matching towel sets and co-ordinated kitchenware while we had one chipped pan and a green-and-orange duvet set that my mum had kept from the 1970s and that smelled vaguely of bananas.

"Winston. DOWN!" a voice shouted from the top of the stairs as I came in through the door. This was Carl. He was Bad Cop. "You mustn't let him do that."

"Oh, sorry, I didn't really get a chance to . . ."

"You must say, 'Down, Winston,' immediately or he will have the better of you."

"Oh, right. Sorry. Winston, down. Down, Winston. Down. DOWN!" Winston bounced around my feet like a hyperactive toddler. He wasn't interested in listening. At least not to me.

"Winston, DOOOWWWNNNN!" boomed Carl, at which point Winston reluctantly perched at the foot of the stairs, still panting frantically.

"Don't look him in the eyes. He has to earn your attention."

"Right. OK."

"He will not respect you if you look at him. Ignore him. Decline him. Reject him, until he does what you ask."

I tried my best not to look at him as I made my way up the narrow stairs to the flat but he bounced up and started twirling around my feet and I ended up stepping on one of his paws. He yelped, loudly. Carl tutted, also loudly.

Their flat was petite, expensive, and immaculately tidy with almost no sign of normal, messy human life. Most strikingly, it was almost entirely brown, like a very chic molehill. The carpets and rugs, the leather sofas, the cushions, throws, the kitchen cabinets, kettle, the wooden floors, curtains, the teak knickknacks bought on foreign holidays, even the mug that my brown tea came in. And the dog, of course. Also brown. Bought to match the decor or the pivotal inspiration for a very bold refurbishment. Either way, Winston was the ultimate accessory for a modern happy family.

Joe was warm and friendly, the Good Cop in the dog-parenting scenario, and offered me the tea while telling me about his PhD. Carl did not smile, not even once, and sat bolt upright on the edge of his brown chair as though there might be something uncomfortable under his bottom. He had the air of someone who might have been bullied as a child for being a bit puny or crappy at PE and then spent considerable amounts of time plotting disproportionate revenge. He was excessively serious, contemplating Winston's welfare with the utmost gravity, and, as such, I was to be given a vigorous grilling.

"So why should we choose you to walk our dog?" was the opener.

"Well, I love dogs. Had them all my life and I really believe I can help give them a good day. Break up the boredom a bit." I was nervous and could feel my hands start to tremble. This was only the second interview I'd had for a position of dog walker, but even the most skilled and experienced of interviewees might have felt a little toasty under the collar in the presence of Carl and his list of questions. I realized almost instantly that my cheerful meeting with Frank's owners was almost certainly an exception and not having prepared even the most basic of backstories was woefully shortsighted. Expect everyone to be aggressive and anal, I said to myself, and then you can at least be pleasantly surprised if they are not.

"Your website says, and I quote, 'I have experience with many breeds, including Labradors.' How many Labradors have you walked?"

"Er . . . a few," I blurted. Walking alongside them as a child counted, surely, even if I was in a pram for some of it? "I grew up with them. So all my life really. And I have recently been walking a very energetic Jack —"

"How many have you walked, *exactly*?"

"Um . . . three?" Three seemed like a reasonable number of Labradors.

"I shall need to speak to the owners."

"Right. Of course."

He didn't take a breath. "What are the

most significant traits of the Labrador and how would you be mindful of those while walking Winston?"

"Well, I —"

"A Labrador has very specific requirements. Are you aware of what those are?"

I thought back to our old Labrador, Sultan, a huge, hulking black dog who lived only to eat and would often dig up raw potatoes and sugar beet from my grandparents' farm just to have something in his mouth. He once ate half a sofa and a Sunday newspaper, supplements and all, in the space of an hour. "Don't sleep in too late," my mother would say as my brother and I approached the teenage lie-in years. "Sultan has only had a light breakfast and is feeling a bit peckish." The Labrador's greed was renowned but Winston was lean and trim, just like Carl, so I decided to mention what I felt were the breed's more appealing traits: loyalty, adventure, and a fanatical love of swimming.

"Winston is *not* to go swimming," snapped Carl, as though I might have suggested taking him clubbing or ice-skating. "He is not to get wet, under any circumstances, and he is definitely *not* to get muddy."

"Oh. OK. That's fine. No problem."

"He is to be kept away from puddles. *All*

34

puddles. And *all* mud. Do you understand?"

"Yes. Of course," I replied, wondering how on earth this was going to be possible in one of the world's wettest countries with a breed engineered almost entirely for that purpose.

He asked a further time if I fully comprehended what he was saying about the mud before I was ushered out of the door so they could "deliberate." As I walked back down the stairs, writing the whole thing off in my head, I looked up to see an enormous five-foot square canvas of Winston on the wall. It was surrounded by a few smaller framed photos of the family all together, cuddling on the sofa, out in a park, and one where they were dressed as the Three Bears. Winston was not only a dog, he was the most precious and prized of children. Looking after a dog was one thing — challenging certainly, but it felt within the realms of my capabilities. A dog-child was a whole other matter.

"It's not going to happen," I said to Finlay when I got back to the flat. "I am a total amateur. They could see right through me. They know I'm a fraud."

At the time, it felt like being a fraud would be the end of my business before it had even begun but in fact it was absolutely the best thing I had going for me. Not having any concrete dog-walking (or, more crucial still, business) experience really just meant ignorance. Sweet, blissful ignorance. The kind of ignorance you still have in your twenties, that piggybacked a ride from your teenage years and is now sitting on the end of the bed twirling its hair and wondering what "net" and "gross" mean. The kind of ignorance that you might generously call optimism but is, in fact, I know now, hopeless naivete. The ignorance that can't possibly conceive of how awful the clients might be, how complicated the accounts, how unreliable the dog walkers you hire, or how difficult the decisions you will have to make on your own on some wet Wednesday afternoon when you can't get hold of your mother on the phone.

Without this ignorance, without the childish belief that all dog owners must be intrinsically kind, good people and that anyone wanting to work with dogs would be dedicated and reliable, I would never have taken that first step or knocked on those first clients' doors. I would have talked myself out of it with great ease and patted myself on the back for having swerved such a colossal nightmare. I would have stayed in that office, shackled to that desk. Luckily, it propelled me out the door and unsuspectingly into clients' lives — clients like Carl and Joe, who looked to me like they knew exactly what they wanted and in fact had everything they needed. Though I'd soon learn that most adult of truths: very few people have everything they want and even fewer know what they need.

"We're all frauds," Finlay said simply. "We are all amateurs. None of us knows what we are doing."

"But the dog is like a baby! He has likes and dislikes and fancy-dress outfits!"

"Well, there you go then," he replied. "They don't know what they are doing either."

An email appeared the following morning. After much discussion I had been "accepted" and was to start next week. It was followed by a separate, longer email about "hygiene" that had a lot of things underlined and the word **MUD** repeated again and again in bold.

During my first week walking Winston it rained solidly and Kennington Park, Winston's local medium-size municipal space, turned into a large, wet bog. It was mid-October and London was pelted daily with stubborn horizontal rain. Autumn had arrived. Winston was thrilled and rolled blissfully in the mire, despite my best efforts to stop him. You would have to be Arnold Schwarzenegger in his prime to hold back a Labrador with its heart set on finding the perfect puddle and for Winston, it was vitally important that each and every one was tested for squelchiness, viscosity, and dankness of aroma. Winston was completely besotted by mud.

Whether Carl had known this in advance and was simply shifting the responsibility for Winston's cleanliness onto his dog walker or had yet to encounter such boggy park conditions was uncertain. Joe had intimated that Winston's previous walks had mainly been street based with the occasional weekend jolly up to Hampstead Heath, so it was quite possible that they had absolutely no idea how devoted to dirt their dog was. A fantastic irony when you are quite so uptight about the cleanliness of your house.

As the months and years went on and I met more and more customers, I developed a good sense of who might be more trouble than they were worth but in those early days I had little appreciation of how tricky people could be and what to look out for. I learned, often awkwardly, which characteristics are not compatible with a stress-free work life as a dog walker. Rudeness, while unpleasant, is depressingly common but usually manageable. As are flakiness and abject stupidity. Cruelty should always be rejected, although this often only presents itself a bit further down the line when it is much harder to extricate yourself. Obsessive traits, particularly ones relating to the home or the dog, are also best avoided. You can never win against an obsession. This was the lesson Carl and Joe taught me.

As we left the park after his first walk, Winston didn't look *too* bad. Soggy around the edges but basically fine. As you would expect a dog to look after a good autumn walk. How a dog *should* look. Once puddle testing was complete, Winston had moved on to his secondary hobby of stick commodities, trading up from twig to branch as he wandered around the park until he had a nice sizable chunk of tree to proudly carry back home. He was tired but seemed happy and content, his tail wagging slowly.

It was only when we reached the flat that it became clear how utterly plastered in mud Winston was. His brownness had, of course, disguised it perfectly. The ultimate camouflage. I brushed some of the mud off with my coat sleeve outside the front door but as he shook himself dry inside the kitchen half a bucket of Kennington Park detritus rained down onto the floor, leaving a thick brown soup all over their shiny ice-white tiles.

The kitchen floor was in fact the only white thing in the entire flat and it dazzled so brightly with cleanliness and prosperity against the multiple shades of tan and russet that you would have happily eaten a full meal off it. I tried my best to clean the mud up with a brown tea towel but Kennington Park mud is tenacious stuff. I had to finish the job with a packet of wet wipes, which I pilfered from the bathroom. Not only are they the perfectionist's choice of post-poo bottom cleanser but can also wipe kitchen floors in an emergency. I had to use the entire packet but, with a bit of elbow grease and a lot of determination, the floor gradually turned from brown to beige to cream and then eventually back to white. It was exhausting.

An email later that day confirmed the obvious: Carl and I had very different benchmarks on kitchen hygiene and even if I had spent the rest of the day on it, it would never have reached Carl's meticulous standards.

Subject: MUD
Kate. I suspect Winston was allowed in

mud today. There were traces in the kitchen. Winston is NOT allowed in mud — as you know. I presume this was an awful accident? Please do not let it happen again. Ever. Carl.

The expectations and demands of clients were always challenging. Further down the line I would encounter dogs who needed a full bath and blow dry after every walk, dogs who only drank Evian and wanted a bedtime story, dogs who absolutely had to walk on the left-hand side of the road or who only understood Welsh. Just when I thought I had seen it all, that nothing could possibly faze me, a client called to ask if I wouldn't mind leaving the lead at home and using the Baby Björn instead. "Toots is *so* tired this morning," the caller continued, "he had a heavy weekend."

Winston's list of requirements now seems minimal compared to some, although Carl's infatuation with order and neatness, his dog's passion for mud baths, and the relentlessly miserable weather made this situation particularly trying. Every walk became a puddle gauntlet as we tried to duck and dodge potential hazards. I became fixated on the weather forecast, the really detailed one: moisture levels and precipitation and rainfall in inches. If it looked very wet, we would avoid the park altogether and cross over Vauxhall Bridge, turning right along Millbank to Tate Britain, where we would sit on the cold stone steps and look back across to MI6 and the scaffolding at St. George's Wharf and wonder what on earth we were doing with our lives. At least on some very basic level, Winston knew he should be in a park somewhere, preferably reclining in a big, beautiful quagmire. I couldn't say for certain where I should have been.

Getting to grips with the new job was proving harder than expected. It wasn't just the walking that was problematic. Yellow balls would be eaten and Labradors would shake buckets of mud onto the floor but that could be dealt with in the moment. A short-term panic that could be soothed with alcohol later if necessary. It was the creeping, longer-term panic that was more of an issue.

As office life faded into the distance and the novelties of fresh air and morning television started to wane, Panic would regularly drop in for a visit. Panic with a capital P — the kind that keeps you awake until three in the morning and then rouses you again at five. Panic that makes you feel sick and dizzy and takes lungfuls of air away, leaving you winded. Panic that easily lets itself in and makes itself at home because you now spend most of your day alone, without human interaction, and your thoughts rapidly metastasize into doubt and self-criticism.

I had met Panic before. We were formally introduced at university but had caught glimpses of each other for years, right back to childhood. I always suspected it was there, tucked behind the door, waiting for its moment. Sometimes Panic would appear when life was tricky, but often, when things were just merrily ticking along, it arrived with little notice and plonked itself on the sofa, giving me a quick rundown of my failures, mistakes, and flaws before settling in for a long uninvited stay. Sometimes it would lurk in the shadows undetected, before pouncing onto my back without any warning, squeezing the air from my lungs and shaking me to the core so violently that I was forced to sit, paper bag to mouth, until the terror and the trembling subsided.

Then it would be gone, just as quickly as it had arrived. I would look for it, try to second-guess it, but it was always cleverer than me. So clever that I couldn't tell anyone else about it. It made me keep quiet, berating myself for being unable to tell it to go away, to leave me alone. So it remained a secret, something dark and shameful, which is exactly what Panic likes.

This time Panic was here to remind me that I had absolutely no idea about how to run a business. It wanted to convince me that I would fail and I fell for it over and over again. There were many times in those first few months that I questioned what I was doing. The future suddenly seemed so terrifyingly unknown, so alarmingly unregulated. It seemed lonely. When you have spent most of your young adult life surrounded by people and cushioned by structure — at school, at work, following timetables and deadlines and familiar routines — the abrupt silence that comes with working from home is utterly unnerving. At work, the chorus of little worries that sings to us throughout the day is muffled by chatty colleagues, mugs of tea, Friday drinks. When you are alone, the whispers of Panic are deafening.

My mother was not helping. She would often call to see whether I had changed my mind. "Have you changed your mind, darling?" No, I would say. Not yet. She would then ask if everything was "OK" between

Finlay and me. "Hang on to him, darling," she would say gravely, as if having a normal, respectable office job meant he was somehow floating off to some higher ground.

In her book, the path to adulthood was straight and narrow and any deviation from the tried and tested route was cause for great alarm. School (private), followed by university, preferably an old one, and certainly not a polytechnic. Then a move to London and an administrative or marketing-type job at a reputable firm where career progress was preferable but not essential as you would want to start thinking about husbands and babies before too long. As I had been generously given the tools and the opportunities to embark upon this traditional, innocuous journey, gratitude was to be shown by toeing the line and any sort of a rebellion was at best self-sabotage and at worst a slap in the face of her parenting and her values.

She would try to steer me back to convention by firing alternative career options at me — something a friend might have suggested, or a cutting pulled straight from the job pages of her local rag, the *Shropshire Star*.

"PR? What about PR? Everyone does PR these days."

45

"I don't know anything about PR, Mum."

"Right. Here we go, here we go: 'Local Enterprise Partnership Support Officer?' It's £25k pro rata!"

"*What?*"

"OK, forget that, forget that. Ah! What about architecture? You've always liked houses."

"Everyone likes houses, Mum. Plus I think you need a qualification for that."

"Fine. Fine. If you say so. What about cooking? I could even help you with that. Show you a few recipes?"

"No."

"Well, you'll never know until you try. You have to give things a go."

"That's exactly what I'm trying to do, Mum. I'm giving *this* a go."

"How's your typing? Is it fast?"

"It's OK. It's two-handed."

"There you go. No shame in being a secretary. You could work up to being a PA. There's good money in that."

"But I don't *want* to do that."

"Well, you have to do something. You can't just do . . . *dogs.*"

Animal care in her view was decidedly subclass, particularly in an urban environment where her need for comparability had placed it somewhere between scullery maid and pet shop Saturday girl.

To be fair to her, dog walking wasn't a proper job in 2006. We hadn't quite caught up with the Americans who have had professional dog walkers in New York since the 1960s and have developed it into a wholly legitimate career for anyone who fancies wielding multiple Chihuahuas in pink sweaters down Park Avenue. If you had a dog in New York, you also had a dog walker, in the same way that if you had parents, you had a therapist or if you had working limbs, a personal trainer. Americans are clever like that. They see a problem and then fix it with a sensible service while we tend to struggle on and tell ourselves we don't need the fuss.

Here, typically, your nephew on his gap year or your unemployed cousin would help out with your dog for a bit of pocket money and the rest of the time you muddled along while your dog crossed its legs, twiddled its paws, and got stuck into an existential crisis. Although dogs were clearly in the ascendant, most owners hadn't elevated them to the level of needing their own carer — an extraordinary omission when you consider that dogs have been our right-hand assistants for thousands of years and we really should have worked out what their basic needs are. If you had a paid dog walker, you most likely found them by chance, say a random meeting with one in the park or your neighbor had one once in a while. And even then you would really have to be desperate to use one. The vast majority of London's dogs were still bored and lonely and sat at home all day.

But all that was about to change. The canines were slowly taking charge, demanding gluten-free diets, weekly grooming appointments, and tartan bow-tie collars. A multimillion-pound pet industry across the pond had started drifting over here and egging them on, encouraging play dates and pedicures and a choice of winter coats. I wonder if dogs ever miss the straightforward days of pack life, where time is structured around the simplest and most basic requirements with no need for overcomplication. Humans really are unparalleled in their ability to interfere, to tinker, and to fuss.

A few weeks after Winston's walks started, he was taken to the vet to be neutered and the walks were put on hold until he had recovered. When our walks together resumed, something was different. Winston was listless and melancholic and kept turning around and around in circles in the kitchen.

Joe and Carl, already racked with guilt about putting him under the knife, were understandably worried and asked for regular updates on his mood and energy levels. Winston didn't seem to be in any pain or to feel unwell and would bound toward the park with his usual eagerness but, once there, his behavior started to become unusual. Instead of looking for sticks or testing out puddles, he spent most of his time frantically digging up random patches of grass or sniffing through the flower beds as though he was searching for something. The hunt would then continue back at home as cupboards were pawed open, the dustbin turned over, and every inch of tiling sniffed and then sniffed again.

"Has Winston lost a favorite toy?" I asked Joe on the phone. "He's definitely looking for something."

"Oh, *that*," he replied. "Yes, we've been keeping an eye that. The vet thinks he's looking for his balls, if you can believe it. It's quite common after the snip, apparently."

"His . . . *balls*?"

"Yes, those ones. He can't understand where they have gone. They are not in the cupboards, I can tell you that much."

On the advice of a very expensive and shrewd dog psychologist, Joe and Carl eventually bought him a pair of fake testicles. As a drastic measure, you can have them surgically implanted into your very confused dog but Winston preferred to use his as chew toys. They were so successful at calming his post-snip distress that they ended up buying multiple pairs in a variety of colors and sizes, all of which could be found in various states of angst-fueled disintegration on the kitchen floor.

They were in fact the only colorful things in the whole flat.

STANLEY, PART ONE

As a child, I spent a considerable amount of time trying to decipher what it was that made a *good* family. What were the essential components, those key ingredients that made some families seem so inviting, so enviable, while my own felt small and somewhat lacking? I thought that if I could just figure out what it was that made the good families tick, then I would know what I was looking for when it came to be my turn.

For years, I thought it was as simple as having a paternal presence. Since I had no real father to speak of, I concluded that this must be the fundamental backbone and, therefore, placed it at the very top of my wish list. Fathers were the jolly ones, the ones who wore silly hats and instigated games and were in charge of the meat. They ruffled hair and told awful jokes and said things like "Just don't tell your mother," before giving you lots more biscuits. They knew about music and garden birds and completely pointless things, like long-range weather forecasts and cricket scores, but they would tell you all the important stuff about life without making a meal of it. Fathers were busy, hardworking, and they often had very important jobs to do around the house, but when you got the chance to sit in their lap for half an hour it was to sit on a golden throne, high above the earth, and to feel like you were the only two people in the entire universe.

Once the father was in place, there would be siblings. Lots and lots of them. I would be the youngest, the smallest, the one they had to look out for but also slightly under-estimated. My brothers and sisters would be clever and funny and all slightly odd in their own way, and everyone would play a musical instrument and collect unusual things like green buttons or bank notes from South America. There would be lots of laughter with the occasional squabble thrown in for a bit of variety, the kind of bickering that happens when you know someone right down to the core. Then there would be those times when we would all fall absolutely silent, for being still with each other would be more than enough. It would be busy during the week while we pursued hobbies, attended clubs, and had friends over for tea, but we would all get together again at the weekends for our secret sibling club, solving mysteries at abandoned railway stations or in old people's homes and saving stranded whales from remote Welsh canals.

I had a mother, of course. Everyone has a mother. But I never pictured her with any light or any color. She was never an integral part of any scene, never a key player. She wasn't in her purple dress or singing ABBA songs or laughing down the phone to her friends. She wasn't doing any of the other things she normally did, the cooking, the cleaning, the caring. I would gloss over all of that and place her in the background somewhere, static, stable, always resilient. She was holding the whole roof up.

There were others, too, when I felt like it, as larger families seemed to be the very best ones, where the noise level sits just on the cusp of reasonable and your elbows all nudge at the table. So I imagined a throng of extended family members, godparents and old, eccentric friends traipsing in and out through the door. With cousins who invite you to the beach and grannies who invite you to wildlife centers; uncles tall and handsome, who return unannounced from far-flung adventures with deep suntans and presents in their pockets. Aunts with red lips who giggle and chain smoke and tell naughty stories and a cheeky bearded grandfather with a wooden leg who keeps tins of barley sugars in his car.

Then there would be the dogs. There absolutely had to be a dog and preferably a few of varying size and color — and always one who would only sleep on my bed. That was the one thing we always got right, my mother, brother, and I, in our small, quiet unit. The one thing that wasn't a daydream. We always had a dog. We had a number of them, in fact. Labradors and Jack Russells, and many a mongrel. There was never a time when we didn't have a dog, despite the fact that life could often be very disorderly and that a number of them got squashed on the road.

My parents got divorced when I was very young and in the years that followed, my mother, brother, and I moved from house to house as various men washed in and out of our lives. Among this upheaval our dog was the constant, the line from one chapter to the next, rooting us to the ground and tying us to the past, the present, and to the future. The bedroom would change, the way the kitchen smelled, the rules, but the dog was solid and stable and somehow glued us all together. When I think of that imaginary house, that frenetic family, with all the siblings and the neighbors and the perfectly orchestrated chaos, the dog was always at the very heart of it all, in absolute stillness, the silent, sage observer. The one that kept it all steady.

As I grew older, I learned that family life is considerably more complex and intricate than head counts or domestic accessories. It can't be itemized or cataloged or assembled from a list of parts. It can't be plotted with characters from late-night story tapes or set in the pages of the *Laura Ashley Guide to Home Decorating*. It's not a fixed or solid or floral chintz thing but an ever-evolving, changeable force, one that both cements and fragments, pulls together and then pulls apart. Families are made by alchemy not design and often what makes them work, what makes them *good*, is fleeting and transitory and almost certainly indefinable.

All except for that dog of course. That's the one real thing. The constant.

Perhaps that is why I stumbled into starting up a dog-walking company. After all, the decisions that feel the most impulsive and whimsical, the ones that just seem fall out of the sky, often have roots so long that they are wrapped around your bones. I was looking for something, although I did not know what at the time. A new job, yes, a purpose, but something much bigger, too. I was looking for answers.

While some families I met while dog walking made me wonder if cohabitation was a sensible course of action, others inspired hope. The unexpected gratification of the job was a privileged insight into others' family lives. There were some homes I would happily sit in for hours, slowly absorbing the layers of happy memories around me; in others, discontent and frustration seemed to be sewn into the very walls. Very occasionally, I came across a family that reminded me of something warm and wonderful, or lit a spark that helped me see the right way to go.

This is how it was with Stanley, one of the first inquiries I had. Stanley was from a good family, the kind you want to be part of, with one of those large, busy kitchens that everyone congregated in. Stanley's owner, Steph, wanted to go back to nursing after taking a long career break to bring up her children but she was concerned what would happen to her beloved rescue dog.

Stanley had never been left alone for very long before but if the right job came up, then the house would be empty for most of the day.

"He's a bit of a funny fish," she said on the phone. "He's a homebody you see and doesn't like that many people. He's always been *my* dog really. That's what I'm worried about."

"That he'll miss you?"

"Well, yes. Definitely that. And he might just refuse to go out with anyone else."

"Ah, I see."

"He will of course, I'm sure. He'll need a pee, won't he? And some fresh air. I just feel bad about it all. Sorry. It's silly really, isn't it? I mean, I never felt this way about leaving my children."

Steph soon got a full-time job at Chelsea and Westminster Hospital's oncology department. The week before she started, I went around to meet Stanley. It was a chilly November evening and the whole family was home, back from work and school and milling around the kitchen, chatting and giggling, grabbing bags of crisps and doing homework. The house was a large, rambling villa in Clapham North, just a twenty minute walk from our flat, filled with books and bags and coats and trainers that been tossed across the wooden floors. Steph was making supper, tea towel over her shoulder, while her husband, Pete, poured a glass of wine and flicked through a magazine.

The house was frenetic and disordered but also warm and loving, and in the middle of it all was Stanley — huge and gray and woolly and looking like a cross between a lurcher, a wolfhound, and something you might find in the Arctic. He was a proper mutt, a hearty and wholesome melting pot of dogs, striding around the kitchen with a big grin on his hairy face, bashing pots and pans with his tail, and sidling up to various legs in the hope of a neck scratch.

"Shall we sit down?" Steph pointed to a sofa by the window. Having felt woefully unprepared for Winston's meeting, I had resolved to bring a notebook with me this time. Writing things down would look professional. It would also give me some- 'here to look if any awkward questions se.

ow long have you been walking dogs ? Must be a great job."

s it is. It's a great job. We've been r a few weeks now." The "we" ut. It sounded right somehow.

e" but more a sense of having an imaginary team of people around me, all of whom knew what they were doing. It couldn't possibly be just me doing this, could it? "And I grew up with dogs so I've had years of experience really."

"Well, you're very lucky. We would all like to be making a living from being outside, wouldn't we, kids?"

One of the teenagers grunted in reply.

"What sort of dog do you have?" Steph continued.

"Oh, I don't have one yet. We rent at the moment and, well, my boyfriend doesn't like them much."

"Sensible man," said Pete, Steph's husband, putting his thumb up. "Wise, sensible man."

"Pete didn't want a dog, did you, darling? But he wouldn't have it any other way now. He won't admit it but he's Stanley's biggest fan."

Pete smiled and wandered over to give Stanley a little stroke before heading out of the room.

"So I presume you are fully insured?" Steph asked.

"Absolutely," I lied. Easily. I shocked myself with how very easy it was.

"OK, great. As I said on the phone, Stanley is *very* relaxed but isn't used to being walked by anyone but me really. With everyone out of the house now and the kids doing all their sports and homework and what have you, he just isn't getting any attention. I thought they might help out when they got back from school but they are not as reliable as I had hoped."

Hearing his name, Stanley came over and started bashing his tail on to Steph's leg, waiting for a stroke. I got out my pen and wrote "sport," "homework," "kids," and then "GET INSURANCE" in very large letters.

"And how old is Stanley?"

"It's a bit of a mystery really. We think around six or seven but it could be much older. He has a lot of energy and loves the park but he doesn't like to be out too long. He's a bit of a hermit really. Not interested in other dogs. Not interested in much — oh, except food. Don't leave any food out anywhere or he will eat it. He can easily jump up on that," she said, pointing to a substantially sized kitchen island. "He was at the vet last month after eating two whole chickens and a pan of potatoes."

"Gosh, was he OK?"

"Oh, absolutely fine. He probably could have eaten double that." Stanley grinned at her. "Are you able to give me a reference for you guys?"

"Oh yes, of course. I can email it over if that is all right?"

"Yes, great. We've met now and everything is fine but obviously when you are giving over your keys . . ." she trailed off.

"Understood."

"Thank you. For doing this." She took my hand and held it for a second, staring intently into my eyes before giving it a shake. "A weight has lifted somewhere."

As those first clients started to come in — Winston, Stanley, and one or two others and quite a few more inquiries — I quickly realized that I would have to hire some additional dog walkers. My initial plan of being the sole walker, briskly hopping from dog to dog on bus and tube, was very quickly dashed as I discovered that not only did everyone seem to want their dogs walked at the same time but getting from house to house took a lot longer than expected. Even addresses in the same borough as each other could take up to an hour to travel between and the slightest delay with a bus or a kink in the traffic could knock all the timings out.

There was, however, a far bigger problem to come to terms with, something that never even crossed my mind. I was hideously, painfully, embarrassingly unfit. Years of student loafing, office inertia, and gym avoidance had withered away all strength and stamina, leaving me aching all over and completely exhausted at the end of the day. It was a bit of a shock.

As a twenty-something healthy person you assume that you will always have a base level of fitness, carried over from the multiple laps around the playing fields you were forced to do at school, the long walks to lectures, and the late-night dancing at university. "I'm young," you say to yourself, "I can walk anywhere and do anything." But asking your body to do something that it's not familiar with, even if that is just walking around a park or two, can be met with such stubbornness and refusal to cooperate that you begin to wonder if you and your limbs are even on the same team. My body was slack, it was weak and very out of shape. A daily saunter to the tube and the office, the odd jog here and there when running late, did not count as regular exercise. Nor did the round trip to the office kitchen or the subsequent carrying of six mugs of tea and however many digestive biscuits you manage to pile up on the side.

Being fast was little help either. The med-

als I won for sprinting when I was ten may
have given my mother occasional drops of
comfort as she anguished over my drastic
change in career but they held very little
sway when walking a large, determined dog.
If a dog decides to bolt, then speed might
give you a slight advantage but what you
really need are muscles the size of cinder
blocks and the endurance and power of a
very patient camel. I needed to be able to
walk and walk for hours on end, often at a
pace that didn't suit my arms and legs, as a
dog ten times more powerful than me
surged toward a park. What I needed was
stamina.

At first I blamed the fatigue on illness. I'd
had a bit of a cold and thought it must have
been some sort of post-viral malaise. But as
the days turned into weeks, it became glar-
ingly obvious that the malaise was simply
my body's horrified reaction to being made
to move farther than the tube station and
back on a regular basis. The shame did wear
off eventually, around the time my muscles
decided to wake from their deep slumber
and began to function like most people's
do, allowing me to move from A to B and
back again without feeling like I needed
resuscitation. But in the meantime, as the

inquiries kept rolling in, I realized I needed help.

As I started to hire those first few dog walkers, I would tentatively ask them about their fitness. "Do you . . . um . . . like exercise?" I would inquire awkwardly, as if it was some strange fetish and not a basic cornerstone of healthy living. Most did, which was reassuring. "Me too, me too," I would reply. "I love exercising!" Enthusiasm is key in recruitment.

At first, the dog walkers were friends and friends of friends, acquaintances from school or university who hadn't quite found their feet and were still trying out various career options. The unemployed, the ones who wanted to retrain, the loafers. The student years were not so far in the past that dream jobs couldn't be pursued for a little longer, so there was no shortage of actors, artists, and musicians kicking around aimlessly during daylight hours and looking to make a bit of extra money. In 2006, it was possible to live in central London and juggle a couple of part-time jobs while settling into adulthood. Rents were expensive but not prohibitively so and areas like Clapham, Fulham, and Islington were still just scruffy enough in parts to allow the average young person to move in with a couple of flatmates.

The first additions to my dog-walking team were Sarah and Matt, a playwright and a guitar teacher, who met at university, fell in love, and moved to a two-bed flat above a video shop in Battersea. Both had grown up with dogs and now had ample time during the day to walk them so were the perfect candidates.

"Right, what's involved?" asked Sarah excitedly when I met them for coffee not long after taking on Stanley. Sarah was the school friend of a university acquaintance and we had been introduced at a party the week before. She was petite and pretty with curly brown hair and front teeth that rested just outside her top lip. She was also mad about dogs.

"Well, we arrive. We open the door. We get the dog. And we take the dog to the park. And then we take it home again." On paper, it is all so simple.

"On the lead?"

"Um, yes I think so. Definitely on the streets anyway."

"What if they run off?" asked Matt. He was less keen, less smiley, and would in fact only end up helping every now and then when Sarah couldn't do a walk.

"Well, we would try and get them back.

Onto the lead. By calling their name. And waving food. Treats, that sort of thing."

"What if that doesn't work?"

"You would . . . well, you would call me and I would . . . I would sort it out."

"What if they get attacked? By another dog?"

"I would also sort that out. All of it."

The truth was that I had no idea what I would do except hope that nothing like that ever happened but as their employer, and owner of the company, I had to reassure them that I had all the answers and would come to the rescue in an emergency. I had to convince them that I knew exactly what I was doing.

"I think I will keep them on the lead," said Sarah, and Matt nodded in agreement, putting a protective hand on her knee. In the end, Sarah's first client was a tiny eight-week-old Dachshund puppy called Pip who lived a few streets away from their flat and only needed some light stroking and to pop outdoors for a pee. He was all ears and paws and had beautiful speckled silver fur that made him look as if he was permanently standing in dappled sunlight. He liked Enid Blyton stories and chopped up fish fingers and, at the request of his owners, Sarah would read a chapter to him from *The*

Faraway Tree at the end of each visit before tucking him into his basket.

When she moved on to walking Stanley, things were somewhat different.

Despite her grave misgivings about my new endeavor, my mother wrote Steph a very detailed, polished reference from a "Veronica Pembleton Smythe" of Cheney Walk, Chelsea, who had a "very satisfied" spaniel called Chops. Veronica Pembleton Smythe was undoubtedly the woman my mother thought she might have been, had her hand played out differently.

"I'm hiring some people, Mum," I said boldly on the phone. "They are going to work for me. As dog walkers!" Having employees gives you legitimacy. It says payroll and contracts and the laying down of rules. It says expansion.

"So how many customers do you actually have, then?" she asked.

"Five! Well, four actually. I lost one. Frank. I lost her ball."

There was silence. And then, "I am sure Sotheby's would take you back, darling."

But there was no turning back now. I had clients, I had dog walkers, and I had acquired public liability insurance from a company who reassured me that my starter policy would cover "most accidentally dead animals." It also covered lost keys, lost dogs, and lost property but definitely not incidents relating to acts of terrorism, so if a dog were to be kidnapped by the IRA or the Taliban then we would have to fork out. I opened a bank account too, a business one, and had the first inklings of what it felt like to be a legitimate grown-up. It felt fantastic.

Thankfully, Sarah started out well. She walked Stanley over lunch while Pip, her main charge, was having his midday nap and her chipper, light-footed approach got him out of the door and up to the park in record time. Before he'd even had a chance to decide how he felt about his alarming change of circumstance, Stanley was in open green space and in sniffing range of both some discarded chicken bones and a beautiful park dog, a caramel Saluki called Pamela.

Steph was thrilled. Unfortunately, her relief was short-lived as the very next day Stanley refused to move farther than three meters from his front door and spent the full hour sitting firmly on the pavement. Having contemplated the situation, he had decided he needed to protest.

"He simply will not move, Kate," said a frustrated Sarah on the phone. "I have been standing here for bloody ages! Pip will be awake soon and I can't wait here all day."

She eventually coaxed him to the nearest strip of grass for a pee, but once that was done, Stanley made it very clear he wanted to go home again by yanking Sarah back to the front door.

"You did really, *really* well," I said to her that evening. "You persevered and it paid off."

"It's only because of the ham," she replied.

"The . . . ham?"

"Yes, the ham. I had my shopping with me. He ate the whole packet."

"Oh, gosh. I'm sorry, Sarah. Well, at least we know what he likes."

"Well I won't have ham with me tomorrow," she snapped. "Or any other day. Dogs should want to walk, shouldn't they?"

Steph was apologetic, refreshingly so, but implored us to persevere. She told Sarah about the day that Stanley came home from the rescue center and hid under the car until it was dark. About how he once ran off when the plumber came over and how their cleaner had to bribe him for over a year with tiny cubes of cheddar before Stanley would let her into the kids' rooms. It took him a while to trust people, to adjust, but as long as we were patient and gentle with him, as long as we were kind, he would come around.

Stanley did come around. They settled into a rhythm and Stanley slowly came to accept his new walking companion. He liked Pamela and he eventually grew to like Sarah. And then, just as everyone had relaxed into their new routines, Sarah was asked by a regular in her local pub to walk their dog, one street away from Pip, a dog who ran and chased sticks and bounded merrily toward the park. A dog whose owner said she would pay more.

I said that I understood but I was annoyed. Very annoyed. I didn't want to let Steph down and I knew that the only way to avoid that was if I walked Stanley myself. There wasn't another walker. I just had a niggling feeling that we weren't going to get on.

BILLY

As the year drew to a close, the little business was looking after ten dogs and many more owners were making inquiries. We had five or six regular dog walkers and a cat called Geoffrey booked in for cat sitting over Christmas. The weather was freezing and picking up dog poo wasn't getting any easier but I was feeling a very small sense of achievement. It wasn't anything to get the stock market excited about but it was *something.* There was progress and, more importantly, there was money coming in.

Two weeks before Christmas, we took on a dog called Billy in Bow. He was a Manchester terrier but not at all what you would expect from a dog bred up north. The breed does not conform to many Mancunian stereotypes, being petite and delicate in stature with a skittish temperament and an inclination to pick its paws up like a show pony. Like most Manchesters, Billy was

71

black and tan in color with glossy fur and fragile, slender limbs and looked like a miniature Doberman. He was devoted to his owners, highly suspicious of strangers, and tended to bark a lot, particularly at men, with a high-pitched woof that sounded a bit like he might have been at the helium.

His owners had asked for a female walker and started out with a girl called Sophie, an in-between-jobs dog walker, looking to make a bit of festive pocket money. I had met her for a coffee in Vauxhall one afternoon as her email had said she was willing to work "any time, any place," just as long as dogs were involved. Her whole life was dogs, she said, the only thing that made her happy and fulfilled and reason for being put on the planet, but she then got offered a temp position in a department store and, frankly, it paid a lot more so in the end she only lasted two days.

Billy's owners were cross but I couldn't really blame Sophie. The extra cash, central heating, and free lunch that came with the temp job were all far too appealing to turn down, however "fulfilling" Billy had been in the short term. As a walker, a dog's charm is somewhat relative to the forecast and your cash flow, especially when it's been sleeting for days and you haven't bought any Christmas presents yet. However cute Billy was, he wasn't going to provide bath bombs and Fortnum's chutney.

With no other walkers available, I was bracing myself for the phone call where I would have to tell the clients that they were stuffed. They had already stressed how incredibly busy they were in the run-up to Christmas with work dos and travel and the imminent refurbishment of their house. I stalled for a day, hoping that a solution might make itself known. In those early days, I just couldn't bear the thought of letting people down. It wasn't just that I hated any sort of confrontation or reprimand, it was that anything going wrong, any inkling of failure, would only stoke those niggling worries about what on earth I thought I was doing. When something didn't go to plan, I panicked.

"I'll do it," said Finlay as I paced the floor of the flat, willing a solution to appear. "Where is it again?"

"It's Bow. Central line. Are you . . . hang on, are you sure?" Finlay was still working at Bart's Hospital, just around the back of St. Paul's, sifting through the files of people who had died of cancer in a stuffy, windowless office alongside a colleague who only wanted to talk about his tuba.

"Should be all right. There and back over lunch. It's only a couple of stops on the tube and it's just till Christmas, right?"

"Yes, yes. Just two weeks. I will find someone else to take over in the new year. One hundred percent."

"No problem."

"*Really?* Are you . . . absolutely, totally sure? You know it's a proper, real dog?"

"It'll be fine. He's only small, right?"

It's hard to underestimate what an enormous act of kindness this was, in its own small way. Finlay did not like dogs. He didn't see the point in having one. They didn't *do* anything, not anything useful anyway, and he had been schooled to believe that unless it was a working dog, they were a predominantly lazy and needy type of animal.

He was also scared of them. There hadn't been many dogs on the scene when he was growing up, certainly not in the family home, which was a place of sparsity and order, run with precision and piety by a formidable Irish matriarch who disapproved of the expense and frivolity of pets. Finlay was the youngest of four boys, an unexpected, Catholic sort of surprise, a golden boy who was still firmly tethered to his mother's apron strings while the older brothers had all flown the nest and his father was working abroad to help pay for their education.

The Irish side of the family came from Limerick, a farm not far from the River Shannon. His grandparents owned a tetchy weather-beaten collie who lived outside in the rain and was boarded at night in an old barn that had a huge roll-across door. Whichever boy behaved the worst, whoever left the most dinner, was tasked with rolling the door open in the morning, an assignment fraught with danger as by the time the sun came up the collie was ravenous, furiously angry, and far quicker than any pale ginger boy visiting from England.

Finlay was only tasked with rolling back the door once, but once was more than enough. The collie launched at him, knocking him to the ground just for the hell of it before running off up a hill and disappearing for most of the day. He was blamed for having scared it off, a most unjust accusation but the kind of thing you have to take on the chin when you are the youngest.

Then there was the unfortunate incident while house-sitting a pair of terriers as a student. After smoking a joint one day (the owners grew it in abundance in their greenhouse and had told him to help himself) he became convinced that the terriers were plotting to kill him and was forced to spend a whole day locked in an upstairs bedroom while the dogs, hungry and bored, scratched and gnawed at the door. One of the dogs needed daily eye drops, so when he finally plucked up the courage to emerge from the bedroom, his first task was to pin the animal down and squeeze yellow liquid onto its eyeball, an experience that neither patient nor nurse was particularly fond of. It thrashed wildly on the floor, snarling aggressively, and had to be restrained with a copy of the Yellow Pages on its chest to stop it biting any fingers off. It had been a traumatic ordeal for all involved and Finlay concluded that, on balance, the canine species was not for him.

Usually, if your boyfriend has contradictory views to you on one of the major pet groups, it shouldn't be a problem. You would talk it through, argue or sulk a little, and then compromise on a cat or a fish or a child. When you have just set up a dog-walking company, it makes things a little more complicated. There is suddenly a chance that a real, live dog might make an appearance as well as a high probability you will be subjected to never-ending dog chat. But Finlay never tried to talk me out of it. He never even questioned what I was doing. He was only ever supportive and encouraging, despite the fact that I was utterly clueless and frequently got into a flap over everything from invoices to income tax. And to top it all off, he was going to walk a terrier.

Finlay really isn't like anyone you would have met before. He's very odd, but in a good way, like a wonderfully intricate puzzle that you can never properly finish but keep wanting to come back to. He's charming too, and silly and very funny and ridiculously clever and his brain works in ways that most other people's don't. It's ordered, linear, and sharp but at the same time also brilliantly jumbled and erratic. Just when you expect him to say one thing he will say the completely unexpected, which may sound annoying but is actually rather intriguing and makes life far more amusing.

We met doing a play in a pub theater, a two-hander written by a mutual friend. For a long time, I had looked for family in the clan-like camaraderie of the theater. Being an actress seemed like the ideal way to have people around you all the time but, despite giving it a respectable and heartfelt slog, the doors just wouldn't open. "You are too tall," I was told over and over again by people far shorter than me in a tone that suggested I might actually be able to do something about it. "You have to be *smaller* than the man. Otherwise it looks weird." I was six foot, so far taller than the average man, and not confident or brave enough to tell them that I was more than a statistic, more than just feet and inches.

For me, the play was the final thread of the acting dream to be unraveled, while Finlay had just left the city job and was looking for something to do. We were both half-heartedly seeing other people, nice people whom we should have been much nicer to, but all we wanted to do was turn our backs on everyone else. We kissed backstage under the dressing room lights and from that moment on I didn't want to leave his side. A whole other part of the world had opened up, one where the lights were turned up and everything looked a bit clearer and a bit more hopeful. I felt bolder, braver, my feet placed more firmly on the ground.

I hadn't always chosen well. For a long time, I would say yes to anyone who showed an interest. For the daughter whose father walked out, an interest was more than enough. There was also the height issue, what with me being a giant and most other people not being giants and that making things tricky at times. Outwardly I would appear intimidating and unapproachable, while inside I would be feeling painfully conspicuous and awkward. Men who approached were either unfazed (cocky), taller (few and far between), rejects (by every woman smaller than me), or wanted me to pass them something from a top shelf.

Finlay was rare. Taller than me by two inches and kind to the bone. He went to Oxford so my mother was on board from the start and almost as soon as we got together she had been urging us to "get on with it." Apart from ticking one of the primary boxes on her rules of life checklist, she knew, better than I did, that despite her own divorce, getting married would help to smooth over some of the cracks. It wouldn't solve everything but it would be a good start. Adulthood was around the corner and it was time to think about settling down.

"Well, you won't be able to domesticate him, darling," she remarked when I happened to mention my growing appetite for a slightly less chaotic home life. Finlay and I had chatted about buying somewhere together and I was concerned that he might not be as ready as I was to put our twenties to bed. "He's far too intelligent to be worrying with things like cooking or the washing up. And I imagine far too busy." She could throw down a slight in the most impressively roundabout way.

But I didn't really mind about the washing up or the burned pasta or the occasional grumpiness and stubbornness, or even the night he disappeared and slept outside next to the bins because he was too drunk to find his keys. He was as flawed as I was and I didn't want to change him. He made everyone else seem dull and tedious. He made me feel that anything could be possible.

Around the time we took on Billy, I hosted an event to try and garner a bit of publicity and rustle up a few extra clients. It was a dating event, a walk in Battersea Park for singletons and their dogs on a Saturday in December and it had gathered a small amount of attention from the local press.

Got a dog?
Need a date?
Come along to a brand new singles
event in Battersea Park hosted by
London's Number One Dog-Walking
Agency. Join fellow dog lovers for a walk
around this beautiful London park and
then have a cozy drink by the fire in a
dog-friendly pub.
<u>MEET AND BONE</u>™
will not only help you find love,
but your dog might get lucky too.
Woof Woof!

I had been somewhat naive about the name. I thought the meet/meat pun was fun and witty and would make people want to come and have a fun and witty time but it turned out to be horribly, disastrously ambiguous and only attracted randy, dogless men who were expecting casual sex in the bushes. The dashing bachelors with the well-behaved Labradors who I had envisaged as the core of my group never sauntered out of their pretty pastel houses in Fulham to join us. Either this tribe is a myth, born from Richard Curtis movies, or they were all out of London that weekend, shooting game. The only single man with an actual dog was a pest control officer from Croydon, whose dog — a lurcher called Spike — had violent diarrhea and was forced to leave early.

The single women who attended, dogs in tow and hair blowdried, were understandably disappointed by the turnout. As soon as we started the walk, the dogless men all mysteriously disappeared one by one, the realization that the no-strings, al fresco sex they had been hoping for was not in fact going to materialize. As the sleet began to fall, the remaining women's disappointment started to turn into belligerence.

Thankfully, there was Finlay. Awkward and reluctant, but very much there, he did his best to cheer the remaining ladies with invented stories of dogs he had never met and listened patiently as they told him about how Muffin had won Prettiest Bitch at the Ascot Dog Show and how Tiger had a fondness for vanilla ice cream. He walked alongside them, guiding them around puddles and complimenting them on their dogs' heinous diamanté collars and fur-lined jackets, and if it hadn't been for the fact that the pub I had earmarked for a post-stroll drink was unexpectedly booked out for a Christmas function, it might not have been such an awful day after all.

With nowhere else to go, we were forced back to the cold, soggy park for a cup of tea in a café with a broken boiler. My total confusion about why on earth they would want to drag out the hideousness of the day even further when they could have all just gone home quickly evaporated when I suddenly realized they had no idea that Finlay was *my* boyfriend. There were three women left and they all had their eye on him.

"Anyone for cake?" I asked, during yet another lull in conversation. The smell of wet dog and neglected libidos hung heavily in the air and we had run out of small talk a long time ago. It was excruciatingly awkward. I went back to the counter to order some conciliatory Victoria sponge, while one of the women, a travel agent from Streatham with magenta hair, inched her chair closer and closer to Finlay under the pretense of adjusting her leather trousers. He had not yet cottoned on to the fact that, as the only man standing, he was very much in demand.

"So why don't you have a dog, then?" she asked.

"A dog?" he replied. "Ah, well, I'm not really dog . . . *friendly.*"

"Dog friendly? What are you talking about?"

"I don't really like dogs. I mean, I like them. I just don't *love* them."

"*What?* Are you joking? You don't love dogs?"

"Well, your dogs are all *lovely,* obviously, but I'm just not really a dog person."

"What about Samantha?" asked the larger lady with Muffin the Shih Tzu.

"Samantha?"

"The dog you met in Thailand? The one you were telling me about. Samantha? You rescued her, didn't you, from the sea?"

"Oh, *that* Samantha! Another lovely dog. I just wouldn't want to, you know, *live* with her, or have her near me on a daily basis."

"So what are you doing here, then?" Streatham woman continued, her tone sour-ing by the second. "Are you not here to meet someone with a dog?"

"Er, no . . . I, um. No. Sorry. I think there might have been a mix-up here." The penny had finally dropped for Finlay as I reappeared with half the café's cake supply.

"So you two . . . you two are *together*? What are we all doing here then?" she demanded, turning her frustration toward me.

"I'm really sorry that it's not been a great turnout," I replied, placing the groaning tray onto the tiny table. "We were hoping for more people. More men. I'm not quite sure what went wrong but some wires seem to have been crossed somewhere. Sorry. Would you like some cake?"

"No, I don't want any fucking cake," she snapped while dragging her poor sleeping dog to its feet. "What a fucking waste of time! Come on, Tiger." And she yanked Tiger back out into the freezing rain as the other women followed in her wake.

We never did another Meet and Bone.

Billy was having a stressful day. His owners had a builder in who had spent the morning hammering repeatedly at the kitchen cupboards. One strange man in the house was already one strange man too many, so when Finlay arrived for his first walk, Billy barked furiously at him for a good twenty minutes before finally letting him through the door. The owners hadn't been too keen on the idea of a male dog walker but with no other viable options and the house refurbishments starting in earnest, they reluctantly agreed. They had seemed persuaded by the fact that he would be wearing a suit.

The journey from St. Paul's to Bow had taken much longer than expected due to a constipated Central line, so once Finlay eventually managed to get in the door, he only had ten minutes before he had to turn around again and go back to work.

"Little dickhead nearly bit my finger off," said the builder as Finlay put the lead on. "I wouldn't be getting close to that mouth without some pretty fucking airtight insurance. Are you in a union?"

"Um, no. No, I'm not."

"You wanna get in a union, mate. Little prick barks at you like that, you've got a complaint. You got rights."

Finlay explained in his very best mockney that he didn't really have any rights as he was "Just 'elping out his missus," and that it was all a "bleedin' nightmare." The builder patted him on the back sympathetically before resuming his cupboard bashing and Finlay and Billy headed out the door.

Things didn't improve after that. Billy cocked his leg all over a Christmas tree stall, spraying at least four spruces and infuriating the vendor who demanded cash for "tree cleaning." After coughing up a tenner to keep the man quiet, he was heckled twice in the park by some kids, one of whom called him and Billy a "pair of fucking city poofs," and he then realized he had forgotten to bring bags so he had to pick up a poo with a large leaf. And all this in just one lunch break.

Fortunately, Billy quickly warmed to Finlay and the last few walks went well. A packet of Bonios and a scratch just behind the left ear and the bark-to-walk ratio vastly improved. They made it as far as the park most days (a good 300 meters away) and, despite the time constraints and the continued heckling from children, they had an all right time. After years of finding men threatening and scary, Billy had been tamed by a man in a suit who didn't even like dogs. It was a curious turn of events.

The owners were delighted and I was giddily proud. Not only had we stepped in at the last minute when Sophie bailed, we had paved the way for the rest of the tradesmen to come in through the door and finish the building work unscathed. But that was the last we saw of Billy. They found a new walker soon after. Extended lunch breaks are barely acceptable in the run-up to Christmas but not at any other time and, despite the fact that the shift in opinion between dog and man might have worked both ways, Finlay wasn't ready to become a full-time walker just yet. One step at a time.

STANLEY, PART TWO

RESCUE MUTT, AGE STILL UNKNOWN, CLAPHAM
JANUARY 2007
NUMBER OF DOGS WALKED: 14

Stanley was not pleased to see me. He was expecting Sarah and, more importantly, ham. As I turned the key in the lock on the first Monday in January I could hear him bounding through the hallway toward the door, tail thumping excitedly on the radiator, but as soon as I entered his head dropped, the tail stopped mid-wag, and he slunk back to the kitchen to find his bed.

He was temporarily animated when I picked up the lead but that excitement quickly faded as we headed out the front door. We had only just made it down the steps and a few yards down the pavement when Stanley stopped dead, paws firmly pressed to the sidewalk, and refused to budge.

"Come on, Stanley," I pleaded. "Don't you want to go to the park?" I tugged gently on the lead but he would not move. After a moment or two, he walked a few more paces and then stopped again. I pulled a little harder on the lead, I changed position, I tried going in the other direction, but it was clear that he really did not want to go anywhere. We then stood for a while, staring at each other, wills battling, as cars sped by and people ambled past us. A woman and a dog just standing there, wondering what to do. I tugged a few more times, I stroked his head and ruffled his chest. I pretended to have seen a squirrel in the trees and called his name excitedly.

"Stanley, Stanley, look! A squirrel, a squirrel!"

It was all useless. The only options were to give up and take him home, or to call Sarah and ask her what to do. So I called Sarah.

"Oh hi, Sarah, sorry to bother you, do have a minute?" She was walking Pip in the park, throwing sticks for him and generally sounding like she was doing everything very well indeed.

"Yes, no problem, what's up?" She had the tone of someone who didn't really want to give me a minute but thought she probably should.

"It's Stanley. He doesn't want to walk. What do I do?" Stanley had now sat down and was casually sniffing the air.

"He just needs a bit of persuading. Do you have any food?"

"No. No food."

"Ah. Well, then you just need to show him who is boss. Once he knows that it's easy. He likes it once he reaches the park. He just needs a bit of convincing to get there."

"Of course. Thanks, Sarah," I said cheerily. "We'll be fine. Have a good day."

But Stanley would not move. Now that he was sitting down he was even more determined not to go anywhere. The more frustrated I became, the more irate I seemed, the more I begged and pleaded, the more he seemed to relax until he was eventually lying prostrate on the ground in a state of absolute calm. Stanley had won.

"Look, Stanley, I know we don't know each other very well. Or at all, really. I just wondered whether you might give me a chance? I'm not that bad. I'm quite nice really and I promise to look after you. Well, I promise to do the best I can."

He looked up at me, blinking through his floppy gray hair, and let out a long, melancholic sigh. The sigh of a dog who was bored by my ineptitude. The sigh of a dog whose life had taken a turn in the wrong direction. We gave up and went home.

The next day was only marginally better.

Stanley barely moved from his bed when I came into the kitchen and if it wasn't for the stash of pork scratchings I had in my pocket, I doubt we would even have made it out the door. As anyone partial to a scratching knows, there are never quite enough in a packet and they only managed to coax him a hundred meters from his front door. As he swallowed the last piggy morsel, his haunches sank to the ground and he settled onto the pavement for a little rest.

The day after, Stanley had a twenty-minute snooze outside an old man's front gate. The man wanted to leave his house and go shopping and was irked to have to step over a large dog to get to his car.

"You can't leave dogs lying around like that," he said, as if I had fly-tipped him. "Public health hazard! This is private property, you know." I managed to drag the inert Stanley to next door's gate where he happily stayed for the rest of his snooze.

As the week dragged on and with progress minimal, it became clear that Stanley was putting me through some sort of initiation. He would let me think that things were improving, he'd trot contentedly in the direction of the park, and then just as I thought we might finally get there, that we might have cracked it, he would plonk himself down on the ground, stretch himself out, and refuse to move an inch farther. I started to take a book to read, fully aware of how unusual I must have looked to anyone walking past.

Steph didn't seem too concerned. She was grateful just to have someone there each day, even if I wasn't exactly fulfilling the brief.

"It's more the company side of things I worry about," she said as I updated her on the phone. "He gets very lonely on his own."

But he didn't even seem to want my company. Despite the variety and quantity of pork-based treats I brought him, my approval rating only seemed to drop further. He would turn away from me as I came into the house, his muscles tensing as I walked toward him.

It was time to look for more backup.

As the friends and friends of friends had begun to run out, I turned to Gumtree's job pages to look for new dog walkers.

London's Number One Dog-Walking
Agency is looking for dog walkers!
Do you love dogs?
Bored of daytime TV?
Want to get fit?
Then why not apply to become a dog

walker and combine your passions into
one amazing, fulfilling job?
Part-time only.
(Must be OK to pick up poo and
be out in all weather.)

Posting the advert in January had its
advantages. A high proportion of applicants
were looking to purge festive excess and
thought that walking dogs would be a
cheaper alternative to a gym subscription.
Some even offered to run with the dogs.
One asked if he could combine it with the
military fitness classes he ran on Clapham
Common. It was hard to know what the
right answer to that was. The new pug we
had just taken on might not be suitable for
circuit training whereas the overweight
Weimaraner from Shepherd's Bush would
absolutely benefit.

January also had its disadvantages. It can
be hard to sell a job based in a gray, wet
park to someone just looking for casual
work. If do you manage to sell it, the challenge then becomes retention, as the reali-
ties of crap weather and dog poo kick in
and evening work at your local pub seems
like a more congenial option. You need to
love dogs above anything else, so much that
the rain and the cold are just one small

component of the job and the sleet and minus temperatures are merely a good excuse to get out your thickest, ugliest winter gear.

While some applicants would send blanket emails to anyone and everyone who posted a job (resulting in many a cover letter to Domino's or Sainsbury's), plenty also professed their eternal canine devotion. But an impassioned response alone was not always enough. The multiple emails that read "I love dog," or "I can care for dog NOW," or the even more explicit "Need job, I can wash your dog, please give me dog job," were often from unsuitable candidates. Some of the clients we were starting to attract would insist on English accents and upper-crust ones at that. Countless walkers were rejected by clients for not being "quite right" or a "good fit" when what they really mean was "foreign," "did not look right," or "the wrong class." It was thoroughly depressing.

One client spent over an hour meeting a very sweet Brazilian walker who had perfect English and years of canine experience only to turn her down as she didn't "get" her dog. "I was hoping for someone a bit more like me," she said on the phone, which not only meant white, British, and university educated, but also someone who loved her dog to the extent that she did. An impossible request. There were always some that were just too exacting. With dog-walking services still in their infancy, it was hard to imagine where and how these clients had spawned their lofty expectations; their incredulity at not being provided with a walker who had a veterinary qualification or a certificate in canine massage was as baffling as it was disheartening.

Criminal records were also best avoided. While it is important to give people a second chance (and I did on a number of occasions), when the walker in question loses house keys, forgets to turn up, or makes off with the contents of a client's fruit bowl, it is awkward to admit that you might have seen something on their CV about time spent inside. One walker confessed to having made multiple hoax calls to the police about bombs planted in hotels but I decided to hire him anyway. The referee overseeing his case was the priest at his local church and he sent me an impassioned email explaining how "God had mended his ways," and made him a changed man. He disappeared not long after he started, taking the client's keys and dog leads with him and was arrested a month later for pretending that he had planted a bomb in the laundry room of the Savoy. The keys and leads were returned some time later, posted in a Jiffy bag with a very nice apology from the priest.

In the end, dog walking comes down to one very simple requirement: to be available during the day. Which was always going to attract the more alternative individual. For the dozens of emails from teachers or office workers or shop assistants hoping to walk dogs in the evening or at the weekend, there would only be a handful from those available when the dogs actually needed to be walked: midday, Monday to Friday, the occasional evening when the owner is out at the pub, possibly a weekend if their mum can't have her.

There was only ever one client inquiry that I rejected without looking into a potential walker. A Staffie living in an Irish pub in Marylebone who was bored and fat and had developed an unfortunate Guinness habit. The owner wanted him out of the pub when the cleaners arrived as this was when he would usually sneak around all the empties, guzzling up the dregs before spending the rest of the day semi-comatose behind the bar.

The owner sounded desperate. She had tried everyone she could think of. "He's a lovely dog," she said. "So gentle. I just can't understand it." I had to explain to her that the reason she couldn't find anyone was not the dog, it was the timing. The cleaners arrived at 7 a.m., an hour that most dog walkers would not be at all familiar with, unless it was at the very end of an evening. The whole point of being a dog walker is that you only get up when everyone else is already at work.

It took a while but I did eventually get Stanley to the park. Step by step, we got closer every day until he eventually surrendered and crossed through the threshold of the park gates. For me, it was a hollow victory. We had forged a necessary relationship but we were not great buddies. I knew there was something wrong.

"You mustn't take it personally," Steph said. "He's a grumpy old sod. I'm afraid he's found me going back to work very hard and is taking it out on you. He ignores me for the first hour when I get back from work, sulking around the kitchen. It's like having another bloody teenager in the house."

Whatever Steph said, it was hard not to take it personally. I wasn't having much luck with many of the dogs I was looking after.

Winston would happily have walked with anyone but my other charges were not so friendly. One nipped my ankle when I put its lead on and another cocked its leg on my trousers, despite having the choice of two lampposts and a tree within striking distance. Perhaps it was just the disappointment of hearing the key turning in the lock and it not being the dog's owner who walked through the door, but I couldn't help but think that there was something more to it than that. Had I completely misjudged my alignment to an entire species?

As soon as Stanley was allowed off the lead, he would skulk off to look for Pamela the Saluki and if she wasn't around, he would just find a quiet corner to sit in for a mope or sniff until it was time to go home again. I didn't have Sarah's chirpy, girl-guide approach but I had thought that the simple passage of time would eventually bring us closer together. I thought we would bond over our shared misgivings and the difficulties in adjusting to such huge changes. So far, it seemed, I was wrong.

Pamela the Saluki was blonde and brushed and of a very high pedigree. She looked like something out of the 1980s TV series *Dynasty*. I could see why Stanley liked her.

Her owner, a rotund, sour man called Roy, took enormous pride in her and, when not caring for his elderly father, he carted her off to dog shows at the weekends. When I was out with Winston — handsome, elegant, and from a well-respected line of expensive Suffolk Labradors — Roy was friendly. We didn't seem to get on as well when I was with Stanley, whose crush on Pamela only seemed to irritate Roy and make him cross and fidgety.

"What is that, then?" he would say with a dismissive wave of his hand. "Some sort of hound?"

"He's a bit of everything, I think. A Heinz 57."

"And he's had all his jabs, has he? Fleas and worms and all that?"

"I couldn't really say. His owners have been busy recently so they might have let one or two things slide. He had a bit of a cough earlier but that seems to have cleared now we are out in the fresh air." Roy winced and escorted Pamela in the other direction.

Roy was a key member of a Kennington Park dog clique, a group of middle-aged to old men, the retired and unemployed, who liked to sit on the benches in the enclosed dog area at the north end of the park and have a good moan. Like mothers with babies and joggers with their fitness, they bonded over their shared interest: being dog owners. Otherwise, lunchtime was usually quiet in the park, the mums having power walked with their buggies around mid-morning and the rest favoring first light or dusk. The kids with the Staffies didn't come out until it was dark.

There were around five of them in the dog clique, with one or two others occasionally dropping in. Winston wasn't a fan of the dog area so I didn't come across them as a group until Stanley and I finally made it to the park. Stanley liked to go into the dog area for a sniff around. The grass was balding, trampled down by the pacing of owners waiting for their dogs to relieve themselves, and the earth beneath damp and soft underfoot. It suited Stanley. Like Eeyore in his bog, Stanley felt safe on muddy ground.

Thankfully, the men mostly ignored me. Roy might throw a few words in my direction, usually something derogatory about Stanley, or an observation about whether I had arrived earlier or later than the day before. I might get a comment about the weather or an occasional "How are you?" but for the most part, we kept to ourselves. Alongside being a woman, I was just a paid dog walker and therefore an outsider. Being as middle-aged, gray, and grumpy as most of the group, Stanley should have really fit right in but he was clearly an outsider too, skulking around the perimeter fence or sitting in the shadows of a tree. Aside from the crush on Pamela, he didn't really like other dogs. He didn't see the point in them.

One of the men, ex-army and not a talker, owned a small ratty terrier called Skull who was always kept on the lead. Skull had jet-black hair, a short upturned nose, and half an ear missing and he spent his park time crouched down at the side of the bench by his master's feet. You might not have noticed him if you hadn't gotten within a few meters of the bench. It was then that he sprang into action, darting forward with teeth bared and barking with such force that his whole body lifted an inch or two off the ground.

"Eh, watch that!" the man yelled, although it was unclear whether he was directing it at me or his dog. I reverted to a very British "Sorry, sorry, sorry," despite having done nothing but stand in front of a park bench. Skull continued to bark, repeatedly lunging back and forth toward my legs like a battery-powered toy as I stepped backward away from the bench.

"Skull, SHUT IT!" the man bellowed, standing up from the bench, his enormous presence towering over his tiny dog, and whether it was the clumsiness, the uneven ground, or the sheer power of his voice, I went tumbling over onto my bottom, legs flying up in the air, arms and elbows in the mud, dignity all but gone.

In an instant, there Stanley was, between me and Skull, between me and the man, larger than he had ever seemed before, brave and bold and full of fire. Stanley growled, not loudly or even aggressively as that wouldn't have been his style, but low and deep, controlled, just enough to send Skull scuttling back under the bench, docked tail pulled firmly toward his back legs, bark silenced. I staggered to my feet. More apologies. I was covered in mud and my cheeks were flushed.

"What kind of dog is that?" asked the man as he sat back down. Some of the other men had now gathered around, Roy at the front, impressed for once, as their dogs quietly looked on. In an instant, the hierarchy had changed. Just for that day, maybe even just for that moment, there was a new top dog.

"Is it like . . . like a *wolf?*" he continued.

"This is Stanley," I said as if I might have been presenting a prizewinning child. "He's a mutt. A rescue dog. There is definitely hound, possibly Afghan. Possibly even a bit of Saluki. He's lovely anyway. He's a great dog."

We walked home in silence. Everything had changed — but then again, nothing really had. I knew Stanley would be just as stubborn and miserable the day after and the day after that. He would still sulk when Steph got home and would still sigh as I came through the door. But I hoped he had sensed that small but vital shift in me. The one that allowed me to start believing, just a little bit, that I might be able to do the job after all. And helped me to realize that it takes time to bond with some dogs and that wagging tails and exuberant greetings just don't suit all of them. But most of all, I hoped he realized how fond I had grown of him and how thrilled I was that he stood up for me.

We got back to the house and I settled him into his basket. "Let's just keep what happened between ourselves," he seemed to say as he looked up at me. "No need to make a fuss."

FABIO

COCKER SPANIEL, THREE, HOLBORN
SPRING 2007
NUMBER OF DOGS WALKED: 22

In early March, just after I turned thirty, we had an Italian houseguest to stay for the weekend. His name was Fabio and he had never been in a basement before. In fact, he had never been south of the river, having only recently relocated from Rome with his owner, Meredith, settling into a nice serviced apartment in Holborn. He had never felt the lingering smell of damp in his nostrils, or slid across cheap laminate flooring, or watched *The X Factor* with his dinner on the sofa. Vauxhall was far louder and rougher than the type of neighborhood he was used to but Fabio took it all in his stride and made himself at home very quickly.

My birthday had been something of a disappointment. Milestones like a thirtieth birthday make you question where you are in your life and rate what you have achieved. As long as you fall vaguely in line with your contemporaries you can feel at ease. Thirty means engagements and first homes and careers taking shape. It doesn't usually mean dogs. My mother's carefully plotted timeline for my future was already unraveled and frayed.

Every single birthday card I received had a dog on it. There was one of a pretty landscape without a dog but the sender had thoughtfully drawn one inside with a note that read, "Sorry! I couldn't find a dog one!" This was my identity now in the eyes of people who knew me. To them I had become a "dog person." The kind of person who might find a picture of a puppy swinging from the 0 of 30 amusing. One person sent a card with a picture of a confused-looking collie on a mobile phone next to a birthday cake. They wrote, "I thought you might find this funny!!!!" which made me a bit angry. I might well have lost some wit and repartee due to the daily lack of human contact but I hadn't become a completely different person.

Then there were the dog-themed presents: the dog tea towels and mugs and wash bags and a sausage-dog oven mitt. Finlay bought me a new raincoat, which was thoughtful and brilliantly practical but not hugely exciting or sexy. I wanted perfume and glitter and makeup and to not look like I was always about to go camping. I lived in wellies and tracksuit bottoms and reeked of mud and wet dog. I was permanently dank — not exactly how I imagined I might look and smell as I entered serious adulthood.

"You won't want to get too close to me," I moaned to Finlay as he leaned in for a birthday kiss. "I stink like a kennel."

"A very lovely kennel," he said, and gave me a squeeze.

I had first met Fabio a few weeks earlier at his flat. He needed a few ad hoc walks while he and his owner settled into London life. Meredith was nervous but brutally efficient, asking for multiple ID documents and references and handing out typed, laminated instructions for Fabio's walks. I was given an in-depth background on Fabio, who, despite being a very young dog, seemed to have achieved more than most adult humans do by the time they are forty.

Fabio was born in Rome, second son of a prizewinning cocker spaniel called Cosima. The family line could be traced back to the Renaissance. The breeder was world-renowned (well, in the spaniel world) and had secured Fabio's introduction to Italy's top dog trainer, a suave and canny Roman named Matteo who had supposedly trained most of Europe's royal dogs and a handful of celebrity ones too. Fabio had lived with Matteo for many weeks before being returned to Meredith and her partner, Arjun, as one of the most "obedient dogs in Europe," complete with a certificate of authentication.

Yet despite this heady accolade, Meredith's bullet-pointed list of instructions included many things that Fabio wouldn't do, or didn't like to do, or refused to do, including an inability to not eat other dogs' poo and his penchant for humping small male dogs. This seemed to be a particular issue for Meredith, who initially asked if Fabio could be walked with a female spaniel and when told that there wasn't one, looked as if she might cry.

"Matteo says it's just a phase," she said, defensively. "He'll grow out of it eventually. Moving to London seems to have rattled him a bit."

"Of course. Poor Fabio."

"He had so many girlfriends in Rome. *So* many."

Fabio was a beautiful dog. He had soft caramel curls, long fluffy ears, and huge brown eyes. There was a slight sashay to his walk, a very subtle swing of his hips that would have looked fine on Via del Corso but worked less well on Kennington Lane.

He was a dog who needed the right back-drop.

"The scavenging is also a problem," she continued. "Matteo was insistent that Fabio eats slowly and chews properly. It helps to center him. We can monitor that at home with staggered eating but it is more tricky in the park. Temptation gets the better of him I am afraid."

"Oh, well, doesn't it get the better of us all?"

Meredith smiled but didn't want to agree. I noticed a bowl of half-eaten dog biscuits sitting aimlessly in the kitchen. Fabio had a wistful eye on it, a small drop of drool forming at the corner of his mouth. He had clearly been subjected to a staggered lunch.

"With his Indian heritage, of course, we are eager for him to respect his food and be thankful for it. It's a core value."

Thankfully, Meredith was referring to her own heritage and that of her partner, Arjun, rather than some additional branch of Fabio's spaniel ancestry. Either way, it was an awful lot to take on board and I was relieved when the first couple of walks passed without incident. Often, when you are handed the longest list of requirements for a dog, detailing the most complicated needs and the most convoluted backstory, the dog turns out to be most pedestrian and normal. The dog is just a dog, carrying with it the burden of its owners' neuroses but otherwise completely ordinary. The client requests, the demands, the many idiosyncrasies: they will have little to do with you or even with the dog and are anchored to much deeper, knottier worries. If you are lucky to know them for long enough, a picture of each life will slowly come into focus and you realize that really, we all have the same worries, the same knots — it is just that some of us like to share them with our pets.

I hadn't given Finlay too much information about our weekend visitor. He knew it was a dog and that was more than enough to be getting on with. Some vague guidelines had been discussed. Fabio was not to sleep in the bedroom; I was to clean up any dog-related mess and Finlay would not be taking him out for any early-morning walks. In fact, he wouldn't really be getting involved at all.

We had not been Meredith's first choice of babysitter. The weekend away was a last-minute thing and, after all family members, colleagues, and casual acquaintances had declined, we were the only available option. I was delighted when she asked. It wasn't just the money that was appealing — though Meredith had been so desperate to find someone that she had thrown a generous amount at it — there was also something else. It was a yearning for something, something I couldn't clarify or articulate at the time but when I thought about how we would be looking after someone, *something,* even just for a weekend, I felt those roots tugging upon my bones.

Meredith arrived early on the Saturday morning with an overnight dog bag bigger than our bathroom and a panicked expression on her face.

"Did you get the email?" she said, hurriedly. A long emotional essay had been sent late the night before about how to care for Fabio, including preferred teddies and how he liked to be stroked. I had skim-read it.

"Yes, yes, all fine."

She kissed Fabio hard on the nose and flapped imaginary tears away with her beautifully manicured hand while her boyfriend, Arjun, impatiently tapped the car steering wheel. "I love you, Fabio!" she called, blowing theatrical kisses from the car window as they sped off down the road. Fabio was unfazed. He sniffed the brisk Vauxhall morning, cocked his leg on the front steps, and then trotted down to the flat, where he settled himself on the sofa and began to chew a pair of Finlay's glasses.

We spent a lot of time out and about. Fabio took to south London surprisingly well. He was a big hit in Kennington Park, an impressive flirt, charming both sexes with his beautiful caramel fur and catwalk strut. One poor bichon frise was the recipient of some particularly enthusiastic bottom-sniffing. "He's Italian," I explained apologetically to his anxious-looking owner. "Ah," she said, nodding her head.

Roy spotted us from across the park and came over with Pamela. Fabio wasn't overly impressed with her, which seemed to annoy Roy. She had on a new sparkly collar that he had hoped someone would notice.

"Where did you get that from then?" he said, pointing at Fabio. "He's not from around here, is he?"

"No, he's from Rome," I replied. "With Indian heritage." Finally, I had impressed him.

Upon unpacking Fabio's enormous bag that evening, I realized that Meredith had forgotten to leave him any food. I was about to head off to Tesco to buy some dog biscuits when Finlay sensibly suggested that he might as well just have some of our spag bol.

"He's Italian, right? It's his national dish!" Fabio seemed to agree that this made perfect sense, so we tied up his beautiful long ears with a hair bobble to stop them getting stained with the sauce and all tucked in while watching the telly. It wasn't one of my best attempts but it was definitely tasty and Fabio ate it at a speed that Meredith would definitely not have approved of. It was gone within seconds.

During his last-pee-before-bed walk Fabio was, alas, violently sick all over the pavement outside the Vauxhall Tavern, much to the amusement and then horror of some very merry transvestites who were tottering around in the queue for the weekly Duckie night. Fabio had a sniff around Spring Gardens, another quick vomit in the shadows of MI6, and then retched all the way back home, hacking out any last remnants of the spaghetti.

I thought that it would be wise to keep an eye on him and moved his bed into our room.

"What's he doing in here?" asked Finlay. "I thought we said no to this?"

"He's been sick. I'm sorry. I think it was the bolognese. Just forget he's here, I'll look after him."

But Fabio, who had already decided that

our bed would be preferable to his, jumped up on the duvet and curled into a ball between us, snoring gently. At around three in the morning, he had a vivid dream, something dark and exhilarating, which caused him to yip loudly for over ten minutes while kicking his legs wildly at the back of Finlay's head. Neither of us got any sleep.

"How did it go?" asked a breathless Meredith on her return the following morning. We met outside as before, the car engine running, her words falling into each other as she raced to get the handover done. She had got engaged the night before and flashed an enormous rock on her finger.

"Really, really, really well," I replied, handing over the lead. Fabio had survived the night and was looking remarkably perky. He'd had leftovers for breakfast and they seemed to agree with him this time as he had asked for seconds.

"I realized just as we got there that we left all his food at home. I am so sorry."

"It was totally fine. We got him some biscuits."

"Oh, thank you. That's so kind. He's a bit funny about his food, as you know."

The words only resonated later. At first I thought she was referring to the poor dog's staggered eating regime but as the day wore on and the lack of sleep started eroding my equilibrium, I became increasingly worried. Was he allergic to tomatoes or Parmesan or wheat? Had he already keeled over from a delayed anaphylactic reaction? Did I put too much red wine in it or forget to leave out the onion? Too many herbs? Can dogs even eat herbs?

I logged on to my emails to reread Meredith's lengthy instructions and there it was in bold, point number eighteen: **"Fabio is a strict Hindu and must not consume any beef. He eats white meat — chicken and fish only, accompanied by boiled white rice or dry biscuits, preferably organic."**

I thought it was best to keep quiet.

Not long after the Fabio weekend, we left Vauxhall and moved farther south, up the river to Wandsworth. Finlay's family had lent us a bit of money and we had managed to scrape enough together to buy a percentage of a shared-ownership flat, a brand-spanking-new two-bedder near the Thames with light and space and a bathroom free from mold. We traveled there in a black cab, our joint possessions easily fitting in the back, and, as we rumbled westward through Battersea, our hands tightly knitted together

114

and a saucepan balanced on my knee, I felt the page turn and settle quietly onto the next chapter. Our first proper home.

A short while later, we had another Italian houseguest. A human this time, Marco from Genova, who was a friend of a friend and stuck for somewhere to stay for a few weeks. Finlay had drunk five too many beers one evening and said Marco could stay for as long as he liked, when what he really meant was absolutely no bloody way.

Marco was a respectful, considerate guest but Finlay did not like sharing his space and, as the days turned into weeks and Marco made himself more and more at home, Finlay became irritated and resentful.

"Can you come to the park with me?" he whispered in my ear, squeezing my hand tight.

"Now?" It was a Sunday evening, mid-July, and after a few glasses of wine I was feeling sleepy.

"Yes. I need to talk to you in private. It's important."

Wandsworth Park was a short walk away and we ambled there as the sun melted into the Thames and the water slapped against the sides of the houseboats.

"Is everything OK?" I asked. "You seem weird."

"There's just something I need to talk to you about."

"Couldn't we have done it at home?"

"No. No. That's just the point."

"What, is it Marco? He's got a lead on a new place. I don't think he'll be here much longer."

"No, no, it's not Marco."

Then, just as I was about to tell him to spit it out and that I wanted to go home and get in the bath, he got down on one knee and again asked me to marry him.

Once, near the beginning, we'd had a fight about "grand gestures." I was drunk and said something silly about how he never did anything romantic. A friend had been taken away for the weekend by her flashy new boyfriend, a "pack a bag and meet me at the airport" type thing. He wore neckerchiefs and matching colored cords and you wouldn't have wanted to spend much more than ten minutes with him let alone a whole weekend but I couldn't help mention it nonetheless. "A weekend away?" Finlay asked, confused. "Is that what you want?"

No, I didn't want that. I didn't need a grand gesture. I like small, quiet things. Grandness wasn't who he was. Who we were. But Finlay then went outside in the middle of the night and breaded a car on my street. Not our car, we didn't have one, but one belonging to a man called Rob, who awoke to find over one hundred slices of Hovis covering his Ford Fiesta. He was late for work and the bread was upsetting, having partially frozen to his windscreen, and he didn't notice the "I love you Kate" Marmited onto the roof slices. I watched from an upstairs window as he chiseled the bread off with a knife, my heart blazing.

"Will you marry me?"

The grass was wet and seeped across Finlay's trousers and the ring — old and delicate and completely perfect — got stuck in the lining of his pocket as he tried to pull it out. It must have been less than a minute, seconds at most, but I held that moment tightly in my hands and tucked it away forever. The mud, the grass, the fumbling in his pocket. It was nothing like you imagine it would be, those twinkly lit scenes you conjure up when you're sad or lonely or when you have just fallen in love. "Let's get married," I said not long after we met, when everything was new and urgent and we couldn't bear to be apart. There would be balloons and flowers and singers galore but when you settle into things, when you are just happy to sit side by side, not saying a word, you don't need anything like that.

No grandness, just a small, quiet, perfect gesture. I couldn't think of anything I wanted more than to be his wife. I couldn't think of a better man.

We received an engagement card a few days later from my mother. It had two dogs on it, smooching. "Congratulations, my darlings," it read. "Walkies up the aisle!"

It went straight in the bin.

118

WINSTON, PART TWO

In a strange and complicated coincidence, toward the end of 2007, Winston moved around the corner from us in Wandsworth. Joe and Carl had separated and Winston was splitting his time between Joe in Vauxhall and Carl's new Wandsworth rental.

The breakup had come to light a month or two earlier. Standards in the flat had started to slip and the familiar order and symmetry seemed off. It started with the odd mug left out here and there but quickly moved to takeaway boxes piled up in the kitchen, cereal boxes not put away, shirts left drying on the rack, and shoes kicked off carelessly on the floor. Normal living for you or me but for Carl this would have been sacrilege. Then one day I came into the flat and Winston was not in the kitchen but stretched out on the sofa, distinguishable from the brown velvet beneath him by just a hint of pink as his deep snoring breaths

119

flapped his tongue slightly at the side of his mouth. It was clear that something had gone very wrong.

Joe, unshaven and gray, came down from the bedroom in his dressing gown for a chat.

"You've seen the mess," he said, gesturing toward the kitchen.

"Oh, I hadn't really noticed," I lied.

"It wouldn't take a genius to work out that Carl's not here. He's moved out. Down your way. Wandsworth."

"Oh? Right."

"We're not together anymore. You probably figured that out already."

"No, I'm . . . really sorry to hear that, Joe."

"Well, that's how it goes, isn't it?" He swallowed hard and took a long, deep breath. "We are going to try and do what's best for Winston. Spending time with both of us seems right at the moment. And having you in his life will really help. It's going to be a bit unsettling for a while and I know how much he loves you. And relies on you."

"Of course. Well, I'm right there so it should be easy."

"But not just there. Here too. In Vauxhall. You'll still come here?"

"Yes. Sure."

"We are going to need all the help I can get at the moment." He handed me Winston's lead and his chin started to wobble. "Life's shit, isn't it?"

"It really is," I fibbed. Such a massive, stonking fib that you could have seen it a mile off.

The next time I saw Winston, he was getting out of a livery cab by Wandsworth Park. The driver, in wrap-around shades and a very bad mood, thrust Winston's overnight bag into my hand and begrudgingly informed me he would be picking him up again the following evening. He hadn't signed up to ferry chocolate Labradors around south London.

The joint custody arrangement was not only expensive and complicated but clearly unsustainable. Dates and times were constantly being changed with the rise and fall of work commitments, and as Joe and Carl weren't speaking to each other, communication was limited to terse, monosyllabic email exchanges, most of which I was cc'd in on. The arrangements for one weekend stretched to over sixty emails, an endless back-and-forth of timings and locations, of shouty capital letters and sulky pauses that left me in the middle feeling somewhat like a couples counselor.

Winston was oblivious to begin with. All

the extra fussing distracted him from the turmoil. There were treats and toys and longer walks and endless cuddles as both Carl and Joe tried to stroke away the guilt. Each owner would try to out-dad the other with bigger, better presents. Giant teddies, Barbour jackets and woolly sweaters, squeaky ducks and chickens, and animal bones sourced from butchers. Walks became more and more scenic. Richmond Park one week, the beach at Whitstable the next, until one of them pulled out the ace and booked a mini-break to a glen in Scotland. Poor Winston just wanted to be at home.

I knew how he felt. Though with my dad it had been chocolate bars, not Barbour jackets or weekends away. Five or six in one go when you saw him, and all the best ones. Boosts and Caramacs and huge purple bars of Dairy Milk. He would pop into the news-agent to get his Silk Cut and a newspaper during a Sunday visit while my brother and I sat in the car fighting. It was thrilling at first. Decadent and naughty. "Eat them now," he would say as we gawped at the time, realizing it was not long since break-fast. But then it started to taste not quite as good. It wasn't chocolate that we wanted.

As time went on, Winston began to suffer. He seemed to slowly absorb the sadness around him until it just became who he was. The novelty had worn off and all he wanted was his old life. Familiar surroundings, familiar smells. His old routine. Stability. I traveled back to Vauxhall as much as I could to cheer him up with the puddles in Kennington but when I walked him in Wandsworth he was morose and completely indifferent. His fur looked dry and ashen as though the color was leaking out of it. His eyes were glassy and blank and he once walked past half an eaten sausage roll that had been dropped on the floor without even giving it a sniff. Worryingly un-Labrador.

Carl's new flat was small but predictably pristine, although not color coordinated, which I know must have grated. It was a short-term rental, furnished, and I had an inkling that Labradors were not listed on the inventory. Carl would occasionally request urgent last-minute walks at specific times of the day and he became even more fastidious about cleanliness. There were endless messages about towels and dog hair and window ventilation, his tone getting sharper by the letter. He also insisted that he actually lived in leafy, upmarket Putney, the borough next door, despite having the same Wandsworth postcode as we did.

"Now Winston is in Putney, he really does

NOT like to be muddy," read one cheery text message. "Please ensure paws are thoroughly wiped down (wipes provided) and spritz kitchen with the anti-pet air freshener (also provided)."

Joe was beside himself with worry and wanted regular updates. "How is he?" he texted me. "When you saw him today, was he all right?"

"He's OK. We walked around the park. He ate a small stick. He's a bit miserable," I replied honestly.

"We are ALL miserable. Miserable beyond belief. It's unbearable."

Joe asked me to keep an eye on things in "Putney." Not just Winston, but the flat too. Vague things like the central heating and the decor but then also very specific things like were there olives in the fridge and had I seen any Swiss cheese lying around. I soon realized that he wanted me to spy for him. I said no, initially. I made excuses. I was in and out I said, always in a rush, not good at spotting things, would make an awful detective.

I didn't like Carl but sneaking around his flat felt like a step too far. I didn't want to be involved. What's more, there was also something about Carl that made you feel like he might be watching you, all the time.

But then, only a week or so later, Winston had some sort of infection and needed antibiotics. I was instructed to do the lunchtime dose, pink liquid squeezed onto pink ham, which meant venturing into the fridge to get the medicine.

The fridge. Even before opening it I knew something was in there. I tried not to look too hard but it was impossible not to be drawn to the enormous block of custard yellow cheese sitting squarely on the middle shelf. Waxy, full of holes, reeking of guilt and unquestionably Swiss in origin. And next to it, a large tub of green olives, the shiny ones that have the little red hats.

I slammed the door shut and pretended I hadn't seen it. It was cheddar cheese, I told myself, a nice solid, sharp English cheddar, and alongside it some very, very small apples. But the more I tried to banish the image from my head, the more it butted in, the holes from the cheese expanding and swirling as they yodeled a tune about goats and the Alps while the olives tap-danced with their pimento hats. Panic then started to join in, clapping along to the rhythm, tapping its feet upon my chest so that the breaths became fast and slight and the room began to spin.

"It's just *cheese,*" said Finlay sensibly as

I fretted about what to do. By the time I got home the panic had mostly ebbed, leaving just a thin film of disquiet. To an outsider, worrying about cheese was the most ludicrous of concerns to be carrying around with you. But Finlay wasn't an outsider. He knew me better than anyone.

"I know, but it's cheese I am supposed to report on. It's significant cheese. *Bad* cheese. It means something."

"It doesn't really. Not to you anyway. This has nothing to do with you. Nothing at all."

He was right. Somewhere along the way I had taken one step too many, let myself get just a little too involved in problems that didn't belong to me. Being in these homes day after day, week after week, watching the stories of people's lives unfold — you can see how it happens. I knew that I must try not to forget that my place was only in the wings, watching the drama play out, and never center stage. These are all somebody else's stories.

I eventually found a new walker for Winston in Vauxhall, a guy called Tom who was slightly odd but completely devoted to dogs and Winston took to him straightaway. Aside from the fact that I felt deeply uncomfortable about being involved in the fallout of their breakup, the journey back and forth was taking far too much time out of my day. But it wasn't long after that Joe decided to move out of London. They sold the Vauxhall flat and Joe bought something in Essex with his share of the proceeds, closer to his mother, farther from Carl, and surrounded by the most verdant, stick-laden fields and woods. Winston visited at the weekends, settling into the more conventional co-parenting arrangement and freely indulging in all his favorite hobbies.

There were a couple of the last-minute Wandsworth walks that I couldn't do and so Carl abruptly replaced me. He always knew I was on Joe's side. While I knew I would miss Winston, it was a huge relief to not be in Carl's orbit anymore. It was only when I stepped out of it that I realized quite how pernicious it had been.

As we rolled into another year — our wedding year — we were walking lots of dogs. There were Frank and Stanley still and a number of others besides, some needing walking five days a week, some only every other Tuesday. The business was slowly but steadily growing. There was a collie in Battersea, a boxer near London Bridge, a Newfoundland in Lancaster Gate, and a husky near Parsons Green, who looked uncannily like Rod Stewart from the mid-1980s. Labradors aplenty, terriers galore, from north and south to east and west, London's dog community was thriving.

More dogs meant hiring more walkers, which meant more people to rely on and more being let down with last-minute excuses. It also meant spending more time behind a desk (kitchen table). More dogs meant more emails, more placating, more organizing, more reports about bowel movements, more updates on the weather, more logistics with keys. More apologies.

I finally got a Blackberry, which allowed me to leave my desk (kitchen table) occasionally and venture out to meet the walkers and clients. It had a minuscule keyboard that took a long time to get used to, caused a crick in my neck, an ache in my thumbs, and produced a few unfortunate typos along the way. One poor dog became Anus for an entire email, which was a long and detailed memo about the dog's weekend itinerary with a dog sitter. His name was really Angus and his owners were very strait-laced. The teeny tiny buttons meant that I frequently mistyped in a hurry, sending many "breast wishes" and "kind retards" and then there was the client I repeatedly called Bev instead of Ben.

But once teething problems were overcome, the new gadget transformed the way I worked. It sounds silly to say it now that smartphones run every area of our lives but being able to spend time away from the desk (kitchen table) was monumental. It not only allowed me freedom but the ability to be hyperactively productive and organized, answering new inquiries within seconds, and rattling through emails expeditiously. "Wow, that was quick!" was the most common response, followed by, "Can you start today?" But I was always happier when busy. Or even a little too busy. I thrived right on the edge of stress — not close enough to the brink that I felt I might fall but still feeling its pull. Being busy, being in demand, helped to keep Panic away.

More dogs and more admin also meant less walking and, most significantly for me, less Stanley. He had a new walker, Tom, originally hired for Winston but now in charge of Stanley, too, and a pair of psychotic Jack Russells who lived near Kennington Park. Stanley adored Tom from the very first day they met, which had stung a little at first, particularly after our run-in with Skull, but quickly felt enormously comforting. I worried about Stanley and it was a relief to know he was happy and settled. There were no problems getting out the door, no problems getting to the park, no problems at all.

Steph aside, Stanley was either just a man's man or he had simply found someone like him. Stanley and Tom were a perfect match, similar in all the right places, their temperament and outlook almost identical. They walked at the same pace, in the same rhythm, slowly but diligently, step by step, as if nothing was ever accomplished by rushing. They liked to sit together on one of the park benches and watch as the world sped by, Tom rolling a cigarette and Stanley blinking through his floppy hair. They had fish and chips on a Friday and occasionally a bone from the butcher if Tom could get his hands on one. Stanley knew exactly what he liked, who he liked, and he couldn't much be bothered with the rest. He was happiest when everything was pared back to the basics.

Tom was similarly disinterested in modern life and had already consigned most of the human race to the reject bin. But unlike Stanley, who sat perfectly happily at the bottom of the pile, Tom raged against the hierarchy and proselytized about government conspiracies and dark shadowy organizations that controlled everything from votes in the House of Lords to the ingredients in baked beans. Humans disappointed him, society confused him, and the only joy he seemed to find was in looking after dogs.

We first met for a coffee in Starbucks, which hadn't gone down too well as a choice of meeting place on account of it being a "corporate twat headquarters." I apologized for the oversight, bought him a hot chocolate, and he told me how he had just been dumped by his girlfriend.

"She's working for Foxtons now. Can you believe it? Foxtons! She's got one of those Minis. Drives everywhere in it."

"That's nice."

"I don't think it is nice. You think you know someone, you know? Then this!"

"Perhaps she just wanted a car? And to be an estate agent."

"No, no way. No chance. There's got to be more to it than that."

He then sold me two homemade, brown rubber disc necklaces with hair woven into the center. I didn't ask whose. It was his sideline business and I couldn't really say no. "They're normally a hundred each," he said. "But I'll give you both for a tenner." He told me it was essential that I had them as they were one of the only ways to ward off the many "evils of society." These "twat repellers," as he more succinctly named them later, were large and heavy and would have looked alarming around a neck but in fact made excellent doorstops.

"I feel like I can talk to you," he said after we had chatted for around five minutes, which only made me think that he was someone who people didn't really bother to listen to. He was the sort of person from whom you might have switched off without giving them a chance. Employees would often give me tiny snippets of their private lives, usually accompanied by an excuse as to why they couldn't walk a dog that day, but Tom was disarmingly detailed and frank from the very start.

Tall and wiry, with long hair and a warm smile that revealed one missing tooth, he mainly favored band T-shirts and ripped jeans and would occasionally wear tie-dye and long dark ponchos if he was feeling particularly disenfranchised. There would be more intense sartorial phases, like the summer he mainly dressed a bit like a pirate and the brief few weeks he was an urban cowboy. He did a few walks as a 1920s gangster and one or two as Freddie Mercury and the clients mostly accepted his aesthetic eccentricities — mainly because he was so brilliant with their dogs but also because they rarely saw him.

This lack of contact was a huge advantage with the more unusual walkers I employed, Tom being a fine example. Once the first meeting is done and the walker starts, the clients don't often see them for weeks or months at a time and their initial impressions tend to blur a little. During his retro cowboy phase, Tom once returned a dog after its walk and scared the life out of the poor owner who had happened to arrive home early from work. She had completely forgotten what he looked like and thought he was a burglar.

But underneath the outfits and the conspiracies, Tom was kind and generous to the core. He volunteered at a youth center, helping kids who had run away from home or who had gotten into trouble with drugs, and also helped to care for his dad, who struggled with severe arthritis.

We talked a lot about his family and growing up with dogs on that first meeting. He had lived alone with his mother as a child and she had always fostered dogs, taking rescue animals in for weeks or months at a time before they found permanent homes. Tom would get attached, fall in love, and then they would be gone. It was the way his mother liked it, he said. Not really having to commit to loving anything.

"So can you maybe get your own dog now?" I asked naively. Things are rarely that simple.

"Nah, nah, can't. I live with my dad now. My stepmum gets rashes."

"Oh, I'm sorry."

"It's all right. Haven't got much time anyway. And I'm going to be looking after them for you guys, aren't I?"

Tom and Stanley favored getting the bus to Battersea for their walks, with the occasional jaunt on the 345 bus to Camberwell and then north to Burgess Park. The awful terriers that Tom walked before Stanley, a brother and sister double act called Mustard and Maeve, had made going to Kennington a little awkward. They had nipped at the heels of most of the regular park dogs and one of them had a full-blown tussle with Skull, which resulted in his owner squaring up to Tom and threatening to deck him. We stopped walking Mustard and Maeve shortly afterward.

Battersea and Burgess Parks were a whole new experience for Stanley. Rather like moving from primary to secondary school, Stanley's worldview broadened so completely that at times he was overwhelmed.

"He's tired tonight," Steph would text. "Dinner as yet untouched. Must have been a good one."

Very little was known about Stanley's pre-Clapham life but as he spent more time with Tom and explored London's green spaces, it became apparent that it might have been very quiet and very small. Kennington Park was as far as he had ever gone with Steph, apart from the one time that she took him in the car to visit her mother in Kent and he spent the whole trip hiding on the backseat. Tom was allowing him to start from the beginning, to see the world as if it was all brand new.

Tom emailed regular updates. One read:

We saw a busker today, Stanley loved the music. And he saw a horse in Battersea! It was massive. He couldn't get over it! A great walk today. He's such a happy lad.

Gradually, Tom started taking Stanley to the youth center with him for the afternoon. He found it hard to leave Stanley alone at home after the walks and so gradually introduced him to the building, to the support workers, and finally to the kids. They would stroke him or chat to him or just lie quietly nearby, and Stanley would sit, soft and still, taking it all in. He was wiser than anyone really gave him credit for.

It was Stanley's transformation alongside the continued growth of the business that helped me to finally understand what people mean when they talk about "job satisfaction." Being "satisfied" in a job had always

136

sounded rather disappointing to me — a sort of feeble acceptance of your servitude in return for the rent and wine and Danish pastries. But this was different and more like the kind of contentment you feel after a meal — the three courses with friends and a bottle or two of wine type meal — or when you can have a lie-in on a rainy weekend morning. It was like the hill you managed to walk up and the cake you didn't burn. It was calming and grounding and uplifting at the same time and, I learned, only really comes from working hard and feeling like you might have helped someone.

CLEO

LABRADOR, FIVE, OXFORD STREET
MAY 2008
NUMBER OF DOGS WALKED: 41

Everyone I knew migrated to London after university like moths to the lightbulb, in search of jobs, flatmates, life progression. When you are from a tiny hamlet near the Welsh borders and don't plan on a career making butter or organizing ponies, then the City is really your only option and that city is always London. It's where everyone else goes; it's what your mother tells you to do — so you go, starting small, aiming big. But it's not an easy adjustment. The scale, the noise, the hard edges. It all takes some getting used to, if you get used to it at all.

Despite now being a homeowner, I only ever felt that I was borrowing London for a while, renting a tiny temporary space in its vast sprawl. I knew I wouldn't be able to stay for too long, not forever, anyway. This seemed to be a feeling shared by many, particularly those with dogs. You couldn't help but picture them running through a wood or a field somewhere, ears flapping as they reached top speed, hurtling joyfully toward the horizon. I wondered if dogs living in cities missed these things, even the ones who had never experienced it. When they squeak and kick their legs in their dreams, are they really just running for the hills?

Cleo's owner, Jess, worked long hours in the City while Cleo sat alone on the sofa in central London getting fat and listening to *The Archers.* Jess was, however, in denial that her black Labrador was the size of a modest suburban bungalow. Cleo and Jess did have something to miss. They had recently moved to London from Brighton and found themselves on Oxford Street, four floors above a sports shop, completely miserable. If you had to circle a focal point of the City on a map, the most central, the vortex, the place least suitable for a dog, you might well have picked that shop, that flat, that small section of a street. All of London was there: half-price trainers next to Big Ben key rings and Diana mugs, coffee and Marks and Spencer, Pret sandwiches and noodles and cheap electronics. Despite the ridiculous convenience in one sense of their location, they found urban living lonely, dull, and ugly and pined for their old home by the sea.

The first email I received from Cleo said:

> My dog is lonely. I feel awful leaving her but I have to work and the hours are getting longer. She's on her own for around ten hours at the moment, which is dreadful I know. We don't really belong here, you see. Can you help, please?

There was a follow-up email that simply read: "Oh, and Cleo is a teensy bit fat."

This was something of an understatement. Cleo was so large she might have been mistaken for a small hippo or possibly even something porcine due to her very low-hanging stomach. Her back was easily wide enough to rest a breakfast tray on and her neck and head, solid and wide like a bear's, hung heavily from her body as her weight pulled her down toward the ground. It was hard to determine at the start whether Jess was simply unsure what was a normal, healthy size for a dog or whether she was just burying her head in a desert's worth of sand. Either way, something had to be done.

The first time we went out for a trial walk, it took at least five minutes to get Cleo to her feet, and then another ten to get her down all the stairs and out the door. The flat was small, dark, and airless, the low hum of the busy traffic below just about audible over the radio, which was always on loudly — Radio 4 misery dramas and serious discussions about the housing market. Cleo lay prostrate on the sofa, snoring loudly. Even when she woke, she continued to snore, her breath straining against the paddings of fat on her chest and lungs and the remnants of her second breakfast lodged somewhere down the back of her throat.

Cleo was one of the most emotional dogs I ever walked. She would have made an excellent "Sad Dog" in one of those charity appeal adverts. Her eyes, wide and deep, expressed waves of unhappiness and her body, drawn down by its weight, seemed to shoulder the worries of a whole city. She was desperate, lonely, and closing the door on her heavy, melancholic face at the end of the walk was almost too much to bear.

After the first one, I dropped Jess a text message: "I think Cleo might benefit from a little bit more exercise. If we can get her to the park and even running a little I think it might really help her."

"Help in what way?" she replied.

"With her weight. And her mood."

"Her weight? What do you mean?"

"She's a little shapely."

"Yes, but only a little? I thought she might have lost a bit recently?"

"She might have done but I don't think she's quite at her target weight."

"Well what's her target weight?"

"Quite a lot less than she is now?"

Telling a client that their dog is morbidly obese or badly behaved will inevitably lead to the taking of offense. Most will flat out deny it and shirk all responsibility. A dog could be as large as a barn or as disobedient as a toddler and the owners will still declare that it is just "the breed shape" or "a thyroid problem" or "you weren't strict enough." If they are willing to acknowledge a weight issue, then it's usually your fault as the dog walker. You didn't walk the dog far enough or fast enough, regardless of the fact that an automatic cat feeder in the kitchen is dispensing an endless supply of kibble and the dog spends the majority of its time with its mouth open underneath.

Oxford Street was too far for me to go daily so I assigned Cleo to my new recruit, the reassuringly double-barreled Caroline Hamilton-Beaver, a posh, headmistressy blonde from Chelsea with hiking boots, a dog whistle, and a very no-nonsense manner.

"Fat Lab? Ha! No probs," she barked

down the phone. "Seen *so* bloody many. Owners just don't have a ruddy clue how to manage them. They're greedy buggers and need a firm hand!"

She seemed to know exactly what she was talking about on a whole host of topics, from Labrador care to messy divorces. Hers had been a bloodbath.

"I know my way around a horse," she announced, boldly, "and if you ever get divorced, I know a jolly good intermediary."

I told her I was about to get married. "Good luck," she snorted, and then offered to keep an eye on the business while I was on my honeymoon.

"You'll need someone to hold the reins and keep the pony straight, make sure everything is tickey boo. People just need to be bloody well told what to and when to do it. And dogs are a doddle compared to children of course. A child will ruin your day, whereas a dog just won't do that. Well, most of them anyway."

"Oh, do you have children?" I asked. She looked around fifty and I had already pictured the offspring at prep school somewhere, dressed in boater hats and sailor collars.

"Lord no!" she roared. "Just babysitting. Nannying. You won't catch me falling into that trap!"

Caroline had a way about her that made you feel that everything you had ever done in life had been completely wrong and she was the only one who knew how the world worked. The Kensington banker clients in particular liked her — the bossiness presumably invoked warm, milky memories of childhood nannies. Her confidence, delivered in short anecdotal bursts with loud interjecting snorts, was impressive and bewildering in equal measure and made my modest measure of self-worth feel rather sparse in comparison. It is easy to be taken in when you don't often believe in yourself.

So I said yes to the offer of honeymoon help. Not only did I feel rather steamrollered by Caroline, I couldn't think of an alternative and time was running out.

We were married in early summer just as the roses were coming out. After days of rain, the sun appeared on the morning of our wedding day, streaming through the stained-glass windows of my home village church as we arranged the flowers, leaving jewel-colored puddles on its hard stone floors. The predictable family bickering about table plans and speeches and what time the canapés might be served had all but fizzled out by lunchtime and the whiskey my mother necked at five past one as I zipped up the back of her dress was just enough to take the edge off her growing panic.

My father walked me down the aisle just after 3 p.m. My mother didn't think he deserved to but it would have been odd if he hadn't. It would have made it into an issue and I didn't want any issues, certainly not ones that were not of my making. My hands were shaking and the vicar tried to get in all the photos. We ate bangers and mash in the marquee on the lawn at home and then a DJ with long hair and a Chaz n' Dave T-shirt played cheesy pop hits while shouting "wicked!" into the microphone over and over again. Everyone got very drunk and my cousin was sick in the flower bed and then it all suddenly finished and everyone went home, apart from the one guest who we found curled up in the Porta-loo the next morning, cradling one of the bridesmaids' bouquets.

I don't remember much else. I only remember the way I felt. Nervous and excited and full of love as if my heart was being squeezed tight. Nobody remembers what order the hymns were or the color of the ties the ushers wore. Nobody remembers the odd snide comment my mother made about my father or Finlay's mother made about the "excess." I wouldn't have thought that being married would make me feel different. You don't love someone more just by becoming their spouse. But there was something there that day. For me, it was everything. It was the start of our own family.

While we were away, Caroline had made good progress, chivvying Cleo as far as Regent's Park. Sometimes they even managed to venture a little farther, down the first long line of trees and back so that Cleo could see grass and flowers and other dogs. It looked like things had started to improve, as at last the weight slowly started to budge and her mood became a little lighter.

But then she collapsed on Great Portland Street in the midday heat. Caroline heaved her into the back of a black cab with the help of some builders and took her to the vet, who promptly declared she was the "fattest dog she had ever seen" and took photos for very important scientific research. Cleo had heat stroke but, more worryingly, she also had diabetes.

I texted Jess on our return: "So sorry about Cleo. How is she?"

"She's on a diet. And insulin."

"Poor Cleo. Poor you. What a shock."

"Yes. Very scary. All my fault of course. I hadn't realized how bad it had all gotten. Sorry."

We spoke on the phone a short while later and Jess told me she had bought the cat feeder to help take the edge off the incessant guilt she felt at leaving her every day. Cleo's two loves were food and Jess and if she couldn't have Jess, at least she could have the food.

Cleo was not used to being left alone. She had always had company. Before Jess moved to London, Cleo had spent her days with Jess's mother and her dog, an elderly collie called Burt, who lived in a neighboring street down by the coast. But then Jess's mother died unexpectedly, followed shortly by Burt, who had pined so badly for his owner that he was dead within three weeks. The survivors headed to London, bruised and grieving, to the most central point they could find, and hoped that urban life would drown out the sorrow and start to heal them.

But rather than distracting them and keeping them busy, living on Oxford Street had only seemed to make matters worse. It was a loud, incessant reminder of their old, perfect life and of how much had changed.

"We'll be all right," Jess said at the end of the call. "Eventually. We're still a family. The two of us."

I had no doubts. Being a twosome can be the best thing in the world.

Aside from the Cleo incident, the business had run smoothly in my absence. But stepping back from it all, even for my own wedding, was harder than I imagined. It wasn't that I thought someone else couldn't manage it — more that I wasn't used to not doing it all myself. To not working. Not checking emails. Sitting on a beach and drinking rum punch with my new husband isn't exactly taxing — unsurprisingly, it was lovely — but it also felt strange, uncomfortable almost, as if I had left an oven on somewhere.

There was a walker who didn't turn up and a client who moaned about her dog's water bowl not being full enough but that was standard, everyday stuff. Caroline knew her way around a dog-walking company it seemed, as well as horses and divorces. But for all her confidence and double-barreled snortiness, it wasn't long after we returned from honeymoon that a wealthy American client called to complain about her.

"Caroline? Caroline . . . Hamilton-

Badger?" It was Beaver but I don't think she noticed. I was surprised she was calling about Caroline because her dogs, a pair of ditsy Dalmatians who lived in the very smart mansion-block corner of Chelsea, just a step back from the Thames, were walked by someone else.

"Yes, Caroline. Caroline with the names. She works for you, doesn't she? I want her fired. And I want her fee back."

It transpired that Caroline had done some dog-sitting for the Dalmatians over a long weekend — a job she had set up by herself through having access to all the client details when I was away. She had contacted them, one by one, and had offered her services at a cut-down price. The canny American was the only one who had taken up her offer, booking her in for three nights while she was abroad. But Caroline had then gotten very drunk. So drunk that she had passed out half-naked on the American's sofa and let half a bottle of merlot seep into the silk upholstery. She had left the windows open and Guns N' Roses on full blast and by two in the morning the Dalmatians' patience had worn a little thin. They barked continuously until the police arrived sometime before dawn, ramming the front door down and taking both human

149

and canine residents into custody. Another thing Caroline knew her way around was a wine bottle. She was an alcoholic.

"I'm very sorry but I don't think I can get you your money back," I said, "as it wasn't actually a job done through me. But I can certainly pass on her contact details though, if for some reason you don't have them?"

She had them of course but sadly failed to extract any dry cleaning or door replacement damages, not to mention that any financial recompense wouldn't have helped to ease the tensions with the neighbors, none of whom had signed up to listen to "Welcome to the Jungle" at volume 11 on a Sunday night and were somewhat tetchy about the whole thing.

I eventually got hold of Caroline. Telling a walker they have been badly behaved and you have to fire them will inevitably lead to the taking of offense. Most will flat out deny it. A walker could be as drunk as a skunk or as sly as a fox and they will still claim it was "antibiotics" or a "misunderstanding" or "someone else's fault." This one was apparently my fault. I was a bad employer, irresponsible for going on holiday, and I shouldn't have left her all the client contact details. It was the Dalmatians' fault too. They were "irrational" and "needy" and had bad taste in music. I wished her luck in the future and she told me to "bugger off."

But there was an upside to the story. Out of the forty or so clients she contacted, only one had been disloyal and that didn't seem like a bad ratio at all. I found Cleo a new walker, one who had a very simple surname and an average level of confidence. When everything is said and done, double-barrel surnames and knowing about horses don't mean very much in the world of dog walking, or any world for that matter. Not if that's all there is. Anyway, Cleo's diet and the insulin were working wonders and she finally had a little pep.

I had been building up the American client base for a while. U.S. dog owners did short stints working in the City with the occasional long-term relocation and, despite the Dalmatian incident, I had managed to accrue some positive word of mouth among this expat community. They liked to bring their dogs with them, shipped over in cargo from New York or Los Angeles or Chicago and installed in their fancy serviced apartments with furniture that was definitely not designed for molting golden retrievers.

The American clients were generally smiley and appreciative at first. They'd tell me that I was wonderful. They'd say "amazing" and "awesome" in response to sentences that from a Brit would call for an "OK" at most. They would occasionally call me names like "sweetheart" or say you are "the bestest." But beneath the gloss and the perfect dentistry and everything being super brilliant, Americans have a steely, uncompromising need for customer service perfection. They expect it, they demand it, and if you can't deliver, if you can't perform, they become confused and disoriented before eventually sulking or sending passive-aggressive emails.

It was never as simple as "please take my dog out for a walk." There were feeding requirements and allergies to ingredients you have never heard of and regular shampooing sessions. Coats for hot weather and coats for cold weather, checks on paw cleanliness, ear hygiene, and teeth that need brushing with chicken-flavored toothpaste. These dogs had spent most of their youth in strict obedience classes and dog summer school and were so accustomed to commands that they hung off their owners' every movement, desperate for the next instruction so they simply knew what to do with themselves.

Having only seen dusty, bald dog runs, dogs that move from New York City get a bit giddy when faced with the wonderful wide-open spaces of London's many parks and tend to either bolt toward the horizon or walk around and around in rectangles as if surrounded by an imaginary fence. A few of the ones from Los Angeles had had surgical alterations, like the Doberman who had its ears pinned back and the vizsla who had its voice box removed. I was never sure whether or not to take on these dogs.

Zeus the Rhodesian ridgeback (surgically intact) was a New Yorker originally but had spent some time in Paris and Amsterdam prior to his arrival in London, rather like an eighteenth-century gentleman on a Grand Tour. With more money spent on his education than most people shell out for their annual holiday, Zeus was impeccably well behaved and from a lineage so pedigree that it made Fabio look a little bit common. Zeus was insured for over $1 million.

"So, you're here to help us with Zeusy-boy?" said his owner, Alexis. I had gone to meet her in their enormous, slick, converted warehouse, tucked around the back of Covent Garden. "He's just the best, you'll love him. We all just love him, don't we, guys?" Some staff nodded dutifully in agreement. There were at least five in attendance, one of whom was wearing what looked like a medical uniform, complete with nurse's watch.

"Well, we've done some looking around and researching and we hear you guys are just *the* best so we know Zeus is going to be in great hands. You *are* the best, right?"

"Yes! I am the best!" However excruciating, that's the kind of thing you have to say to Americans. They like boldness.

"Great. Awesome. Great. Mandy, can you bring Zeus in please?"

Mandy, one of the staff, slunk off and Alexis shifted in her seat slightly. She was a honey-blonde, tanned, and nail-polished Californian with a face at least half her age and a mesmerizing row of polo-white teeth. She was almost perfect, the only real flaw being that you wouldn't want to leave her out in the sun for too long.

"Zeusy just arrived last night from the plane so he may be a little jaded today. If he is, I don't want you to worry about it, he can get like this sometimes. Don't take it personal. We just wait for it to pass and give him his space and it's all good. You'll see."

"Oh. Right. Where has he been?"

"He's been in the States on a training course but flew in on transfer from Amsterdam. He just loves it there. It's sort of his place, you know?"

Before I could think of a suitable response, or wonder what exactly Zeus loved about the Dutch city, from another part of the building a low, echoey howl could be heard, followed shortly by thundering gallops as what sounded like a small herd of ponies approached the room.

"That's my boy," said Alexis, standing up as a huge orange dog crashed through the doors and bounded over to his mistress, long legs flying up to the table and knocking a jug of tulips onto the floor. Mandy followed in his wake, panting.

"Sorry, Alexis, he was just so excited to see you," she said, gripping the doorframe as Zeus bounced between them, woofing loudly.

"Wow, he's big!" I said, trying not to sound too alarmed.

"He's not quite full size yet," said Alexis, as she ruffled his enormous neck and ears. "They were bred for taking down lions, y'know? Out in Africa and places. Still do, I'm sure. But this one is just a big ol' softie, aren't ya? Yes you are, you are, you are." She then began kissing his face. He licked her hungrily in return.

A lion killer. Just what you want in a dog when you live slap bang in the center of London. But then again, is there any dog really suitable for urban dwelling? The small, shivery hairless ones, the tiny terriers in Aran sweaters with weepy eyes and legs like twigs still need to go out. They still need air and light and a patch of grass to have a pee on. They still need walks.

Alexis handed me a typed schedule of exactly when she wanted Zeus to go out according to the other appointments he had with his trainer, his masseuse, and the groom. It looked far busier than my diary but I took it with a massive smile on my face and said, "Super. Awesome. No problem at all," because that is the kind of thing you need to say to Americans right before you head home and have a minor meltdown about how you will source an enormous, strapping dog walker with a PhD in advanced client services. Not surprisingly there wasn't anyone who really fit that description so I sent along Gabriella, a petite, soft-spoken Brazilian girl who had experience with Chihuahuas and seemed excited to be going to Covent Garden. If all else failed, I thought she might be able to ride Zeus to the park.

That summer had seemed to go on and on. The weather had stayed fine for most of it, days and days of light and warm yellow sunshine, lolling on the grass in the park, lolling in bed, long lazy weekends, and endless bottles of wine. We worked long hours too; Finlay was promoted to a new job in cancer research and I was busy as I had ever been with the business. It finally felt like hard work was paying off, a realization so deeply satisfying that it occasionally trumped all the other good things — being a newlywed, being in love, being a team. We somehow managed to allow ourselves a whole season of feeling good about almost everything, enjoying life without questioning or doubting it or wondering what lay ahead. We were exactly where we needed to be. At least until it all changed again.

Little did we know that the big, beautiful bubble that the Americans lived in was about to go pop. It burst on all of us, ripping through the foundations and crumbling our old lives into dust. We were in Barcelona for a friend's wedding when Lehman's collapsed. "It's bad," everyone said, without really explaining why. "It's the banks. The mortgages. Subprime." We read the papers, trying to make sense of it all, but only got lost in terminology we didn't understand and the back-and-forth of blame. We watched the news but everyone was either angry or sad or confused and we realized we were only watching it to hear someone say everything would be all right. They didn't, but we concluded that it couldn't be that awful and tried to carry on as before, hoping that everything would all just blow over and we could all talk about something else. But then the emails started to come in.

I'd imagined a recession to be a slow-moving creature, dragging itself painfully along the ground for months and years, secreting tiny morsels of misery in its wake until it eventually died of exhaustion or crossed a finishing line. But the effect of this crash on my business was instantaneous and brutal.

A client from New York who was due to move to Notting Hill emailed almost immediately to say that she was no longer coming due to her job being "paused." A lady called to ask if she could delay her weekend dog sitting as her husband had just been made redundant from Lehman's and a gourmet tour of Venice didn't feel quite so palatable anymore. Almost everyone wanted to put their walks on hold. Apart from the lawyers and the doctors, most people feared for their jobs. The cull began, slowly at first but then picking up speed as we limped toward the end of the year, with redundancies handed out like Christmas cards and contracts failing to be renewed. Then the Americans started to head back home, their dogs repacked into cargo and shipped back to their dusty dog runs.

I should really have guessed that Zeus and his family would remain unscathed. Dogs that tour Europe and live in houses with staff don't tend to find recessions overly trying. Alexis called in early December to see if someone could walk Zeus over Christmas as she and her husband would be in Barbados.

"I hope you haven't been too affected by what's been going on," I said. "It's so worrying, isn't it?"

"What is? What's happened?" she replied, startled.

"The crash. The recession, the banks . . ." I trailed off, hoping she would pick up from where I was going.

"Oh, that," she said, cheerfully. "Geez, you gave me a real fright then. I thought you were going to say something terrible had just happened!"

Fortunately, Gabriella was available and was as reliable and efficient as Zeus was disciplined so as we headed into the Christmas season my only concern was whether or not I would be able to offer her — or any other walker — work from the new year. There was barely a handful of clients left and, while the business's annual festive closure was to be a welcome stopgap, I knew I couldn't put off making some fairly crucial decisions forever.

The call came just as I had started to wrap presents. It was three days before Christmas but I could tell it wasn't going to be a festive conversation from the outset as the very first sound I heard was of Gabriella wailing.

"He's gone, he's gone. He's disappeared into the crowds. Completely gone!"

"What? Who? ZEUS?"

"Yes, Zeus, he ran off. Bye-bye, Zeus."

"What? Where? What happened?"

"He just disappeared. He was there. And now he's not there. There and then not there. Gone! Bye-bye."

They had been walking in Lincoln's Inn Fields, a park Zeus was very familiar with, when he suddenly just bolted and disappeared into the streets. He was so quick that Gabriella hadn't even seen exactly in which direction he had gone. She presumed it must have been toward home so that's where she headed, only to find the house completely empty, the remaining staff having all headed out to the pub.

"Go back to the park," I told her as calmly as I could. "I'll come and help. We have to find him. He's very expensive."

Images of Zeus being bundled into the

back of a van by balaclava-clad dognappers swam around my head as I remembered Alexis telling me how very, very pedigree he was. Losing dogs due to a recession is one thing but simply *losing* them is a whole other matter, even if they were insured with Lloyd's of London. I called Finlay and asked if he could help. He was at an office mulled wine and mince pie event so he readily agreed.

There were about five of us looking in the end, squeezing down streets thronged with Christmas shoppers, down the sides of large office buildings, and around the back of restaurants. A policeman said he thought he'd seen a large dog with a couple of tipsy-looking women outside the pub and one man thought he might have gone down the tube but in the end Zeus was found hanging out in a clothes shop, five minutes from home, snoozing behind the till and utterly oblivious to the chaos he had caused. He'd just wandered in apparently, had a little browse, and then decided it might be time for a nap. Alexis would have been horrified. It was a Fat Face clothing store.

"Maybe he just wanted to go shopping?" said Gabriella, matter-of-factly. She had eventually calmed down after a very large gin. "Covent Garden is very good for shop-

162

ping." It was more likely that he was looking for a mate or his owners, I thought, or perhaps Father Christmas to ask for a more normal dog life. Either way, I doubted we would ever be trusted to walk him again.

Finlay and I sat in the pub until closing time. They kept playing *Cliff at Christmas* and I could feel my festive spirit sink with every single swig. There wasn't much to celebrate.

"Do you think I am a bit like Zeus?" I asked. "Running around, a bit lost, out of my depth, needing more training, or even less training, just needing to be a bit less *shit*?"

"God, no," he replied. "You're not worth nearly as much." He smiled and put his arm around me.

"But I am a bit shit, aren't I? I have let you down. I've let everyone down, fucked it all up. We just got married and my business has gone tits up, I haven't got a job, and I can't even look after the dogs we have left. One just nearly got a job in a bloody clothes shop and he was the well-trained one! They are all just going to run away, back to their homes and never come out again, or they're going to get as far away as they can, to escape, to run to the fields and the hills and I for one can't really blame them!"

163

I was a little tipsy. It had been a long, disappointing week. The day before I had drafted an email to the remaining clients and told them the business would be folding. It was the recession, I said, the banks, subprime. Two-thirds of the clients had left since September and the rest had cut down their walks. Zeus would follow soon after. The Covent Garden shopping expedition had exposed some "minor flaws in his education" and he would be spending most of the next year back in training.

I couldn't bear the thought of letting anyone down, of letting a dog down, but the miserable daily tide of recession facts and figures, the job losses, the cuts, the sheer size and scope of it all made closing down seem not only inevitable but somewhat easier to accept. All you ever heard being discussed was budgeting and austerity and belt tightening. If anything was going to be erased from the family outgoings, it would be the walks, not to mention the recently redundant, all of whom would now be walking their own dogs. I would simply have to get another job, a new career. My mother had already kindly sent me a brochure for secretarial college with a perkylooking woman dressed in a suit on the front cover. She had drawn an arrow toward the woman's face and written "YOU" next to it.

But there was something that stopped me sending the email. Something was making me cling on, even when it made no sense to do so. Letting go was so much harder than I thought it would be. The business was a part of me now and I couldn't give it up.

"Perhaps I am not even a dog person after all," I continued as Finlay patiently listened. The pub was clearing out and everyone was heading home.

"Perhaps I am not a businessperson for that matter. Or any kind of person. I should have just listened to everyone and become one of those marketing women, or some sort of caterer. A secretary! That would make everyone happy, wouldn't it? If I was a secretary?"

"I think you would be a very bad secretary," he said rather bluntly.

"But mothers are always right, aren't they? Even when they're *wrong* they are always somehow right, their whole purpose in life, their single fucking objective is to tell their daughters, 'I told you so.' I was right, you were wrong; why did you *ever* think you could do something different, something out of the ordinary, something different from me? Maybe I should just retrain to be a plumber or something. Something useful. Something skilled. An electrician perhaps? People will still need electricity in a recession, won't they?"

"They'll still need *you*. Maybe not right now, maybe not next week, but one day very soon when the rain is coming down and their dog has crapped on the rug, they are going to need you again. And not just anyone, but *you*. Because you are good at it. You're really good."

We sat silently for a while, our drinks now empty. The barman cleared his throat. He wanted to go home.

"I think we should get a dog," Finlay said eventually.

And that was how we got Mabel.

MABEL, PART ONE

JACK RUSSELL, THREE MONTHS, WANDSWORTH
FEBRUARY 2009
NUMBER OF DOGS WALKED: 7

It wasn't that Finlay *disliked* Mabel. It was more that he wasn't prepared for all that having a dog entailed. The hypothetical dog, the one Finlay suggested we get, was entirely different from the *actual* dog we did get. Anyone can easily get on board with a hypothetical dog. It doesn't repeatedly poo on the bath mat or eat your cushions or cry when the lights are turned out. It doesn't shed multiple white hairs into the ether — hairs that inexplicably make their way into your cereal or knit themselves so ferociously into the car upholstery that highly skilled valets from Poland are left pained and sweating after tackling only one seat. The hypothetical dog does not require you to turn the other way when it has a pee or ask for a snack at three in the morning. The hypothetical dog is one you think will solve a problem and cheer up your wife, while the actual dog just creates a whole host of other ones.

It wasn't that he disliked Mabel. How can anyone dislike a puppy? Everyone likes puppies, even really awful people. And she was a very, very good puppy. One of the best. A Jack Russell made of soft, stumbling paws, crisp white fur, and a dappled piglet-pink tummy. She had a black teardrop spot on her back and neat brown ears that fell in perfect triangles above her eyes and she smelled rather curiously like a tin of buttery biscuits. Her head liked to rest slightly to the right as if she might be in the thick of solving a murder and when she napped she would curl so tightly into a ball that you might have mistaken her for a tea cozy.

So, yes, it wasn't that Finlay disliked Mabel. It was more that he disliked the responsibility, the constancy, the unfathomable thirteen-to-sixteen-year tenure. Being tethered to something, however loose that tie may be, had made him extremely grumpy. He wasn't ready to be depended upon, not by something so young and helpless. Marriage hadn't fazed him in the slightest, nor had the mortgage, the pension, or the recent foray into cod liver oil capsules, but for Finlay, the addition of a small, incontinent animal had tipped him over the edge into the dark depths of serious adulthood. Having a dog had made him realize that carefree youth was now behind him. This was now the age of commitment.

"I'm not walking her," he would say, sternly.

"That's fine."

"She will be *your* dog."

"Yes, yes, I know."

"*You* wanted her remember, not me."

"Yes, yes."

"*Your* dog. Not my dog."

"My dog that *you* suggested."

"Yes, I did suggest it. But for you. For *you,* not for me. I don't like dogs."

"Right."

He then might google things like "Help! I got a dog by mistake," or "will my wife love my dog more than me?" or "how long do Jack Russells really live for?" although he never quite found the answers he was looking for.

"Bloody hell, there's a Jack Russell in Wales who lived to twenty-three!" he announced one day, utterly horrified. "Twenty-fucking-three? I'll probably be dead by then!"

Once the decision had been made, it all slotted into place with such serendipity that it was hard not to imagine that Fate herself had got out of bed and done a good day's work. A dog was already waiting, at the right time and in the right place, the last of a litter born to a notable Jack Russell in Shropshire, five minutes from my mother. Previous litters had been snapped up by various friends of hers, who loved to boast about their superlative temperament.

"She won't have any more litters," my mother said down the phone as I pretended to be mulling it over. "I can't emphasize that enough. This is your very last chance."

"I thought you wanted me to get a job?" I said. "A proper job. As a secretary."

"Well, yes, yes, but I am sure you will manage. Finlay must be after a dog, isn't he? It is about the right time."

This was apparently the time in your life where you should probably acquire a dog, alongside a mortgage, pension, and marriage certificate, especially if it was a dog with county cachet. It was the natural order of things. The timeline. Damn the logistics, the recession, and the geography, people just had dogs as far as my mother was concerned, particularly men. Men had dogs, usually large sporty ones, although terriers were permitted as they had spirit. Men needed dogs to walk up hills with so they could ruminate on problems and have someone to open up to. They needed to be able to train a dog so that when it came on command in front of their friends, the man could feel a deep sense of pride and accomplishment. They needed a dog so that they could say, "I'll just take Spit out for his business," when what they really wanted was a pint, an illegal cigarette, or ten minutes' peace. Men needed to be able to do these things because in my mother's world, men were still king and women were still secretaries.

"He's doing this for me," I replied, the full weight of the gesture hitting me hard. He did it for me so that I wouldn't lose hope. He did it for me because he saw, far clearer than I could, that the business might just be OK. He gave me a reason to keep going. "Finlay doesn't really like dogs."

"He doesn't *what?*"

"He doesn't like dogs. Not really. Not yet."

"What sort of chap doesn't like dogs?"

"Well, I should think quite a lot of them! My *chap* in fact."

There was a pause as this news sunk in.

"Maybe you shouldn't have one, then," she said, sulkily. "Although I have put your name down now and it would mean letting them down. Very badly." She couldn't bear to let people down. Not those sort of people, anyway.

"I want a dog, you know I do, it's just the work thing. The business is in a tricky place. I am going to have to work very hard."

She sighed but thought better of stating the obvious. "This is the very last litter. The *very* last."

However much you want to forge your own path, however much you want to rebel, it's hard to fight against the matriarch's wishes *all* the time. Plus, this was a very easy one to go along with. I called her back an hour later and said yes.

In my mind, Mabel's role would be to help me with the business. Spur me on. She would earn back the huge amount of trust and love and sheer optimism placed on her impending residence with us by helping me get the business back on track. The winter had been a predictably bleak and barren period. Just as dog walking was shedding its last few detractors, it was consigned back into the frivolous and unnecessary bin. We had gritted our teeth through the initial stages of shock and panic, the painful streamlining and the stringent cutbacks, always braced for more catastrophe, more redundancies, more collapse. The email I had written to my remaining clients re-mained in my draft folder, for now. Disillusioned and mistrustful, the country now shuffled quietly through the cold, frugal months, hunkering down and hoping that it would all soon be over.

The first few weeks of the year had been freezing cold and torturously slow. We had acquired just one or two new American clients who had flown in for the mop-up job. Some of the old ones had stuck with it, including the likes of Stanley and Fabio, but the business was limping along, lugging the promise of what it might have been behind it through the gray sleet and snow. I woke up every morning wondering if this would be the day when I would finally pull the plug, the day when the silence of the phone and the stillness on the screen would become too much and I would go crawling back to a normal job.

Going back to an office was out of the question, not just because the job market had imploded but because it would feel like being sent back inside — an airless, desk-bound imprisonment where I would be held captive by filing cabinets and jammed printers and badly made tea and all those things that I had so desperately wanted to get away from. The only thing to do was to cling on until things picked up or I was unexpectedly offered an amazing new career doing something so totally brilliant and completely fascinating that I couldn't possibly understand why I hadn't thought of it before.

But just as winter started to pack itself away, London began to slowly pick itself up once more. The headlines started to feel a little more palatable, the newsreaders a little less gloomy, and the City's inhabitants began to tentatively emerge from their belt-tightening hibernation to face the world again. They realized that some things still needed money to be spent on them: broken boilers and flat tires and the tap that won't stop dripping. And that there were other things that it felt good to spend money on, little things that helped to cheer us up and give us a little hope: red lipstick and bars of milk chocolate, pink nail varnish and mini skirts, baking and knitting and repairing, something homemade, something to warm our stomachs, and something to nourish the soul.

There are a few things in life that are worse than a sad-looking dog but not many that are better than a happy one. To see your dog bounding blissfully through the park is to come close to understanding what life is all about. We had been through turmoil and upheaval, a national crisis that rocked our confidence and made us question our priorities, but once all that dust had settled, once we remembered who we were again, we saw our dogs standing there, steady, dependable, their breath still awful and their farts just as bad, and we knew that, when all was said and done, our dogs make us happy. *Really* happy. Looking after them and loving them and giving them a rub on the tummy makes us feel good and so we would continue to spend our hard-earned money on walks and treats and a new tweed coat because they are a symbol of everything that is wholesome and right and true in the world: constancy, loyalty, love. We all needed reminding of that.

Just as the sun started to warm and the daffodils pushed through, Mabel arrived.

"Funny things happen in recessions," said my mother as she dropped her off in an old Pampers box lined with newspaper. She had gotten divorced during the last one. "Unexpected, wonderful things that turn out better than anyone could have predicted."

I looked down into the box and thought she might be right, *again.*

Dogs seemed to arrive in boxes, especially Jack Russells. It's funny how we root around in the past, digging up the old bones of memories to bring with us as we go. When we were young, my brother and I were given a Jack Russell in a baked beans box who we called Heinz. When he was killed on the road shortly after his first birthday, we were promptly given another one called Heinz as we needed to believe that tragedies like that don't really happen and if we closed our eyes tight enough, everything would be back to normal. But then the new Heinz was run over a short time later and we never got another Jack Russell. Until now. She was curled up tightly, impossibly small and impossibly mine. I was eight again and felt like this was the start of the most exciting adventure.

I fell in love instantly, the kind of love that just crashes straight in, elbowing everything and everyone else out until there isn't a single space left. In those first few weeks of Mabel, with the novelty as fresh as her sparkling white fur, I could have been abandoned, divorced, or widowed and would have barely mustered a frown. Poor Finlay, his wife was there one minute and the next she just suddenly disappeared into a thick puddle of saccharine mush, saying things like "cooocheeeee," and "pooochy-pooochypooooochy," and "moooomoo-mooooo" and all other sorts of incoherent nonsense. The intoxicating giddiness of owning your first puppy was as potent and fervid as any narcotic, and just as addictive. When something so small and so adorable needs you so wholeheartedly, it's hard not to feel utterly undone. I was completely smitten.

There will be no other time when you will find puddles of urine charming or think of chewed-up cushions as "just one of those things." For no other reason would it feel rewarding to stand in the park multiple times a day in all weather, waiting for your dog to do a poo so you can reward them with treats and tell them how exceptionally clever they are for not doing it inside. It's a reminder that deeper reserves of tolerance, patience, and humor are not that far from the surface, and that it only takes something small and vulnerable to shake the best bits out of us again.

The house-training process, while consuming and repetitive, did allow me plenty of opportunity to show off Mabel to the many dog owners, pram pushers, and fitness enthusiasts who frequented Wandsworth Park. If you ever need to make friends in a hurry, then the best course of action is the use of a puppy. They instantly attract people, eliciting smiles and gentle conversation from even the most ill-tempered of human beings. It is in fact one of the few instant litmus tests we have on the state of humanity — if you cannot summon up even a minuscule morsel of joy on seeing a puppy, then you might want to rethink your entire personality.

Our first few outings, with Mabel at her most cautious and inquisitive, fortunately proved that most people had not been completely hardened by life, recession and all. A steady procession of admirers showed up every time we ventured into the park, scooters discarded on the grass by eager children clamoring for a cuddle and striped businessmen on their way to work cheerfully risking trouser creases for a short scratch of those soft brown ears.

"A puppy, a puppy!" squealed a middle-aged woman with a border terrier. She clapped her hands in childlike excitement while Mabel indulged her by rolling onto her back and proffering her soft tummy for a rub. "She's completely delicious, isn't she, Rufus?"

Rufus was unimpressed and sat on his bottom waiting for the fuss to be over. He was gray around the muzzle and knew that his best years were behind him.

"Poor old Rufus was nowhere *near* as cute as this, were you, Rufus? No he wasn't, he wasn't, he wasn't, not as cute as you, was he? No he wasn't, he wasn't!"

In addition to the daily doses of puppy adoration, there was also plenty of opportunity to observe the unique social hierarchies of the park. As a fully legitimate dog owner, you are now free to join a number of exclusive "park groups," a variety of which can be found at your local green space. Dog owners, the largest subsection of the park groups, assemble themselves into smaller groups according to sex, age, wealth, and, occasionally, breed of dog.

The Labrador owners often stick together, usually under the misapprehension that they all have a similar amount in the bank or have been to the same schools. The rescue-dog owners like to think they are morally superior, as do the French bulldog owners, who try to outwit each other with their hilarious choice of dog berets and Gallic names — Pierre, Baguette, and Bisou being typical of this oeuvre. In our local park, there was also a small group of older divorcées with a collection of petite fluffy dogs, the type that all end in "oodle," and a very small subgroup of the retired, who often looked a little bewildered at how busy the park was or how fast everybody was walking.

Mum dog owners come in two subcategories — those who wear Lycra and those who don't. The latter usually have a bored-looking spaniel attached to the buggy, while the former always move at too fast a pace, a panting dog following in their wake. "Mums" was the largest of the park groups and the most consistent, meeting most weekdays to moan about their kids or their husbands, sharing tales of sick bugs and homework and last night's telly.

The safest course of action was not to pledge allegiance to any one group but to hover vaguely between all of them, therefore having the opportunity to collect plenty of park gossip without actually being the subject of any of it.

But there was also work to be done and little time to hang around now that Londoners were finally peeking over the recession parapet. As well as a comprehensive leafleting tour of most of central London's veterinary clinics, I planned to flood Wandsworth Park with flyers advertising our services. Starting local seemed like the best idea.

London's Number One
Dog-Walking Agency
(founded by GENUINE dog owner).
Local Walks. Affordable Prices.
"It's not your dog's fault
that the banks crashed!"

Mabel was to play a key role. She was to be a mascot, a muse, a motivator. A physical sign of legitimacy and wisdom. With a Jack Russell puppy at my side, members of all park groups would take my flyers and look at them pleasantly rather than scowling and then putting them in the bin. Veterinary receptionists would now smile at me as I came through the door. Dog walkers would marvel at my hands-on experience and clients would roar with laughter as I shared amusing puppy anecdotes while simultaneously proffering snippets of information from my limitless canine knowledge. Most importantly of all, I could tell them all I was a genuine, *bona fide* dog owner without it all being a big, fat, furry lie.

I was one of them now. Well, sort of. They were still "them," the clients, and I was still "us," me, the business, but at least we were now in the same Venn diagram, "dog ownership" in the middle bit, the consolidator.

It wasn't long after that the phone started to ring again. The first call was from a new mum with a tiny, cream-colored Chihuahua called Rabbit who lived on the Putney side of the park and was finding the challenges of juggling motherhood and dog ownership increasingly difficult. Having been the center of attention for at least four years, Rabbit was also finding it challenging. He had not adjusted to the new arrival and spent most of his days sulking in his basket or aggressively chewing baby toys that had been dropped onto the floor.

"I am afraid Rabbit has been a bit tricky recently," she sighed, rubbing her forehead. I had popped over to meet her and to give my verdict on the Chihuhua. "He hasn't warmed to his new sister as much as we would have liked. We have tried everything. Buying him more toys, more treats, a new collar . . . we even tried buying him his own baby toys, rattles and all sorts of teddies, but he only seems to want the baby's. He's been through at least ten this week."

Despite the pressing need for a new client, I found myself siding with Rabbit on the matter, as being in the giddy first flush of dog ownership, I couldn't really understand why she'd even bothered to have a baby. She seemed to have brought the whole situation on herself.

"I'm sorry. How awful," I sympathized, which seemed to do the trick. "As a dog owner I *fully* understand."

"Thank you. It is very upsetting," she sniveled back.

In the corner of the room next to Rabbit's basket was a small graveyard of deceased teddies, stuffing ripped from limbs and lying in cloud-like balls on the floor while chunks of brightly colored plastic animals were spat violently on his bed like trampled confetti. It was hard to imagine how such a small, fluffy dog could be quite so angry.

"We thought that if we left all the mess there, he might see it and feel bad about what he has done. Show some remorse." She held up a disintegrated stuffed cat who had been virtually decapitated. "He humped this one. It was brand new last week."

"Oh dear."

"You see, Rabbit? Look at what you have done. DO YOU NOT FEEL BAD?"

Rabbit did not feel bad. He looked as if he wanted to rip the whole world apart.

"Right, well, we will do our best to help. Perhaps making a few new park friends will be the answer? Getting out in the fresh air. Exercise!"

And so Rabbit came out with Mabel and me three times a week, his relief at being taken away from the baby and out into the park palpable. He skipped joyously through the grass, darted in and out of the bushes, and rolled on his back in the cool spring sunshine. He was also instantly taken with Mabel, not only because she was the only dog in the park whose bottom he could get remotely near, but because her puppyish, playful bouncing seemed to match his own jubilant mood. He was on day release and couldn't have been happier.

The companionship was also good for Mabel — regular socializing, learning the rules. She took Rabbit's lead on how to behave, which dogs to greet, and which to avoid. He introduced her to Squirrel Corner, a collection of firs at the southeast end of the park where squirrels liked to snack and chat. Rabbit would try to forget he was small and pretty by charging at them full pelt like a lion into a herd of gazelles, but he also taught Mabel the more successful technique of stalking up on them slowly, like a game of grandmother's footsteps.

"I think Mabel has a boyfriend," I said to Finlay after one particularly amorous walk. The dogs had spent several minutes licking each other's faces by the park gates before we dropped Rabbit home.

"What, already?" he replied.

"A Chihuahua called Rabbit."

"A Chihuahua? Is that . . . *normal*?"

"Well, size-wise it is. There's a four-year age gap but I don't think that matters."

"But that's twenty-eight human years, isn't it?"

"I don't think dogs worry about these things. They get on, that's the main thing."

I took the fact that we were even having this conversation, and others quite like it, as evidence that the tide might just be turning. After Mabel had been with us for a few months, there were definitely signs that Finlay's defenses were dropping. He no longer called her "it" or "dog" or "you." "Oh, it's *you*," he would say as he came in the door from work to find her waiting, tail wagging. "I suppose *you* want a stroke." He'd started to call her Mabel, he'd even give her the odd treat, a scratch behind the ears, and, when he thought I wasn't looking, he'd pat the spot on the sofa next to him so that she would jump up and snuggle into his leg. She had gotten to him bit by bit, day by day, managing to wear him down just like I'd hoped she would.

One weekend in early summer, I had a friend's hen do booked in and would be away overnight. I had promised to walk her before I left and as soon as I got back but in the days before I left, Mabel seemed out of sorts. She was gloomy, indifferent, ratty even, and spent most of the day moping about on the sofa like a sulky teen. I started to worry that I might not be able to go.

"I think she's ill," Finlay said. "It looks serious. Maybe you shouldn't go."

"I think she knows I am leaving," I replied.

"She senses it. Dogs know things like that."

"Don't be silly! She's clearly very, very unwell. Far too unwell to be left."

"That's exactly what's going on. Look at her! She's depressed at the thought of me leaving. Dogs are very sensitive. They get all sad before you go away and then, when you have gone, they revenge poo on your bed."

"Revenge poo?"

"To show you how upset they are."

"Well, shouldn't we be avoiding that?"

"Yes, I suppose so. You will just have to take her out a bit more. Make sure she goes outside."

"I meant by you staying here. *Not* going. So she doesn't get distressed."

But as much as I would have liked her to be lamenting my imminent departure, it turned out to be something far more rudimental. Biological. Mabel was in heat and by the time I left for the weekend, she was up off the sofa, flush with hormones, and desperate to get out and meet some men.

"I'm not sure I can do this," said a worried-looking Finlay as I headed off to catch the train. Mabel had been scratching and whining to go out all morning. "This feels very dangerous. What if something . . . *happens?*"

I stood at the door looking back at them,

186

bag and train ticket in hand, and wondered for a moment if I should go. They both looked slightly unhinged.

"You'll be fine. Just keep her on the lead."

"She's your dog, remember?"

"She's *our* dog."

"She's your dog when there's a problem. Especially if it's a 'woman's problem.' "

"Just keep her on the lead, OK?"

The unexpected thing about a bitch in heat is that they actively want to meet a mate. It is not just a case of standing your ground and fending off the advances of southwest London's virile dog population while your dog demurely hides behind your legs. Your dog is not defenseless. She is not scared. She is one hundred percent up for it and the task at hand is as fraught and challenging as any father of daughters will face.

It was a sunny Saturday morning and the park was heaving. Finlay pulled her in close but it wasn't long before noses had started to turn and various male suitors had made their interest known. Mabel was skittish and flirty, twisting around on the lead as she tried to show herself off and by the time they had completed one full circuit, a small pack of four or five determined admirers was circling around them like sharks. At the very front of this pack, the most determined and shark-like of them all, was Rabbit.

Teeny, tiny, fluffy Rabbit. He had already seen off a few much larger dogs, bearing his miniature teeth and nipping one poor Staffie on the leg who yelped rather pathetically and then ran back to his owner. Mabel was suitably impressed. She gave Rabbit a few coy turns of her head before suddenly jerking it clean out of her collar and belting off into the bushes with Rabbit in very hot pursuit. Finlay stood there shocked, collar and lead in his hand, as a small gaggle of disappointed dogs began to slink off embarrassedly.

They were tangled up in the rhododendrons, fortunately still in the figuring out how it all works stage, when Finlay found them a few moments later. He scooped Mabel up, much against her will, and marched her out of the bushes like an angry father at a school disco. Rabbit's owner caught up with them shortly after, baby strapped to her chest, having run from the other side of the park.

"Sorry, sorry," she panted. "I thought he was with me. Has he been bothering anyone?"

"My dog is in heat!" Finlay exclaimed as Mabel squirmed in his arms, desperate to get down, while Rabbit skulked out of the

188

bushes looking distinctly sheepish. "Your dog was *in there,* after her."

"Is that . . . *Mabel*?" she asked. "We know Mabel. This is Rabbit! They're walking friends. Well, he has a bit of a crush, I think. It must have been why he ran off."

"Right. Well. Hello, Rabbit. How are you? No harm done. We just don't want her to be . . . you know," he said, awkwardly. "We don't want puppies."

"It's fine. He's been snipped. Not sure he would be able to reach anyway now she's grown so much! Well, nice to meet you, Mabel's dad. Good luck."

And there it was. "Mabel's dad." The horror of it, but also the utterly unexpected but totally unmistakable feeling of pride.

The funny thing about the Rabbit incident was that it hadn't just knocked down those last stubbornly held defenses, those little remaining niggles Finlay had held about owning a dog. The overwhelming surge of protectiveness that the skirmish in the bushes had produced smashed through it all, leaving him bewildered and doubtful. Suddenly, all dogs had approval. Well, nearly all. Chihuahuas were never going to cut it but all dogs of a decent size were now wholly acceptable. These dogs could have a stroke or a pat if they came over to say hello;

their names would be inquired upon and compliments would be given to their owners on their appearance or temperament or ball-catching skills. He would understand the gratification that these compliments would propagate as he now felt it too. Even though he couldn't quite believe it himself, he understood what some of the fuss was all about.

When quizzed on his change of perspective, he would shrug casually and say it was just one of those things, like becoming a goth or giving up meat. People change their mind. They adapt. That's what life is all about. If he'd had an elk or an otter move in, he would probably have softened to them too, given enough time.

"But this is huge," I said. "A complete turnaround. People will write about this in journals. They will study you and use you as an example of how men *can* change, even on really fundamental issues."

"It's not a fundamental issue," he said. "It's a dog."

Soon after, Mabel went to the vet to get spayed. I dropped her off at ten and went home to sit by the phone. I realized quite pathetically that I desperately missed her, even in those short few hours. How quickly and effortlessly she had knitted herself into our lives, to the point that I couldn't even remember life without her and worried what might unravel if even one small thread was unpicked. I'd had a small taste of what family life might look like and I was hooked.

I collected her again at time end of the day, her stomach stitched up like a rugby ball, sore and groggy with her tongue lolling cartoon-like from the side of her mouth. She lay mournfully on the sofa, immobile and whimpering, and a huge wave of guilt and remorse washed over me.

"I've made a terrible mistake," I said to Finlay tearfully as we sat beside her, stroking her head. "She's going to hate me for this. She'll never forgive me."

"Of course she will. She's not going to remember it for a start."

"Will she be the same? We haven't changed her forever, have we? I liked her just the way she was."

"Well, she'll be less of a tart. And I guess she might have better taste in dogs."

"Thank you. I know you did all this for me. Keeping it all afloat. Keeping *me* afloat." I realized that I hadn't said this before, even though suggesting we get Mabel was the most unselfish, wonderful thing that anyone had ever done for me. We say thank you all the time for the little

191

things — for a cup of tea or a kind word — but often not for the really big things, when someone does something for you that completely changes your life. I wasn't sure I could be quite so benevolent.

"Well, it was a business decision really. Tactical. Like a very high-maintenance loan."

"Thank you. Thank you for everything."

"And I did it for Mabel too," he said, leaning in for a kiss. "We all know that if we hadn't had her, your mother would have and Mabel would be wearing some sort of tartan waistcoat by now."

STANLEY, PART FOUR

Stanley had been on strike for most of the summer. Tom had taken some time out of urban living to tend poultry on a smallholding commune near Ipswich and, reluctant to get anyone new involved, the family had tried to muddle through. When the teenagers of the house couldn't be roused, Steph had asked Sarah to do the odd walk here and there but, having finally found someone just like him, Stanley found the whole arrangement completely unacceptable and wanted everyone to know he was not at all impressed. He knew that we would buckle in the end and bring in the ham — or, better yet, a different walker. He hoped it would be Tom.

Sarah was equally unimpressed. She was now used to dogs who actively wanted to walk and along with a burgeoning career as a freelance journalist, did not have the time or patience for canine sulking.

"If he's not going to walk, Kate, then I am not going to walk. I haven't got time to be hanging around street corners with difficult dogs."

"He's just missing Tom, Sarah. It's a protest, that's all. He'll come around."

"He's snoring outside a bookmakers."

"Perhaps he just needs a bit of encouragement. Have you got any meat by any chance?"

"No, I do not have any *meat*. I don't just randomly carry meat around with me. What I have is a deadline and I need to get on."

But by mid-September, an unfortunate incident involving a chicken over in East Anglia meant that Tom was suddenly back in town and reunited with Stanley by the first day of autumn.

"Ipswich is a dump," he declared. "And chickens have *major* issues."

Life on the commune had turned somewhat sour after Tom had tried to introduce a meditation program to the chicken coop in an attempt to procure more eggs. It had sadly backfired when the majority of the chickens escaped in fear and he began to realize that he was actually far more suited to dogs than poultry. He'd also missed Stanley and, as they settled back into their old routine of fish and chips and leisurely

194

walks in Battersea Park, in this very small pocket of south London, order was once again restored.

Tom was also assigned a pair of French bulldogs who lived around the back of Harrods, a white-stuccoed and box-hedged enclave of unimaginable wealth. The owners were Russian, an oligarch's ex-wife and her various children, staff, and security guards. Having recently been through a mega divorce and become overwhelmingly rich, she not only refurbished her entire six-story home but also bought the property next door, the one next door to that, and the mews house behind, and was about to knock it all through to make a family home the size of Kent. The press said she craved privacy and seclusion but it seemed far more likely that she wanted to spend as much of her ex's money as possible.

The dogs were mottled black, plump as piglets, and incredibly lazy. They ate sardines and cubed cheddar out of crystal dog bowls and spent their days lazing about on purple velvet beds in a corner of the library. They had been promised their own room once the renovations were complete, although they could probably have had a whole wing and not been seen from one week to the next. The Russians wanted an immediate start and with nobody else available to do it, I reminded myself how happy Stanley was and tried to set aside any concerns. Tom had assured me that he wouldn't tip up in any French or Russian outfits, discuss politics, or try to sell anyone a hair necklace. I hadn't met many Russians but I had seen the security guards and I suspected they wouldn't be overly keen on being sold things, or being talked to at all, for that matter.

I had asked Tom if he would rather just stick to south London, familiar neighborhoods and all that, but he was keen to pick up as much work as possible and while the business was still getting back on track, he had to take the work where we found it.

Plus, he said, he was learning French.

"Self-improvement, Kate. We need to keep learning, keep growing. It's the only way forward, the only way to beat them all." His stint at the commune had apparently set him back "emotionally" and he was redoubling his efforts. Memorizing the periodic table was next on the agenda.

"I don't think the dogs actually speak French, Tom. It's just their breed name. They came from Hampshire somewhere. And the owners are Russian."

"Don't let setbacks hold you back

though," he said, his voice rising. "Challenges are just opportunities wearing different hats. Knowledge is power, Kate, knowledge is power."

With the recession bounding toward its first birthday, this was exactly the type of client we needed — ridiculously rich, bulletproof from adversity, and cocooned in glorious luxury. They were foreigners mainly, buying up entire sections of streets so they didn't have the indignity of having to mix with their neighbors or speak to the natives. Belgravia was their preferred locale, strolling distance from diamonds and caviar and a selection of mink coats, and only a short chauffeur-driven ride to the Russian Orthodox church in Knightsbridge where they could thank God and the Motherland for all their good fortune.

Having spotted one or two other sleek-looking hounds in the neighborhood, I imagined I was about to hit the dog-walking jackpot and that Finlay and I would be in the inner circle by Christmas, sipping vodka and eating blinis with a snoring French bulldog on each lap as choirs from Oxbridge took requests for carols. We were quite broke at the time. Less broke than we had been but still feeling the pinch at the end of every month. You realize how large the broke scale is and how far down you are on it when people are buying up Knightsbridge mews houses just for some extra storage space. Dog by dog, things were getting better but a few oligarchs here and there would have helped things along nicely.

"So basically, no talking to anyone, except the dogs, who don't speak French but might know some Russian," Tom said down the phone as he prepared to do the first walk. "No selling, no chat, no hats."

"No berets, no KGB costumes, but you can tell them how great we are," I replied. "They might tell all their rich friends."

"I do that anyway," he replied. "Of course we're great. We love dogs!"

Just like Tom, Panic was also back, popping in and out like an annoying neighbor. Panic wanted to remind me that though I had a dog and a husband and a business that might just pull through, it wasn't done with me yet. It didn't come when the banks collapsed and the business faltered. It didn't come when I was trying to decide whether I could carry on, when I tearfully watched the clients drop off one by one. It waited until things were calmer, till there was a lull, when my guard was down.

I should have really seen it this time, coming off the back of the summer months and tapping into that melancholic Sunday evening, back-to-school feeling that September often brings. There had also been a few domestic rows, nothing awful, just bickering really, followed by a bit of sulking. We were over a year into married life and the top, shiny layer had rubbed off a little bit, just enough to see what was underneath: routine, a regular rotation of seven to ten evening meals, and small wars over the washing up. We were settled, happy, but as you shift into the overly familiar there is a period of adjustment, uncertainty even, as the questions start to come again — were we where we should be, did we make enough money, do enough things, see enough people, would we ever leave London, and when should we have kids?

Perhaps this is where it all starts, I thought, the downhill tumble into acrimony, bitterness, and eventually estrangement. Did it start with a squabble over taking a bin out and then build from there, each argument stacking one on top of the other until there is an impassable wall between you? Was that what happened with my parents? I never really knew the full details as nobody ever wanted to talk about it. You didn't talk about those sort of things, according to my mother, even to your own children, as it was far too upsetting and blame might be unfairly apportioned — except for the fact that it was all his fault and he had slept with a Swedish au pair, among other issues.

Among this uncertainty, Panic crept in. It can squeeze in through the tiniest of gaps, gaps you didn't even know were there, the ones right in the corner that seem far too small for anything but light to get in. But then there it is, already established and happily breeding and you berate yourself, once again, for having been so foolish as to have not done something about those cracks, to have found them and sealed them all up once and for all.

The business was much harder to run when Panic was in residence as I doubted every decision, every email, every word. The day-to-day challenges were far harder to navigate with Panic on my shoulder, whispering in my ear that I was doing it all wrong, that everything was a mistake and that I had let everyone down. Panic seemed to smother any sense of instinct or intuition, it blurred judgments and rearranged facts so that even simple dilemmas became impossible to solve.

I started to wonder again what on earth I

was doing and why I was doing it, an uncertainty made far more potent by the fact that my mother had temporarily stopped asking when I was going to get a new job. She had a new bridge foursome and a new boyfriend and so was inevitably distracted. She didn't call as much to see how badly it was all going or ask if I had considered a career in nannying or teaching. For me, it was so much easier to feel self-assured and determined when I had an opposition, particularly a maternal one. Nothing was more invigorating, more inspiring, or more fulfilling, than trying to prove her wrong.

But there is no guide for any of it, no page at the back of the textbook with the answers all written out, no one of vast experience who you can call upon to help you out. There is also the fact that humans and dogs don't often follow predictable patterns. They like to keep you on your toes, even the good ones.

Stanley's Steph and her husband, Pete, were going on holiday. The kids were all safely back at university and they were heading off to Greece, just the two of them.

"It's so important to do things on your

own, don't you think?" she said down the phone.

"Is it? What sort of things?"

"Well, we've been married for over twenty years and going away together is the one thing we do every single year. Sometimes a week, sometimes just a weekend, just as long as there are no kids. Not that you need to be worrying about all that at your age. Free as a bird, you can just take off at the drop of a hat!"

"We have a dog now," I said. "Not quite so free anymore."

"Gosh, don't let that stop you," she continued. "Once little ones arrive everything becomes a lot harder to organize. Plus, you really don't want to get on a plane with them if you can help it, so get all that foreign sun now, while you can."

We had a week in North Wales booked for the end of the month. There was nothing sunny or foreign about it, except perhaps that most people spoke Welsh.

"So you talked him around?"

"Sorry?"

"Getting a dog. You talked your husband into it. Well done, you. You won't regret it. Neither will he. They help to carry you along somehow."

The arrangements for Stanley were that

an elderly neighbor would be popping in to feed him twice a day with Tom coming in as usual to do the walks. Being an old home bird, Stanley would be just fine on his own the rest of the time.

Everything started out all right; the neighbor remembered to feed Stanley and Tom was on time but after a couple of days, things started to unravel.

"Stanley's not happy," said the first email from Tom. "He's lonely. I'm staying longer. Will keep you posted."

"Stanley miserable," came the second. "Lonely. Sad. Not sure what to do???"

"I am sure he's fine," I replied. "You know what he's like. He probably just wants to nap."

I'd never met a dog more autonomous than Stanley. That was what was so intriguing about him — his committed undoginess. He was the only dog who seemed happier when left alone. Even his very select group of humans were too much sometimes now that he was approaching his senior years. But when the elderly neighbor arrived the next day, she found the house empty and a note left on the kitchen table. Tom had already taken the situation into his own hands:

TAKEN THE DOG.

IF YOU WANT HIM BACK,
YOU NEED TO DO WHAT I SAY.
To be fair to the neighbor, she did try to remain calm for a moment or two, calling Tom and leaving a polite message on his voice mail asking whether Stanley might be back for his tea. However, she then dived into full-throttle panic mode, calling the police, the fire brigade, the RSPCA, the BBC, Battersea Dog's Home, and finally Steph and Pete in Greece, screaming down the phone, "STANLEY HAS BEEN KID-NAPPED!" It wasn't long after this that they called to tell me.

Knowing Tom to have a flair for the dramatic, I immediately pictured him teetering on a rooftop somewhere, wired and red faced, veins bulging as he screamed into the wind about social injustice or chicken meditation while clutching a bemused-looking Stanley by the scruff of the neck. He was in fact at his dad's, calmly eating a takeaway and watching telly with Stanley snoring at his feet.

"Oh hi, Kate," he said down the phone like it was any old day of the week. "What's up?"

"Just checking on Stanley, Tom. Is he . . . OK?"

"Yeah, yeah, he's good. Tired. We had a

long walk this morning. We went down to Brockwell Park. Cor, he just loves it down there!"

"Well, the thing is, Tom, that you've caused a bit of a panic. Everyone's worried about Stanley. The police have been called."

"Fair enough."

"And the owners, of course."

"Right."

"Did you say you had . . . *demands*? In the note, I mean?"

"Well, just one really. That they look after their bloody dog!"

There was silence down the line as I tried to work out what the right thing to say was. Panic wanted me to shout, to get furiously angry, to tell Tom that he was wrong, catastrophically wrong, and that he had been far too interfering. It wanted me to tell him that he was fired and that I wouldn't be able to trust him again because you can't just go around taking dogs willy nilly when you think they might be a bit down in the dumps for goodness' sake. Panic would have loved the drama, the yelling, the fallout.

But then I thought of Stanley, alone in the dark in an empty house wondering where his family had gone and if they were coming back and I knew full well that I might well have done exactly the same. Perhaps not a year or two ago, but now that we had Mabel some of my more sensible, logical convictions had been swept clean away. I would have seen Stanley looking sad and lonely and I would have wanted to help. And then there was Tom of course, who was in many ways just like Stanley, and I wanted to help him too.

"Look Tom, I understand where you are coming from. I really do. And I love that you care for him that much. He's a brilliant, special, amazing dog. But he's not yours. You can't just take him."

"Yeah, yeah, I know."

"You'll have to take him back."

"I know, I know."

"And I will see if I can straighten this all out. I can't promise but I will try, OK?"

He paused for a moment and sighed. "I'm sorry, Kate, I really am. I know it's all wrong. That's not what people do, is it? Take dogs and cause problems. I know you have to follow the rules and do what you are told to do but that's not always right, is it? The rules aren't right, are they? And they're not made by people like you and me. They're made by people looking after themselves."

"But aren't we all on the same side, Tom? You and me, Steph and Pete. Stanley. I don't think we are the ones you want to be upset with really."

"Tell them he's on his way home, will you? Oh, and tell the neighbor that he's had his tea. Chinese tonight. Chicken chow mein, one of his favorites."

I felt sick about calling Steph. I pictured her in a taverna, draped over Pete with the sun in her hair and a glass of wine in her hand, their twenty years of marriage wrapped around them like a blanket and I couldn't bear that I might ruin it all, even for one moment, when I called to tell her that the police had turned up and the fire brigade were outside their house for half an hour while the whole street came out to see what the fuss was about. I didn't think I could possibly explain that it wasn't just Stanley who was lonely, but Tom as well.

"Oh hello, Kate, how are you? What a palaver! Is he home safe and sound?" She was calm, chirpy even.

"He's on his way and he's fine. He's happy."

"Oh good. Well, the police have been on to me. I said it was all OK and just a misunderstanding. It is, isn't it?"

"Yes, yes, I think so."

"Well, as long as he's happy, it's all fine. These things happen, don't they? No point in panicking."

No point in panicking at all. Panic has never had any point to it. I marveled at Steph's composure and chastised myself for ever getting in a flap about anything small and silly. I decided to leave it up to her to decide what to do next. I didn't want to get rid of Tom but knew that they might once the ouzo had worn off, what with having their dog kidnapped and all. I had been dropped for far less. But as soon as they returned, Steph emailed to say that they would rather keep Tom than try someone else and would he mind having Stanley the next time they went away?

Back from Greece. Feeling guilty. I underestimated Stanley and I feel terrible about it. When you realize that the person who knows your dog best is not you or anyone in your family but the person who walks him, you have to hold your hand up and say that you're wrong. Very wrong. We got used to seeing Stanley as part of the furniture, like a grumpy old man in a chair, but we realize now that even if he is quiet or solitary he still wants to be with someone. It's an important lesson to learn, isn't it, about the elderly? Well, about all of us really. Dogs included! So please say thank you to

Tom. We are very lucky to have him. And sorry. For not being better owners.

It seemed like such a sensible reaction, so wise and so measured, and yet I still read it with surprise. If only they could have all been like Steph. The ability to see the best in people, to see the best in everything, and to always be learning from your mistakes seemed like the best way to live a life. That and an annual jolly to Greece.

However, it turned out that in the world of dog walking, taking a crap in someone else's downstairs loo is a crime far worse than kidnapping, particularly when it's an oligarch's loo. After a particularly taxing walk where Tom had only managed to get the French bulldogs as far as Beauchamp Place and back on account of their staggering laziness and outright inability not to roll gleefully in their own wee, he had got caught short himself and needed the bathroom. In a house of seemingly innumerable bathrooms it's hard to know which one to choose and unfortunately for Tom, he chose the wrong one.

Hello dog people. Dog walker left very bad smell in lady's toilet today. Not nice. Lady of the house very upset. Please do

not come again. No more walks. Goodbye.

Tom was surprisingly sanguine about the
whole thing. It was the perfect "accidental
anarchy" he said, a small, silent protest
against the wealthy. Plus the journey to
Knightsbridge was taking far too long. I
reminded him we had lost one client,
however awful, and could have easily lost
another and, while he reassured me that he
would not step out of line or misjudge the
use of a client's bathroom facilities again,
he wanted to remind me that very occasionally the world can sometimes tilt toward the
common man, or even the common dog. It
was hard to disagree.

Finlay, Mabel, and I went off on our holiday
to Wales, to the beach where we went as
children — my mother, brother, and I with
the family dog and our buckets and spades
and the resolute determination to have a
normal, jolly family holiday. Out of London
and onto the sand, Finlay, Mabel, and I
were jollied along too, the change of scene
and salty air a welcome respite, and, as the
days ticked by, I felt Panic start to slowly
wash away with the tide. We walked and we
cooked and we watched Mabel racing over

the dunes and it was simple and easy and perfect and I didn't need anything more. That top, shiny newlywed layer might have rubbed off a little bit but everything underneath — the routine, the familiarity, the seven to ten meals — that was the really good bit. This was the best of everything and I was finally starting to see it.

JELLY AND BEAN

Suddenly, it seemed as if everyone wanted to be a dog walker. At least twenty emailed a day, which was either a sad reflection on the state of the job market, a reminder that the seasons were changing, or a clear and positive sign that employment as a dog walker was no longer seen as an enormous embarrassment. Or, as I think was the case, all of the above.

Along with the usual round of actors, dancers, students, and eccentrics, a new breed of applicant had emerged. The Recession Dog Walker — a professional type whose CV covered more than one side of paper and knew how to use an iron and a spreadsheet. This new breed was naturally happier in a corporate environment but, displaced by the barren job market and having been spurned one too many times, had grown mistrustful of offices and wondered if they might be happier doing something completely different. Groomed, soft-handed, and not at all used to mud or fur or slobber, these wide-eyed hopefuls had fallen into the dangerous trap of seeing a cute dog in the park on a sunny day and then letting their unemployed imaginations run riot. As the long-term implications of the recession began to settle in, many had concluded that people were not the answer to anything anymore and that the only way forward was dogs.

Procurement managers, HR specialists, junior lawyers, travel agents, gallery assistants, event organizers, PAs, EAs, and maître d's, all seeking fulfilment and finance through dogs. Shattering any remaining illusions of what life might have to offer them by telling them that the pay was crap and that some dogs can poo up to five times on just one walk was an unfortunate duty but it was important to give them the facts and to weed out the time wasters. It was either going to be far better than they could have imagined or the worst job they had ever had and it wasn't until they were out in a gale walking a dog with a dodgy tummy that they would really get the measure of it.

"I just think that working with dogs might be the best thing for me at the moment," they would say earnestly. "I've always liked dogs and I am good at walking."

"The weather is bad," I would reply. "And

the clients can be difficult."

"But animals seem to really like me. They understand me."

I hired a few of them and sent the best-dressed ones on trial walks in the rain. None of them made it past the first day, citing excuses such as "my aunt has just broken her leg," or "my perfect job in fashion just suddenly appeared," or "I forgot I have to move to Abu Dhabi in the morning." It never failed to amaze me what concoctions people expected to pass for the truth.

The ones that were left seemed like a hardy bunch and with the walker stock replenished, I set my sights on the other side of the Thames. Business was perky in the southwest but lethargic in other areas and with the north London walkers all ready to go, I ordered some new tasteful and arty Islington-esque flyers with a no-nonsense credit-crunch slant that I hoped might appeal.

London's Number One
Dog-Walking Agency
(owned by genuine dog owner)
WE JUST WALK DOGS!
One dog. One walker. One price
(competitive!)
One love.

It wasn't long before we had a bite, and a big one too. A gang of six friends, three married couples, who lived in Islington and all had dogs. They were friends at university who had all coupled up and then migrated down to London, living mere streets away from each other. They bought big flats with big windows and extensive wooden floors and owned things like lawnmowers and picnic hampers. They were seemingly unaffected by the recession, though they certainly knew how to use it to their advantage.

I met them as a group, all six of them on sofas, legs entwined as they drank wine from a real wine shop rather than the newsagent and dipped things into hummus. They were disarmingly grown-up for a Tuesday.

"We're en masse, I am afraid," said Henrietta as she opened the door. She had been the one to make initial contact and we met at her large flat that she shared with her large husband, Mike, and their not very large Scottish terriers, Jelly and Bean. "Book club after this. The Help. Have you read it?"

"No, no, I haven't."

"Brilliant book. Totally recommend it," she said as she ushered me into the enormous sitting room. "I think we all gave it a nine, didn't we Team?"

The "Team" mostly mumbled in agreement while giving me a quick once-over.

Henrietta sat down while I hovered uncomfortably in the doorway, intermittently patting the dogs. Nobody offered me a seat.

"Dan gave it a two but the only book he's ever given a nine to is *War and Peace* or *Anna Karenina* or one of those other huge Russian bricks. So he says, anyway."

"Mike, you are such a *massive* dick."

"Did you actually read it, Dan, or do you just crack the spine every now and then and leave it out in the loo for everyone to see? Anything he wants you to see is kept in the loo, including all those prep school certificates for ball throwing and crocheting and flute playing. Grade two flute wasn't it, Danny boy?"

"Very funny, Mike, you are very, *very* funny."

"Oh, and don't forget all those *Men's Health* magazines," chipped in someone else. "There are *a lot* of those." This was also very funny, apparently.

"Of course! Who could forget the magazines! I think there was a yacht one in there once, wasn't there? And the art, of course. We mustn't forget the art. You're going to need a bigger bathroom, mate."

"My bathroom is bigger than your whole fucking flat, *mate,*" Dan snapped, which everyone thought was hilarious and they all laughed very loudly for quite a long time. Still nobody offered me a seat, even when I was asked to give a quick summary of the business, and I stood awkwardly for the whole thing as if I was giving a public service announcement. I wondered for one tiny moment if the whole thing was some sort of elaborate hoax or a complex initiation test.

"We want a deal," Dan said, butting in at the end of my spiel about being a genuine dog owner. He sat in the corner with one arm casually draped over the sofa and the other placed proprietarily on his blonde wife's knee. He had a misguided, early hipster era beard and was the only one not in a suit, preferring to show everyone he was some sort of artist by wearing ground-down mahogany cords, a burgundy tie, and a pair of slippers.

The room dutifully fell silent. This was clearly a prearranged line of inquiry and he was the appointed interrogator, the man in charge. "I'll handle this," he would have said. "You guys are all *bloody shit* at negotiating."

"A deal?" I asked.

"Yes, a deal. There's six of us here, four dogs. We all say yes, then there should be a discount. Group booking and all that. Times are hard, as you know."

"The rates are already discounted," I replied, softly. "They are very competitive."

"The thing about these dogs is, they're all mates," he continued. "Solid, solid mates. They like being together. They're a tribe. Their own little team. So we'd like to keep them together if we can. But that would mean a discount, wouldn't it? I mean, that's quite a lot of business for you."

Dan was picking up steam now and was clearly enjoying himself. I tried to shift awkwardly while I gathered my thoughts but one of the dogs had settled down for a nap on my foot and I couldn't move.

"There are a lot of other companies out there but I am sure *you* know that. What we're after is a little sweetener, a little something to make us go with you and not with one of the others. How does that sound?"

"Well, I will have a think about it and see if there is anything we can do."

"Marvelous. Well, we will wait to hear from you, then. In the next day or two perhaps? You wouldn't want to leave it too long."

He turned away from me and whispered something to his wife and she giggled like a doll when you pull its string. The conversation was over and I was meant to leave.

It was difficult to understand what could have happened to these couples to make them quite so awful. They were, give or take a large inheritance or two, essentially Finlay and me. Married, pre-kids, pro-dogs, drinking wine on a Tuesday evening, and chatting about the size of their flat. Except that they weren't us. They weren't us at all. They were an entirely different breed.

It was hard not to compare yourself to the clients, particularly the ones of a similar age. It was hard not to picture yourself in that house, wearing those shoes, that necklace, putting that hideous painting of a sailor in the bin. Even if it was only for a second, the smallest of thoughts, you might just wonder why you were standing in a doorway with a dog asleep on your shoe and they were on the sofa drinking wine and eating crudités. The myriad tiny steps you take to get where you are; the thousands of decisions you make along the way; the things you have power over and all the many things you do not — and all of these choices, these things we sign up for, the commitments we make, are done before we even know who we really are.

Finlay liked to compare in black and white, facts and money: how big was that house, how expensive were those shoes, that necklace, that painting. Whereas I looked at the finer print, for signs of happiness, of confidence, and the promise of family. Did they bicker as much as we did and was it about the same sort of things? Did they still hold hands when they walked in the park and leave each other little notes? Should I be hosting book clubs and buying vases and having people over midweek? Did I have the right jeans, the right hair, the right face? Could I be a better cook, a better dog owner, a better human being?

As Henrietta led me back to the front door, laughter escaping from the sitting room behind me, she said, "God, you don't know how long poussins take to cook, do you? I can't for the life of me remember!"

This was second-level adulthood and we were way off the mark. These were the people who sent back food in restaurants and knew a good plumber, a good butcher, a good dealer. They emptied dips into small dishes rather than leaving them in the plastic pot, regularly checked their bank account, and had at least three different types of insurance. They had solid, recognizable job titles and nice, clean career paths with mortgages and allowances for cars; cars they could actually drive on account of having taken and passed their driving tests. Their dogs were grown-ups too, not just in age but in their appearance, their behavior, their pleasant moderation. They had matching beds, which they actually slept in, and didn't bark when someone knocked on the door.

Just when you think you have reached a sensible level of maturity, achieved several recognizable adult milestones, you find that your contemporaries have made wills or bought shares. They ask you what your "five-year plan" is and when you laugh as if it were a joke they then proceed to tell you *their* five-year plan, including when they are having children and the names they like and the nurseries they have signed up for. Having a dog and a mortgage and a marriage certificate was only basic adulting in comparison to this.

It wasn't just the "Team" that was making me feel like this. At an early spring barbecue held by an old school friend of Finlay's, the hostess shivered in the cool evening breeze. Her husband put his arm around her and, without a shred of shame, he said, "I think you are long overdue a North Face fleece." I wondered if there would ever be a time when I might need or even want a North Face fleece. Even in my darkest thoughts, I couldn't see it happening until I was at least the age when I also needed a tartan rug over my knees. Some people seemed to reach their North Face fleece-buying age a long, long time before others, accumulating the props and habits of advanced maturation way in advance of my timeline.

Did just owning these items propel you into an adult sensibility, drawing you into a world of rational decision-making and forward planning, or would you only ever consider buying a raincoat or a Filofax if you were already that way inclined? I hoped it was the latter, not just because I suspected that I might always be muddling through life but because I didn't have the space or the energy to buy and store all these things.

However, if I wanted that big, chaotic family, if I wanted a full house and all the busyness and accoutrements of family life — and I was beginning to realize quite how much I did — then I would have to do a bit more about getting it. I didn't need fleeces or extensive, year-by-year plans but I did need to start thinking about adding to the head count. I just needed to get my head around it all.

"Before you have any babies, you will need a steamer," my mother said not long after we got married. "And a nest of pans."

"We have one pan. Is that not OK?"

"I wouldn't have thought so. Do you have spare towels?"

"What for?"

"Guests. Entertaining. To put in the cupboard."

"I think we were given some at the wedding."

"Well, what about a casserole dish? And a gravy boat? Were you given one of those? You must have a gravy boat."

"Why?"

"Well, that's what you put the gravy in. When you have a roast."

"But there's only two of us here. And we live in a small flat."

"But what about when you do beef?"

"Beef ? I don't like roast beef."

"What?"

"I don't like it. We've got a toastie maker, we'll be fine."

"Well, what about Finlay? You have to feed men beef!"

"What? Why?"

"You just do!"

Her father was a beef man, a farmer who bred cattle, supported Norwich City, and was allowed an extramarital affair. Beef was tradition. Beef was patriarchy. Beef was Sunday lunch and table manners and stiff

223

upper lips. It was a symbol of order, of success and class, of being better than everyone else. It was also the man's way of reminding everyone who was in charge, who had bought it, who was allowed to cut its flesh with the orange electric carver, and who ordered everyone to eat it, all of it, until your plate was clean, or it was a terrible, shameful waste and you may as well sit in the coal cellar for the rest of the week.

After our wedding, my mother bought us a traditional twelve-person dinner set, despite the fact that our table could only fit four at a push and we barely had any cupboard space. She was also trying to coax us toward domestic maturity, a more nostalgic, class-riddled version where people had large dinner parties with at least three courses, molded mousses, and roulades and a selection of savory biscuits. Proper entertaining was one of the signs of official adulthood, and the larger the hunk of meat served on the table, the more upwardly mobile the adult. But I didn't want her traditions or philosophies on meat or on society. I wanted to push back against all of it, not just because that is what you do as an offspring, but because so much of it felt like nonsense for this day and age. Plus, I wanted to forge my own traditions in my own time and then try to foist them upon my own children.

"It's good to have something to look forward to," she said as she piled the dinner service back into her car to store at her house. "Aim high, darling. One day, you and Finlay will be serving twelve."

After a brief Google of the local competition (primarily a man called "BowWow Brian" who drove a gaggle of dogs up to Hampstead Heath in an old maroon Saab) I gave the Islington "Team" a small discount and hired them a red-haired ex-PA Recession Walker called Felicity. She'd been made redundant by a small hedge fund who'd had to do some recession streamlining and was the kind of girl who had taken it personally and felt vengeful about the whole thing. In taking a forced break from the City, she had concluded that she wanted to work with toddlers, or failing that donkeys, but with donkeys being in short supply in north London and toddlers requiring a qualification, dogs were a satisfactory third best.

I was immediately scared of Felicity, which I suspect was the main reason I hired her. I didn't want to say no. She was remarkably aloof for an interviewee, particularly off the back of the many desperately keen applicants. The blatant indifference, the crossed arms and challenging stare, might have actually been what drew me to her and I felt a need to extol the many advantages to walking dogs over working in childcare or donkey rescue.

"The fresh air is just great, and the exercise of course. I mean, there's no need to bother with a gym membership. You basically get paid to be fit! And you meet so many people. Adults mainly. Occasionally children. Dogs, obviously. Are you . . . happy with most dogs?"

"Most dogs. Some dogs are awful, of course. Like people I suppose."

"Are there . . . any in particular that are *awful*?" It was hard to imagine what an awful dog might look like. It was such an unexpected choice of word. Not all were aesthetically pleasing but you could always find some redeeming features, especially after you got to know them. That's the wonderful thing about dogs — that they are not like people. The more you come to know them, the better they get, which is not always the case with the human race.

The Islington Team's dogs were the two Scottish terriers, a mimsy poodle, and a nervous boxer — a varied bunch, but all perfectly *nice.* The terriers were a bit high maintenance and had a habit of peeing on each other but aside from that, they were distinctly average dogs and it would be hard for even the most opinionated to form an extreme view of them.

"You just know when you meet them. Like people."

"Right, so no specific breeds?"

"No. Just individuals. Like people."

It all started out fine — turning up on time, dogs taken home alive, house not ransacked or burned down. It always starts like that. I knew that now, nearly four years in. The walker wants to show you that they can do the job, that they are trustworthy and reliable. But then they go either one of two ways. Around half continue to turn up on time, continue to be trustworthy and reliable, and around half fuck it all up. They don't turn up, they turn up late, they fall asleep on the client's sofa and then lose the keys, they drink their cognac and eat their bananas, and some of them don't even like dogs; they're rough with them, they yank their leads and shout at them, and they always, always think they will get away with it. They never think they will get caught.

Felicity didn't like dogs. I suspected she didn't like donkeys either, or children, but she was quite adept at being angry and irrational. When Henrietta and Mike questioned whether she was definitely walking Jelly and Bean for the full amount of time on account of the dogs being restless and peeing all over the kitchen floor, she said, "I have no idea what the fuck you are talking about," and put the phone down on me.

In hindsight, that might have been the moment to let her go, but Dan had emailed at least twice to tell me how wonderful she was, how caring with his mimsy poodle, how punctual and efficient and how much they all liked her. He was at home all day painting and could attest to her timing, her dedication, her commitment because he saw her, all of the time. I was often left as piggy in the middle, trying to work out who the liar was. It is generally best to hedge your bets until someone drops their guard, and they always do.

A few months into the Team's walks, Mike had surgery on his leg and was working from home. Felicity came to collect Jelly and Bean and didn't see Mike in the bathroom, changing the dressing on his stitches. She returned them fifteen minutes later, an hour earlier than arranged, before they had even made it to the park.

You would think that presenting someone with irrefutable evidence of their wrongdoings might humble a person somewhat, squeeze an awkward apology from them, but not Felicity. Telling her that she had been caught red-handed enraged her. She screamed violently down the phone and sent furious, sweary emails but not once did she admit to any offense.

"Mike was there, Felicity, he was in the bathroom. There just isn't any way around that."

"Mike is a lying CUNT," she yelled, before hanging up again.

It wasn't the first time I'd had to fire someone but it was certainly the hardest. The disentanglement took a while, what with the shouting and all the emails, and then the calls that came from Dan. This is when it headed into unchartered waters. Felicity was at his flat in tears, he said. She was a good person, a loving person, misunderstood perhaps but passionate about animal welfare and customer service. She had only wanted to help, to help dogs and to help people, and why was I being mean to her?

"She called Mike a cunt," I said.

"But not to his face! I mean, we can all get a bit grumpy sometimes, can't we?"

"Well maybe you should have a chat with Mike," I said as the realization of what might be going on started to hit home. "He's your friend and I am sure he can explain what happened. Oh, and if you still want the walks, we will have to stop the discount I am afraid as the other guys are not going to be using Felicity anymore. But I imagine you already know that."

The Team disbanded a short while later and Dan's wife and their mimsy poodle moved in with Henrietta and Mike. I found them a new walker and life moved on, although the book club did fall apart, the final chapter in this small Islington tragedy. No more burned Tuesday poussin, no more stale crudités, no more pretending to be perfect grown-ups.

Mabel, Part Two

Mabel had become both fat and badly behaved, a double victory for Finlay who, after a period of being quite enamored, was enjoying calling her "your dog" again.

After having to wade through a lake in his underwear in Battersea Park to stop her from harassing some nesting ducks, his patience was rapidly running out. With it being a mild, dry Saturday morning, there had been a sizable crowd at the lake and it was the second time that week that he had been forced to strip off in order to retrieve her, not to mention the dozen or so times he had chased her around Wandsworth Park. Squirrels were still her first love but she was now also enjoying some water-based hunting.

Jack Russells are naughty. A grubby knee and playground naughtiness, adventures and mysteries and a bounding sense of mischief, one that is born from the all-

231

encompassing need to have fun. They don't mean to spoil your day, or your pants, but they simply can't help it as the world to them is one enormous amusement park where every tree, bush, hedge, and water feature holds the promise of a thrill-inducing ride. That's why you can't ever be properly cross with them. There is no shred of malice or ill will, only a desire to live as magnificently as possible. If only we could be so lucky.

"Mabel needs boundaries," Finlay said firmly, as if he might be talking about an errant child. He never normally spoke so seriously, which was a sign of how far up the naughty scale Mabel had climbed. "We should have done it a long time ago and it's probably far too late now but we have to do *something*. We have to be *firm*."

A stout, forthright woman, one of the crowd on the shore of the lake, had told him that he should never have got a Jack Russell in the first place as they were usually far more trouble than they were worth.

"I said to each and every one of my children that you get a terrier at your own peril. None of them listened to me of course, and then they all came back saying that they wish they had taken my advice. Every single one of them has been a disaster.

Absolute disaster. Terriers will not do you any favors. At all. They wear you down, you see, little by little. Unless you are firm and take them in hand. You must be *firm.*"

She had a neat, quiet Norfolk terrier on a very short lead — at least that's what I concluded it was, based on Finlay's description of a short and furry gingery dog who looked a bit like Fergie. This one must have already been taken in hand.

"We have to prove that woman wrong," Finlay said. "We're going to train *your* dog and then take it back to show her."

I was tasked with finding a trainer, dispatched to the park to make inquiries among the Park Groups. A few of the Labrador gang suggested an out-of-London residential place run by an angry farmer but the unanimous recommendation was a chap called Monty Shears in Fulham.

"Have you got your name down?" one of the Lycra mums asked. "Monty gets very booked up. I hear he's not even doing one-to-ones anymore. We were lucky to get Champ in really but then Monty and I used to play tennis together *yonks* ago."

Champ was staring into the middle distance while Mabel was already thirty meters away, hassling a squirrel.

Monty was indeed booked up. His wife

answered the phone and enjoyed telling me that I should have enrolled Mabel prebirth, or possibly even before that. Most dogs on his list had been registered before there had even been any fornication, a possible litter based on when a prize-winning bitch might possibly be in heat. For the serious-minded owner, correcting your nonexistent dog's future shortcomings required as much dedication as getting your firstborn into Eton.

In the end, it seemed the only dog obediance classes available were run by a man named Dave in a room above a pub in Elephant and Castle. He had a space starting the following week and so we reluctantly booked ourselves in. In the meantime, Mabel's collar was fitted with a small gold bell, the type a geriatric's cat might wear, and we started getting the bus up to Wimbledon Common so she could stretch her legs out a bit and try to drop a few pounds.

Since being spayed, the weight had slowly, insidiously clambered on and she now had three necks and an extra stomach to go along with her new attitude problem. I had barely noticed it happen — partly due to the fact that it had happened quite slowly but mainly because an enormous pair of rose-colored glasses arrived when Mabel came to live with us. To me, she was perfect.

"She's fat," the vet said as she plonked herself down on the scales at her annual checkup. He didn't mince his words and I was reminded of Jess and poor Cleo and how utterly unbelievable I had found it that she couldn't see the padding, the rolls, the morbid heaviness. I understood so much more now.

"She's very fat," the vet continued. "Well, obese I'd say. She needs more exercise. She needs to run."

Wandsworth Park is beautiful. It's elegant and charming with its long avenue of plane trees curving gently toward the Thames, blushing pink rhododendron bushes and lilac trees, little clipped flower beds, and bright green bowling lawn. It's perfect for an afternoon stroll, nothing too strenuous or taxing, but for a fat Jack Russell it's far from ideal. You would have to spend all day in there to have any hope of dropping significant calories.

Wimbledon Common is an altogether different kind of walking experience. It's huge and rambling with large thick-wooded areas, steep banks of overgrown bracken, patchwork squares of purple heather, and open grassy areas that swish pleasingly in the breeze. With its winding paths, sandy tracks, lakes, ponds, and streams, it's the closest thing to rural and can, albeit temporarily, give you a small, bolstering dose of the countryside you left behind as a child.

It's also a terrier's paradise, with an abundance of small, furry animals to annoy, huge expanses of green to get up to top speed on, and plenty of opportunities to give your owner the slip by disappearing into the undergrowth for an hour or so. This is where a bell comes in handy.

"It's like being followed around by a tiny Morris dancer," Finlay said. "And that's definitely not a good thing."

But there was also another advantage to avoiding Wandsworth Park. I had a rival.

Her name was Agnes and she was German, a student at Roehampton University, and the first time I met her she was power walking a Chihuahua around the park, arms pumping furiously as the tiny dog trotted furiously along behind her.

It was Rabbit and he was supposed to be on holiday in Cornwall.

I knew there were other dog walkers out there. I'd seen the vans, the flyers, and the blokes with four dogs on each arm. People loved to tell me about the walker in their neighborhood with a T-shirt or jacket on that said "Regent's Bark" or "Merry Go Hound" or "Mutt above the Rest." Paying someone to take your dog out had not only become an acceptable way to spend your disposable income, but an expected one. Society had come a long way in a few short years, at least where recognition of animal sentience was concerned. Leaving your dog alone all day while you were at work was now seen as just as archaic and antisocial as picking up the phone to call someone when you could just as easily send a text.

Alongside the one-man bands like Bow-Wow Brian and Penny's Pupz, there were also larger, professional outfits, companies with branded vehicles and catchy slogans and the offer of long rambling walks in Richmond or Hampstead. A north London woman in an old air stewardess outfit drove a dog-packed mini bus with "Paws to Manual" emblazoned on the side, while down in Brixton a man on a bike with a "Waggin' Wagon" trailer attached to the back attempted to ferry dogs from park to park without them jumping out into the traffic.

And why not? Presuming you have some basic social skills, a passing interest in animals, a half-decent dog pun, and the motivation of a weekly salary, then most people can, at the very least, give it a go.

For a service that barely existed a few years ago, it was a remarkable evolution. A whole new industry had developed in London and at its very heart was the care of dogs.

I tried not to think about it too much. While delighted for the dogs of London, too much information on the competition might let Panic back in. In this instance, however, it was rather difficult to avoid.

"Oh, hello, sorry to bother you," I said as I finally managed to catch up with Agnes. "Is that . . . is that *Rabbit*?" You can never be completely sure with Chihuahuas.

"Yes, this is Rabbit." Rabbit's lead was attached to her waist on a pimped-up fanny pack. It had spaces for treats, a tennis ball, and poo bags and looked extremely professional. Rabbit noticed Mabel and did a small tail wag. He was too exhausted to do much else.

"I thought so. Hi, Rabbit! I used to . . . well we used to know Rabbit. A bit. Is he back from holiday early?" I asked, trying to put all the pieces together. I was supposed to have started walking him again the following week.

"He is not on holiday," she snapped. "He is standing there!"

"Right. There he is. Hello, Rabbit. How are you?"

"He is fine. Very fine. I walk him," she said bluntly and whipped a flyer out of her fanny pack.

THE <u>VERY</u> BEST DOG WALKER IN SOUTHWEST LONDON
<u>Agnes Müller, Pet Expert</u>
Covering Putney, Barnes, and Wandsworth
ALL BREEDS CONSIDERED
(except Dachshunds)

"Oh, great," I said, immediately noticing that she had used much thicker, glossier paper than me. " 'The very best' . . . gosh. How brilliant. A dog walker!"

"You need help?" she asked. "With the weight?" She pointed down to a reclining Mabel who had made a large indent on the grass. She was too lazy to greet her old friend Rabbit.

"Oh, no. We're fine. That's very kind, though, thank you," I waffled. "We are working on it, actually. She's in training. And on a diet. And we are seeing people who know about these things. Very good people."

"She is too fat. Very bad."

"Yes, yes, I know."

"She is *obese.*"

239

"Yes, yes, thank you. Well, it was really great to meet you, Agnes. And to see you, Rabbit. Right then, off we go!"

I started to haul the enormous Mabel to her feet so we could make a quick exit but Agnes had already power walked off in the other direction with Rabbit frantically scampering along behind. I didn't know how or when she had done it but there was no doubt that she had stolen my client.

"She's a thief," I railed to Finlay that evening, showing him the flyer. "She's taken Rabbit off me and she called Mabel fat."

"Your dog is fat."

"She also had a fanny pack. Do you think I need a fanny pack?"

"No, I shouldn't think so. Why doesn't she walk dachshunds?"

"I don't know. Maybe it's *too* German, you know, too much of a cliché? Or maybe she was surrounded by them as a child and developed a phobia."

"Well, either way, it's obvious why she's walking Rabbit."

"Why?"

"Because your dog is fat and badly behaved. It's hardly a good advertisement."

I had been dreading the training but after the run-in with Agnes, I started to count down the days. All of a sudden, there were a lot of people I needed to prove very wrong. I wanted to show Finlay that I could be a responsible, admirable parent, to a dog or to a child, and that meant a rapid behavioral and dietary turnaround. Plus, we were seeing my mother at Christmas and the thought of her disappointed face when she saw that not only was I not pregnant and still walking dogs but also that I had let a Jack Russell from such a distinguished line become fat and disobedient. Being married for two years and not having anything to show for it other than the brand new, unopened steamer in the cupboard, was not going to pass under the maternal radar for much longer. I knew I wanted a baby. I knew I wanted a lot of things. I'd just had rather a lot going on.

Dave the dog trainer was clearly a no-nonsense type of guy. Cockney, ex-military, with a rash of tattoos and a German shepherd called Barry, he was dressed in a tight camo T-shirt and shorts, despite the fact that it was freezing cold outside and there was only one working radiator in the pub's upstairs room.

There were five of us there — an elderly man with a springer spaniel, an uptight couple with a delicate silver whippet, and a young bloke with a bull terrier. Everyone looked scared.

"Right then. I presume you are all 'ere because your dog has stepped out of line. They've been taking the mick. Am I right?" he bellowed, gripping Barry's lead tightly. "Course I'm right. We're here to teach your dog who's the boss. There is no point to your dog wandering around the place thinking he owns the bloody joint. That dog, however bloody cute it thinks it is, however fancy, however dainty, however much you bloody paid for it, it needs to know that you, *you* are the boss. Your dog ain't the bloody boss. *You* are. You crack that, and I mean properly crack it, then you'll have a best mate for life. Like Barry here. Any questions?"

There was stunned silence. The elderly gentleman eventually put up his hand.

"Will we be learning any tricks?"

"Tricks? Tricks? What sorta tricks?" Dave replied, rather defensively I thought.

"Well, I had wanted her to roll over really, oh, and er, play dead. Bring me a newspaper. That sort of thing."

"Nah, nah, nah, mate. This isn't what this is about. We don't do tricks here. This is about RESPECT. It's about boundaries. It's about listening. First lesson of dog ownership, learn how to listen. If we can't hear what our dog is telling us, and I mean really hear, then we may as well just chuck it all in now. Do you want to chuck it in now?"

The elderly man shook his head. He looked deeply uncomfortable and kept glancing at the door as if he wanted to leave but Barry was sitting in his way and he clearly decided not to risk it.

"Right. Let's get stuck in. First lesson of dog ownership. Learn to be social. And I don't just mean having a little natter and a gossip. I mean RESPECT. Learning respect for your fellow dog. If your dog can't crack that, then you've got a real nasty problem on your hands. This is the real deal, this is. This is the absolute bloody cornerstone."

We were split into pairs and rather confusingly asked to role-play meeting another dog in the park. I was paired up with the whippet couple who had been taking notes and looked very serious about the whole thing. They questioned Dave as to whether their spindly whippet, Madonna, was the right "match" for Mabel — presumably because Mabel was double her width and could have quite easily squashed her — but Dave didn't seem the type to change his mind in a hurry.

"You two are together for a *very* good reason," he said to Madonna's owner, although he never clarified what that reason might be. I suspected it was because we were sitting closest to them.

Pretending to come across each other on a walk, we approached from opposite ends of the room while Dave and Barry watched. Madonna was jittery and nervous and tried to back away from Mabel's playful, bounding advances and it wasn't long before their leads were completely entangled, someone trod on Madonna's paw, and a drink had been spilled onto the floor.

"What's going on over 'ere?" barked Dave as he marched over. Madonna had yelped loudly and the lady was trying to console her with a piece of chicken she had produced from her pocket. "Wait, wait, wait, wait, wait, wait. What do you think you're doing? Your dog's being a twat and you're giving it a treat! What sorta message do you think that's giving off?"

"She was upset," said the lady, quietly. "The large dog jumped at her." She meant Mabel.

"She's upset because she hasn't learnt yet. She doesn't know what's what. She's all over the bloody place, here, there, and everywhere, dancin' about. She's gotta learn to listen. To respect!"

"She's frightened," the woman snapped while picking up the dog. Madonna was now shivering violently. "This is not the right environment for her."

"It's a big old world out there," said Dave, lowering his voice as he leaned in close to Madonna. "What's she going to do when she's in a park? Or out on the street? There will be dogs far fatter than that one, dogs that want to bite her head off! What's she gonna do if she can't handle a bit of role-play, eh?"

"We'll manage," she said, dragging her husband out the door with her. The elderly man stood as if he was going to make a run for it too but Barry intercepted him again. Barry was deeply intimidating.

The rest of the class was a little more subdued. Nobody wanted to speak in case it upset Dave and so we played a game in silence where the dogs had to walk past some chopped up Spam without eating it. Mabel had scarfed the lot and Barry looked disappointed with her. It was only the first class but I felt keenly that Barry would be disappointed in us at every subsequent one.

"I'm sorry," I said to Dave at the end. "Not sure we are cut out for this. She's probably a bit of a write-off."

"She's just fat," he replied, flatly. "That's it, really. Fat."

"Yes, I know about the fat thing but the

behavior side, is that . . . irretrievable?"

"Nah, nah, nah, mate. *You* are the problem, not her."

"Oh?"

"It's your first dog, you're being all wet about it, a bit pathetic, when you just need to be a bit firm. Say no every now and then. Give her a bit of a bollocking if she's being a twat. She wants to learn from you. All dogs do."

"Right. Of course."

"It's all right not to know this stuff. That's how we learn. By making mistakes."

He bent down and started to give Barry a stroke on his neck. Barry looked up at him, his eyes as wide and open as the night sky, before gently resting his head on Dave's leg. Dave had rescued Barry when he returned from Afghanistan, when adjusting to civilian life was hard. They'd helped each other to fit back into the world.

"You don't write any dog off. This one was rehomed twice before he came to me. No one could cope with him, you see, but they just hadn't given it a proper good go. They'd given up on him before Barry really had a chance to show them who he was. He's not just going to do that straight up, is he? He needed to feel like he was secure, and loved, like he was in the right place. It

246

took a bit of time — these things do, don't they? But we got there. Course we did. He's my buddy now. Couldn't be without him, not even for a minute."

I stood for a moment, watching as they leaned into each other, their bodies using the weight of the other to support and balance each other. It was as if they were sharing the same core.

"You got a good dog there. A fat one but a good 'un. She just needs a bit of a kick up the arse. And a lot less food."

HUXLEY

January is the same as any old month really, except for all the leftover cheese and the bottles of wine you are not supposed to drink and the desperately annoying obsession with order and organization that your mother adopts until sometime around Epiphany. My job status was still high on the agenda, but there was something far more pressing now.

"Right. We need to talk about your fertility," she said down the phone on New Year's Day. "Time is ticking. You are not getting any younger, plus older mothers have a much harder time making friends, you know."

"What? *Why?*"

"They just do," she snapped, annoyed to have been questioned on something unrelated to any fact whatsoever but that she knew to be absolutely true.

"I'm in my early thirties, Mum. I'm not

sure that would make me an older mother anymore."

"Well, we all know your fertility drops off a mountain around your age. You only have to read the papers to tell you that."

"I thought it was a cliff?" I asked.

"What?"

"I thought it fell off a cliff."

"Does it matter what it falls off? The point of the matter is it falls a very long way down and it doesn't meet a happy end at the bottom."

We had been trying for a baby for a while. Six months at least. Not long in the grand scheme of things but the waiting was far harder than I expected it to be. Alongside the frustration and anguish in having to accept that something as vital and transformative as creating a new life is so utterly out of your control, I was berating myself for having wasted precious time. I realized I had been putting it off, for a year at least. I was stalling. Making excuses — not to Finlay, who was fairly relaxed about the whole thing — but to myself. Every time the thought popped into my head, every time I felt my body clock tick and chime, I would bat it all away again, stamp on it until it retreated. It had been all too easy to pass it off as busyness, growing the business, dieting a Jack Russell, and navigating the many entanglements of adulthood, but it wasn't any of those things. Not really.

I was scared. I didn't want to get it wrong, to mess it up. I didn't want it to be right but realize it wasn't enough, somehow. I didn't want anything to change between Finlay, Mabel, and I in our safe little unit, yet I wanted it all to change, to expand, to grow, to push out into the corners and into new, wider spaces. I wanted to be a good mother, the best you could possibly be, but I didn't know how. Was loving them more than you had ever loved anything going to be enough? Would it protect them from the storms, the earthquakes, life's many peaks and troughs? Would it ever live up to the family that I had in my head, the one I dreamed of, the one I clung on to when it felt as if there was no glue in life, nothing to hold everyone together?

My brother had kids already, which had helped to assuage the granny urges for a short while.

"*Leaders* have girls," she had crowed as my sister-in-law pumped out three beautiful blonde daughters. My brother was a successful entrepreneur with an enormous house. "It's evolution, apparently. Girls don't challenge the dominant male." She then turned to Finlay and I and said, "You two will have boys. Which will be *lovely.*"

Boys or girls, just how many grandchildren does one grandmother need? But the issue lay in the fact that as "secondary granny" only (my sister-in-law's mother already in the primary position), she was keen to be promoted to the leading role as soon as possible, boys or not. After marriage, dog ownership, and serving twelve for dinner, having children was next on the list of things you absolutely must achieve if you were to be seen as any sort of acceptable adult woman. It was all the more pressing if your employment was still somewhat awkward to discuss with friends on account of it being ridiculously out of the ordinary, as there had to be *something* that could be bragged about to friends. Her son-in-law's former university, the Jack Russell from the notable line, and her son's perfect girls had all run their conversational course and she was hankering after another grandchild.

"We're working on it, Mum," I said wearily, but I already felt I had failed her because I felt like I had failed myself.

There are so many different ways to count success in life. For some it is work, promotions, money, and a car that costs as much as a house. New boots or goals scored, grade A's and star of the week. The numbers and lists we like to log, of partners bedded or teapots collected or days without having a drink. Measures of success can be as big as a yacht and as tiny as a seed or as dismal as wanting others to fail. Facing another morning, taking another step, making someone happy, or helping them when they are sad — success could really be about the smallest of things.

I could have measured my success in dogs, the stacking up of clients, the money in the bank, Labrador by Labrador. There were momentum and growth and enormous obstacles that had been overcome and a mother nearly proved wrong. I could have measured it in love, and a home, and a dog that smelled like biscuits — and I did, when I could. But for a while now I'd measured it in months, in cycles, in tests with one line, not two, and I forgot about all the rest. Life had utterly shrunk.

I was back in Wandsworth Park, Mabel a little lighter, a little leaner, and without a bell. A balanced diet of squirrel chasing and "neutered dog" biscuits was doing the trick and there was finally a hint of skeleton beneath the layers of fur and fat. The training was still a work in progress but Dave hadn't called her a twat in at least two weeks, so that was something. We were planning a walk around the lake in Battersea Park when the weather got a bit warmer, the stout, terrier-hating woman still very much needing to be rebutted.

Even Agnes noticed a change. She now walked four local dogs and wore a lime green top that said "Pexpert" on it, alongside a picture of a very serious-looking spaniel.

"Better," she said as she marched past, which was almost certainly the most generous and effusive she had ever been. Agnes now knew I was a dog walker and was enjoying the rivalry immensely. She liked to introduce me to new dogs she was walking ("This is Nugget, well behaved, good weight, five walks a week, and often needs dog sitting") or hand me new flyers she'd just had printed on extra-thick, glossy paper.

THE <u>ONLY</u>* DOG WALKER IN WANDSWORTH
<u>Agnes Müller, Pexpert</u>
"I can't trust anyone else at all,"
Domino, pug, aged four
ALL BREEDS CONSIDERED
(except dachshunds)
*other dog walkers available
but not as good

I had started walking a new dog, Huxley, an off-white West Highland terrier with a penchant for biting children. It was the sort of client I had started to turn down as, having rebuilt a healthy roster of hounds by this point, I was finally able to politely decline any that sounded too vicious or too demanding. "Stress is a sperm killer," my mother liked to say as often as she could, another wildly untrue philosophy of life, handed down without interference from feminism or biology. "It makes your womb all angry."

But I was curious. And desperately petty. With Agnes having completely cornered the park market with her potent mix of firmness, cunning, aggressive flyering, and professional fanny pack, I wondered why Huxley's owners hadn't chosen her. They were certainly in her catchment area and what with the dog having a few issues, Agnes's no-nonsense approach would have been ideal. Rabbit was a completely changed dog. He was knackered and slightly defeated but he wasn't humping everything or ripping the heads off inanimate objects. If there was a dog who needed walking and I could get in there before Agnes, then I absolutely had to do it, savage or not.

Huxley lived near Putney Bridge with his

owners, Penny and Jim. They were accountants, only mid-forties, but seemed to have settled on late sixties to early seventies as a preferable age bracket. Penny was small and sweet with a bushy silvery blonde haircut that made her look a bit like Judith Chalmers while Jim was wheezy and balding and had tucked his trousers into his socks. They had reclining chairs and glass ornaments and we had tea in proper rose-patterned teacups. Penny wedged a slice of homemade lemon drizzle onto the saucer while we talked about the weather and how she always saw Nick Clegg in her local supermarket and what a lovely man he was. We talked about Agnes too, who they had met already. I was there for nearly two hours.

"Oh yes, Agnes," said Penny, smiling. She always smiled, even when a smile was not called for. I suspected she felt the need to balance out the misery that was her husband. "We liked her, didn't we, Jim?"

"The black one or the German?" he asked bluntly.

"The lovely German lady from Bavaria, doing the economics degree. Agnes. We liked her, didn't we? I didn't think she was quite the right match for Huxley but she seemed *very* sweet, though. Wasn't she sweet, Jim?"

Jim didn't reply and picked up a news-paper to read.

"Sweet" wasn't the word you would natu-rally reach for when describing Agnes so I felt a little nervous when she went on to describe Huxley as a "softie," a "mummy's boy," and as "calm as a cucumber." He was in training to become a therapy pet, one of those dogs who wears fluorescent vests and hangs around hospices. Penny was very proud.

Huxley had his own reclining armchair, which he liked to sit in while snarling at people. My first impressions of him were not great but I had learned to try not to give up on any dog quite so quickly. They often act differently when a stranger is in the house and you could clearly see mo-ments when he was trying to live up to Penny's high expectations of him, to hold his head a little higher and his ears a little perkier as she proudly told us of how well he was doing with his training and how he was conquering his fear of children.

"Oh, is he scared of all children?" I asked.

"Well, he can be a little jumpy, can't he, Jim? I think it's the noise mainly. The size. And the sudden movements. He's not so good with sudden movements. But then, who is?" She laughed, nervously.

Wandsworth Park, their local green space, was hemmed in by primary schools that used its wide open space for sports activities and general jamborees. The whole area, from Battersea to Barnes and back again, was swarming with babies and toddlers. They may as well have lived in a crèche.

"The thing is, we have to try and get him over this silly phobia if he is to pass his training. I am sure he can manage it. He's an absolute sweetie really and so wonderful with old people. And the disabled actually. He loves the disabled. He's just in need of a bit of encouragement with the little ones."

"Encouragement?" I asked, wondering if a bit of extra stroking or telling him what a good boy he was might suffice.

"A bit of acclimatization. Exposure. You know, getting him used to everything. We don't . . . well, we won't have our own children. As you can see." She smiled again but it was different this time as she held out her hand to indicate the child-free, Saga-friendly space that was their living room. The recliners, the glass ornaments, the husband behind the newspaper. The practiced smile.

"Neither do I," I said. I had meant it as a fact only, to let her know where I stood on everything and that I wouldn't be offering up one of my own offspring for her dog to chew on, but I could feel the worry and the sadness trying to get out and I had to look down at my feet. Penny leaned over to take my teacup but for a moment I thought she might be about to take my hand.

"Well, we must let you get on, mustn't we, Jim? I am sure you are very busy with everything. If you would consider walking Huxley, we would be so delighted. He really is the sweetest boy."

Jim stayed behind his newspaper as I said my goodbyes and made my way out. I told Penny I would think about it but as I walked back home, I felt more keenly than I had ever done that I needed to make this one work.

A few days later, Fabio's owner, Meredith, called. We hadn't walked Fabio for a while as she had been off work. Meredith was pregnant. Not just normal, common, or garden pregnant but more pregnant than anyone has ever been ever. I got a complete rundown of the how, when, who, and where; doctor's instructions, vitamins she was taking, due dates, possible names, what her mother-in-law said to her about how she shouldn't be using Flash bathroom spray, and, most pressingly, how Fabio was taking it all. Badly, it would seem.

Due to his "superior spirituality" (on account of being Hindu, of course), Fabio was completely in tune with Meredith's body and was finding her hormonal changes "challenging." In other words, living with her was a horrible, awful nightmare and he needed someone to come and rescue him.

"Could someone have him for a little while?" she asked. "Until this *ghastliness* is all over."

"Have him? For how long?"

"Thirty-five weeks?"

"Thirty-five?"

"Actually, better make it forty, just so I can settle the baby in."

"Forty?"

"Forty should do it. Give or take a week. You just can't tell with babies, can you?"

"Right."

"We love Fabio *dearly,* we really do, you know that, Kate, but this is such an important, precious time for us and we just don't want anything to take away from that."

I wondered if all women reacted this irrationally to becoming pregnant or whether poor Fabio had just been monumentally unlucky with how his owners had turned out. Everyone knew about the morning sickness and the aches and pains and the doughnuts for breakfast parts but nobody ever talked about the getting-rid-of-the-dog bit, the part when you are so consumed with hormones and your own cleverness that you lose all sense of perspective and decency.

Pregnancy seemed to me as if it might be one of those weird, out of character episodes where people ate logs or punched their husbands and everyone thought it was quite funny in a "isn't nature fascinating?" way. I had been told on more than one occasion that getting a pet was always a precursor to having a child, a "gateway" responsibility that always leads to stronger, more addictive commitments. But in these scenarios, it definitely seemed as if the dog stayed put — the baby joyfully adding to the family, rather than pushing someone out like a deranged cuckoo.

"You'll be wanting a baby next!" people would say when they met Mabel as if it might be anything to do with them whatsoever. Who's to say I wasn't going to get recliners and multiple terriers and live a life of furry, doggy bliss? Who's to say I could even have children, that everything worked as it should, or that I wasn't carrying around the pain of a loss? When it came to the "natural" order of things and climbing those well-worn steps of adulthood, people really had no qualms about sticking their nose in.

But annoyingly they were right of course. At least, they were for me. I desperately wanted a baby and as soon as we started trying for one it was all I could think about. Having a taste of what a family felt like was deliciously, painfully tantalizing, a small glimpse as to what might lie around the corner. Being needed is so utterly, perfectly seductive. What they don't tell you is how it all takes over, how Failure holds hands with Panic and rents out the largest room in your brain that it can afford, which is the biggest and most expensive one because you have been paying it a fortune over the years, feeding it and indulging it. Failure at a task where you have tried, where your limits are set by your talent or your effort, always carries hope along with it. But failure by your body, when it's not doing what it is meant to be doing and there is nothing you can really do to change any of it, makes hope a bit harder to find. As the months wore on and we kept trying for a baby, I couldn't think of anything else.

Finlay thought I was being ridiculous but was too kind to say so. The doctor thought I was being ridiculous but was too polite.

He told me to take some vitamins and have a holiday. Deep down I knew I was being ridiculous. Even though I was in the thick of the torment and the angst and the daily berating there was still a part of me that knew how completely silly it was to get in such a state about something you can do very little about and, if the statistics were to be believed, would most likely turn out all right in the end. But then I had spent great swaths of my life berating myself for things that had nothing to do with me. I knew how to do it well.

Mabel took an instant dislike to Huxley who, for a dog keen on savaging children, was unexpectedly put out by this minor slight. He sulked for the first walk and then snubbed her on the next. It's hard not to be swayed by who your dog takes umbrage against. It's all too easy to see their choice of park friends, or park enemies, as considered and accurate judgments of character, a natural extension of your own views, rather than simply down to which bum smells best or who wagged their tail. We like to think that our dogs have the same good taste as us and, as they are part of our family, the same principles and outlook. We forget they are not human.

Huxley's principles were a little questionable, particularly for a dog who had been earmarked to comfort and amuse the small, the sick, and the marginalized. It turned out that it wasn't just children on his hit list but anyone who was not of Anglo Saxon, preferably English, heritage. And all black dogs. A week into our walks, he bit the leg of a charcoal gray lurcher and then launched himself at a young black man on a bicycle, causing him to wobble so violently that he in turn nearly ran over a toddler on a trike. What a double victory for Huxley that would have been.

"Fucking white dog bitch!" the man yelled as he finally regained his balance and cycled out of the park. It wasn't entirely clear which of us the comment was aimed at.

We decided to stick to the streets for a while, zigzagging up and down Putney's Victorian terraces. Occasionally we would walk the perimeter of a local primary school in the hope that regular doses of screaming children might eventually soften him to their charms but it only seemed to rev him up even more. He'd catch a whiff of them on the breeze, hear their joyful screeches in the playground, and his gums would start to curl back to reveal a set of sharp, eager teeth. If you had placed a fresh, plump child in front of Huxley in that moment, he would have absolutely eaten it, book bag and all.

I decided that I needed to have a word with Penny.

"Oh yes, there is one black dog he doesn't like," said Penny when I asked her if there was anything else I should be aware of on top of the kids, the other dogs, and all ethnic minorities.

"Just one black dog?" I asked.

"I do believe it is just one!" she giggled.

Unless the lurcher had multiple owners, hairstyles, and an ability to change shape and size, it was definitely *all* black dogs. Penny seemed unfazed.

"What a silly sausage!" she said. "And there I was thinking all dogs were color-blind!"

"He just seems to have a few *minor* issues here and there. A few *dislikes*."

"*Poor* Huxley. I do worry about him."

"I am sure it can be worked out. It's just that at the moment, we are coming across some problems."

"I see."

"Maybe you could do some proper training? Get back to basics. Start all over again. I am just not sure the park and playground approach is really working. It seems to be making him *more* angry."

"Oh dear, dear," she sighed.

"Have you heard of dog trainer Dave? In Elephant?"

She hadn't. She was going to try Huxley with a reflexologist she had read about on an online forum for "stressed-out dogs" — I hoped she had looked into their ethnicity first. Dave would have been perfect for Huxley but not so good for Penny. I sensed that a large bloke in army gear shouting "twat" at her dog might have sent her over the edge because this wasn't really about Huxley at all. It was about what Penny needed to do to feel like she hadn't failed.

"Look, I know he's not an angel," she continued. "I know he has some problems. But he's a good boy at heart. He's sensitive. Kind. He looks after me. I think he just gets flustered sometimes, and panicky, like we all do. He just really, really wants to be a therapy dog. If there is anything you can do to help him pass, we would be so grateful. This means so much to us."

I persevered for another couple of weeks, hoping, praying that Huxley might turn it around. I thought that if I could just get him to the test, then I could extricate myself from the whole thing knowing that I at least tried to help. The day of the assessment came and I crossed my fingers that all of southwest London's children, ethnic minorities, and black dogs were out on a day trip somewhere but sadly that was not the case. Huxley failed on nearly every count, including growling at the assessor, jumping up in an attempt to bite, snatching a treat, and lunging angrily at a black postman.

They call it "deferment" so as not to rub the failure in too much and he would be able to try again in six months, but Penny and I both knew that even if Huxley had six years, he was not Pets as Therapy material.

"Well, we tried!" she said chirpily as we met to hand back her house keys. I wouldn't be walking Huxley anymore. I wasn't sure our insurance would cover it.

"Maybe it's just not for him. Not everyone can be a therapy dog. I'm not sure Mabel would be very good. She's far too naughty!"

Penny looked down for a moment and sighed, the sigh of a mother coming to terms with the fact that her child is not different or special but just the same as everyone else — if a little worse.

"Thank you. For helping me. I am sure you think I was completely bonkers about all of this! Jim certainly does. I think I just got a bit carried away."

"No, no, not at all." I really didn't. Of all

the perplexing aspirations the owners liked to project onto their pets, I understood this one best of all. Penny just wanted to be proud of Huxley. She wanted to be like every other mother.

"So silly really. He's just a dog at the end of the day. Just a dog."

The next time I saw Penny in the park it was spring, April, and I was six weeks pregnant. She was enrolling Huxley at a film and television agency in the West End. He had a screen test coming up where he had to do an improvised scene with a Labrador and she was confident that he was going to do very well.

I didn't tell her that I had seen Jim a week or so ago kick Huxley sharply in the side and tell a child who whizzed past him on a scooter to "fucking watch it." I presumed she knew who he was. She reclined next to him, night after night. Sadly, it hadn't been much of a surprise to me either.

I had also managed to sort the Fabio situation. By a stroke of luck, a retired lady in Stoke Newington had been in touch to see if we needed any help with dog sitting. Her dog had died a few years previously and while she couldn't quite bring herself to get another one of her own, she desperately wanted some time with one. I asked how she felt about Fabio and explained the tricky situation with Meredith.

"I'd absolutely love to have the poor boy," she said. "I always had a soft spot for Italians."

"He loves meat," I said. "Especially steak. And bolognese."

Everything seems to have its own cycle, even the business. As summer flounced in once again, the easy coming and going of the clients and the dogs felt as familiar and as rhythmical as the seasons themselves, or the in-and-out breaths of a pulsing, transitory city. There were new dogs on new streets in new neighborhoods, puppies and rescues and dogs needing weekend sitters, while others were saying their goodbyes, leaving for new jobs, for babies or fresh starts elsewhere. There was old age too, old bones and old joints and the white-muzzled faces of the dogs who couldn't make it to the park anymore, where walkers became companions, comforters, nurses, and darkness crept silently into bodies that had worn out. There was life and there was death and the turnover felt like the natural order of things, as though we were a part of a wider rhythm of the world, the City's vital and constant ebb and flow.

Human error, in all its extraordinary forms, was the only thing that jarred. The clients we lost to laziness, to apathy, or through sheer stupidity always niggled for a day or two. And very occasionally, in moments of sharp clarity and boldness, you might decide that some clients were not worth having at all.

Agnes had been walking Winston for a while. I'd seen them in the park a number of times, Agnes's distinct fast-paced walk with Winston lolloping along behind. He used to stop and say hello, wiggle over, and give me a nudge with his pinky nose, but Agnes soon put a stop to that. She was perfect for Carl: neat, firm, punctual, and adept at following instructions, and I knew the fanny pack would have impressed him too. I could picture Carl eyeing it up, wondering where he could get his hands on one and if it came in brown.

Carl and I hadn't exactly fallen out but things had become awkward. After I stopped walking Winston, he had tried to avoid me as much as he could, which is tricky when you share the same park. At first we would say hello to one another, then politely smile, but before long we had moved to outright ignoring or pretending to be on the phone.

I saw him in Sainsbury's a while later, sniffing fabric softeners in the laundry aisle, and I awkwardly waved hello but he just turned the other way and walked off.

The details behind the breakup had trickled out slowly, mainly from Joe who had gone from miserable and heartbroken in Vauxhall to relieved and reinvigorated in Essex. Carl had run off with their personal trainer, an epicurean from Geneva with a penchant for olives and native cheese who had been trying to help Joe get into shape. Getting in shape quickly turned into Carl suggesting that they all get into bed together and then that turned into Carl just getting into bed with him. He had denied it all, saying he just needed some space, some time away from the relationship, but the contents of the fridge had given the game away. Carl was far too vain to eat cheese.

As the fridge detective, I felt terrible at being so instrumental in their breakup but Joe insisted that I had done him a favor and called Carl a "dark, bald cunt," which seemed fairly definitive. A few months later I set Joe up with another client, a PR man with a yellow Labrador in Highgate, and although it hadn't worked out romantically, they became great friends and spent quite a bit of time together. Joe got a new dog, a schnauzer called Eric, and while he still saw Winston at the weekends, his ties to London, and to Carl, were far looser.

But by the spring of 2011, I hadn't seen Winston for a good few months and I eventually got around to asking Agnes how he was.

"I don't know," she snapped. "He has moved. I do not see him anymore."

"Oh, right. Do you know where he has gone?"

"I don't know, somewhere that way," she said, pointing downriver toward central London. "I only do this park now." She had five dogs with her at the time, all of whom looked bewildered and weary. I was nearing my second trimester and, while rather weary myself, I was full of all the joys.

"Well, thanks, Agnes," I said. "Is everything OK with you?"

"It is fine," she replied, slightly bemused. She'd had a new haircut, a blunt black bob with a fringe that cut her forehead in half and made her look like she was wearing a helmet. It suited her.

"You look very nice," I said, and I meant it.

Usually, events with great anticipation often turn out to be a letdown — New Year's Eve, birthday parties, visits to the zoo — and it's all those unexpected, under-the-radar things that turn out to be the most memorable. With such an enormous amount of expectation placed upon it, pregnancy should have been gearing up to be the biggest letdown of them all. Except that it wasn't. It wasn't at all. It was magnificent and shocking and overwhelmingly exciting and, despite the sickness and the fatigue and the alarming aversion to chocolate, for the first time in my life I felt utterly invincible.

There was simply no room for Panic or any other such nonsense because all the space had been taken up with hormones, baby names, and pram confusion. There was no greater sense of purpose or focus than knowing I was going to have a baby; no stronger feeling of contentment or surety than my certainty that what we were embarking upon was the absolute best thing in the world. Despite the precariousness and delicacy of such new and developing life, I felt strangely stable and strong, as if the very foundations were being poured beneath me. The unfathomable wonder of actually creating something within my own body, the incomprehension of how I was able to do this while also brushing my teeth or making an omelette would lead to moments of such complete bewilderment and stupor that I was forced to rebalance myself by eating another kilogram of mashed potato on the sofa. These were the months of carbohydrates and wonder.

For the first time in my life I felt completely, wholeheartedly happy all of the time. A happiness that spread out into the farthest corners, to the fingertips and the toes and the very pit of my stomach. Even if I was to really search for the sadness or the worry, to challenge it to come and find me, it just wouldn't be there. Happiness was usually fleeting and unpredictable or had to be coaxed to the surface with alcohol. It certainly didn't just turn up and plonk itself down.

"I have a positive pregnancy test," I had said to Finlay on the phone some twelve weeks earlier with the stick in my hands, the two dark lines as solid and definitive as they possibly could be. But I couldn't bring myself to say, "I'm pregnant," not after wanting it so much for so long. That seemed far too bold. Presumptuous even. It would take at least ten to fifteen more sticks and many a quizzical look from the local pharmacist to allow myself to finally say that. I liked the digital ones the best, the ones that said "PREGNANT" on the screen because, despite my expensive education, I still needed it laid out in easy-to-read letters like a Speak and Spell toy.

"A positive pregnancy test? What does that mean?" he asked, an entirely justifiable question, all things considered.

"I think it means we might be able to have a baby after all," I said, and I peed on five more that day alone, just to be sure that my petulant biological clock hadn't conjured up some sort of mirage. That is all you get after all, just one word on a tiny screen, a simple line on a white plastic stick to represent the end of all those months of anguish and doubt. I looked at my tummy and imagined the burrowing cells, the flickers and sparks of hormones wildly surging as the body begins to wake to this new, monumental undertaking. I instantly wanted a large, round belly and the huff and the puff of a heavy, waddling walk. I wanted the aches and the pains, the weird cravings and the stretching skin. I wanted a popped belly button and the kindly smiles of the elderly. But all you have is the plastic stick, and the challenge of learning to have faith in your body once again.

Fortunately, when the endless nausea rolled in a week or so later, a period of contentment and gratefulness settled in with it, the delicious secrecy of what was going on under the surface making me feel almost childlike again, where secrets were precious, magical things that you felt honored to be guarding. It might have been all those hormones that led me to tell Agnes she looked nice, to tell my mother what a fabulous primary grandmother she was going to be, and even drop Carl an email to see how he was doing and to check whether Winston needed a walker. He wrote back almost immediately: "Yes. Please have someone for tomorrow."

Luckily, there wasn't much time to regret being so foolishly led by misplaced goodwill and giddy hormones. Carl and Winston were now in Pimlico, not far from Vincent Square, and I asked Tom if he could fit in Winston after Stanley but he said no as his bike was playing up and he would also rather not be that close to the "dark forces of Westminster."

Ideally, I would not have used a new walker. Carl is not the sort of client you want to foist upon a first timer and there would also be the interrogation I would be subjected to on the new walker's experience. But there was something a bit different about Rupert and I suspected Carl would like him.

Rupert was in his mid-forties, mostly single, wore a cravat and brogues, and handed me a business card with just "Rupert" on it and then six ways of getting hold of him, including two landlines and a fax machine. He dabbled in multiple, vague careers like "finance" and "film" and "intelligence" but also seemed have a lot of time on his hands, time he wanted to spend with dogs. He'd had cats growing up but told me they were large for their breed and had "dog-like tendencies," plus during a brief spell with an "elite unit" he'd had a "moment" with a wolf up a mountain.

"So, do you know much about dogs?" I asked.

"I have never met an animal that didn't love me," he replied and, instead of giving me a nice animal anecdote to round it all off, he proceeded to tell me all about the girl he was dating, a dental nurse from the Czech Republic who did triathlons and cooked amazing dumplings. There were other vague details about time spent training in Singapore and a run-in with some goats in Lincolnshire but I switched off at some point, as sometimes you have to gloss over the finer, vaguer details and look at the bigger picture — which was that he was the only walker available at such short notice and he lived around the corner.

Fortunately, Carl was delighted. Whether it was the brogues or the business cards or the posh wheeler-dealer looks, I had an unprecedented "thank you" email which even concluded with a kiss after his name and was sent during normal office hours, which meant there was no chance of it being a two-glasses-of-wine-down kind of kiss.

It is at times like these that you must be wary of being lulled into a false sense of achievement, of thinking that you might have finally cracked the enigma of a successful client and walker match. A happy client (particularly a difficult one) who actually acknowledges that you have done something of benefit to them is so unbelievably rare that even a simple thank you can lead you down a misguided road of self-congratulation. You may start believing you have advanced people skills or superior intuition, rather than it being about luck, timing, convenient geography, or simply the fact that Carl fancied the pants off Rupert.

Carl seemed to temporarily forget all his rules about Winston not swimming or playing in puddles. Considering that he'd gone for an entirely cream palette at his new Pimlico flat, this was particularly remarkable. The fact that Winston hadn't been replaced with a pug or a Pomeranian or some other pale dog seemed to suggest that Carl had relaxed over the years, discovered he was more cream than brown, and become a happier, nicer person — though perhaps this was hormones talking.

Within the first week, Winston had not only been for a dip in the lake at Battersea and a mud bath in a large puddle around the back of Channel Four, he'd had a long nap on the new cream sofa, curled up between Rupert and Carl as they had a post-walk cup of tea. After the confusion of the breakup and the rigors of Agnes, Winston must have felt as if he was finally getting his London life back on track.

But a short while later, a month or two at most, Rupert called with some concerns.

"How are you getting on?" I asked. "Is everything OK?"

"The dude's a bit off, but it's nothing I can't handle."

"Carl?"

"Yeah, Carl. Strange dude."

"Is there anything in particular?"

"Well, there's the flat of course. He started getting a bit weird about where I put things and how clean Winston is."

"Perfectly normal," I replied. "That's par for the course I am afraid."

"There's more. He's annoyed because he's tried it on a few times and he hasn't got what he wanted. He keeps asking me to go places with him, clubs and that sort of thing. I said no, of course. I don't like the dude and I'm not gay, by the way."

"OK. Well, that's fine. Either way."

"I just wanted to call and let you know that if he touches me, if he touches me at all, I am going to have to take him out."

"*Out?* Where?"

"Out. Like down. Take him down."

There was a pause while the words sunk in and in that moment I suddenly felt the baby kick. I'd felt little kicks before but this was a real thump. This perfect, tiny leg kicking my stomach with all its might, turning and somersaulting, and then I had a vision of Carl and Rupert thumping each other on Carl's immaculate cream carpet before an elite team of other brogue-wearing idiots stormed in and piled on top. I chastised myself for not taking in more of the vague details and for even thinking for one moment that working with Carl again would turn out all right.

"Please don't do that, Rupert. That would be ridiculous. Let me have a word with him. I am sure it's all just a misunderstanding."

"I know a misunderstanding when I see

one. I've been trained extensively in misunderstandings and this, *this* is not a misunderstanding."

"I'll have a word with him, OK?"

"He's not the sort of man who will take a word. He needs a smack."

"That's not our job though, is it? We don't go around smacking clients. We are supposed to be walking the dog! Look, why don't we just move you off Winston and on to a different dog. A different client."

"I'll give it one more week," he said, which essentially meant that he was actually quite enjoying the whole thing and hoped it would come to a head.

I thought back to when Winston was a puppy, so eager and excited by the world, his tail wagging his whole body left and right, so loved and so adored, and however tricky the flat was — the cleanliness, the brownness, the rules — for Winston, everything was perfect. Life lay ahead of him like one of their beautifully ironed, fluffy towels, a straight and safe path, cocooned in comfort and not yet tarnished by human hand. We had figured it out together, walk by walk, how to navigate it all. Everything had looked so promising, so easy.

I sent Carl an email. As delicately as I could, I told him Rupert felt a little uncomfortable and wondered whether there had been some wires crossed along the way. A simple, solvable misunderstanding.

Kate. I have just returned from the vet. He clearly hasn't mentioned it but Rupert allowed Winston to carry a very large branch of a tree back from the park the other day which may have caused severe damage to his mouth. While I understand that my dog likes sticks, I do not expect him to be put in such a dangerous position. Winston was also BLACK from having rolled in a stagnant, filthy puddle. I explicitly told Rupert not to allow him into puddles and as my instructions have not been met, I must request that he does not come again. Winston is my dog and he is to be walked as I see fit. I am enclosing the bill from the vet (£335.76), which I expect to be paid ASAP. Carl.

The baby kicked again, harder this time, right into the stomach walls and the force of it made me take a sharp intake of breath. I read the email again, over and over, trying to process each individual word, but none of it seemed to make any sense. Another kick, an elbow up into the ribs. I put my

282

hand on my stomach to try to calm her, to let her know that everything was OK. We had found out that we were having a girl. Perhaps I could be a leader after all.

"Dear Carl," I wrote, the apology predictably, routinely moving from my brain to my fingers. I could write these in my sleep now.

"Dear Carl . . ."

She kicked again, an enormous wallop that forced me to my feet. I held the side of the table and took some long deep breaths but the kicking did not stop. It got stronger and quicker, it was determined and brave and so full of life.

It was the most amazing thing in the whole entire world.

I sat down and started to write again.

"Dear Carl," I wrote. And then I wrote, "FUCK OFF!"

Winston was fine. I never heard from Carl again but Joe emailed to wish me luck with the baby and told me not to worry about any of it as there had been a tiny scratch at the most. The branch was more of a twig really, something a dog twice his age and half his size could have managed with ease.

But the puddle had been black. It was black and very, very muddy.

MABEL, PART THREE

As the year came to a close and my due date inched closer, my mother called daily to remind me that we were "harboring a killer."

"You will never forgive yourself if Mabel eats the baby," she said in a tone so grave that I wondered for a moment if she might actually be serious. It wasn't unheard of for her to be right, on occasion, and, like all mothers, it was usually about something that you really don't want her to be right about, like putting money aside or wearing the right winter coat. When mothers are vehement about something, when they nag, it's hard to completely ignore it. We are conditioned to take their words on board, to ruminate on them, to either accept or reject them, and then pass them down to our children regardless.

On this particular subject she told me she had "read things" and, on top of that, she "knew things."

284

"I know things, darling. I know a lot of things," she said at least three times. "I really would urge you to think about this because I can see a tragedy lurking on the horizon. We all love Mabel but she may get very jealous. You just don't know how she will react."

"Well, what do you suggest we do?" I asked.

"I don't know, darling, it's your decision at the end of the day. I am only here to advise. If I don't tell you these things, nobody else will."

"So what do you advise?"

"I advise you to think about it."

I thought about poor Fabio, recently returned to his family and clearly struggling with the enormous changes at home. Ignoring the fact that he had been expelled from the house for an entire human gestation, Meredith was concerned about how different he was and often emailed for advice. He was off his food for one thing, which could have been a sign of his inner turmoil but was more likely due to the fact that his foster carer had fed him regular portions of beef and dry vegan dog biscuits just weren't going to cut it anymore.

While Fabio may well have longed for those heady early days in Rome, trotting down the Via del Corso, the apple of his owner's eye, I suspected it was just Meredith who was different, not Fabio. She was a mother now and would never be quite the same again, priorities, judgments, emotions had all shifted. Fabio was still Fabio, a reluctant Hindu who couldn't help but love his family unconditionally. He got a new walker, the lovely Juliana, back from traveling abroad, and he slowly adjusted to his new position in the pack.

Mabel had been distinctly uninterested in my growing stomach and, aside from the occasional sniff, she had largely ignored it, which was either an encouraging sign that she would find the baby very dull or that she was going to get an enormous shock. Her life was so simple and perfect, led by a wonderfully reassuring routine of food and sleep and park, that she would never have been able to foresee the enormous wrecking ball heading her way. But however much I thought about it, however many worst-case scenarios I envisaged, there was never one where Mabel retaliated, where whatever jealous feelings she had took over. I just couldn't believe she was capable of it. The books all said to play baby sounds, crying and squeaking and gurgling, so that the dog would be more prepared for what was about to arrive, but we couldn't seem to find any. So we improvised by watching *Three Men and a Baby* and *Look Who's Talking* a few times at top volume. Mabel slept through it all.

"She's going to be fine," I said to Finlay, who, as a relative newcomer to the canine world, still wasn't completely convinced that dogs weren't all biding their time, secretly sharpening their teeth.

"She's got teeth," he said. "I've seen her with a Dentastix. She means business."

"That's because she's scrupulous about dental hygiene," I replied. "She's trying to get the back ones, the ones we all forget about. Those are the ones that get you in trouble. Ask any dentist."

"I'm scrupulous about dental hygiene but I'm not bred to rip things limb from limb!"

We had started prenatal classes and they were making him grumpy. Ten couples in a church hall talking about milk and poo and bleeding would tax even the most convivial among us but forced social gatherings with strangers and without alcohol was Finlay's vision of what the worst room in hell might look like.

"We don't have to be friends with them just because we all had sex around the same time," I said as we left the first meeting.

"Well, at least, you don't have to anyway. I might need to chat about boobs and colic with the other mums."

The men, fresh from their office jobs and still in suits, compared jobs and schooling and then tried to out-dad each other. It was an unusual setting for competitiveness but you can never underestimate the human capacity for one-upmanship, even when it concerns your unborn child.

"I want mine to be good at rugby," the men barked when asked what they hoped for their future child. "And to like watching rugby. Cricket in summer. More rugby. A high achiever. Lawyer. Banker. Squash. Rugby."

"I want mine to be a bit funny and silly," Finlay said, to which everyone hastily agreed so as not to appear *too* awful. I think it was one of the best things I had ever heard. He knows how to be a human being better than most.

But he was worried about becoming a father. About getting it right. He was a perfectionist about many things — work, tracksuit bottoms, scrambled eggs — but he could also quite happily put a navy jumper in a white wash or a mug in the bottom rack of the dishwasher. He didn't worry about the little things like I did, a comment someone made or the party you weren't invited to, and he always stayed calm during the big things too — the baby that we seemingly couldn't have or the business that nearly fell apart. He was somehow able to see a way through to the end, past all the unnecessary worrying about the things you can't change, right through to the point when none of it matters anymore. You either get to where you want to go or you don't, and the middle bit is just life. But this was something totally different. Being a father was the middle bit — it was all of it.

It's easier for the mother-to-be, the baby already there, weaving themselves into you, but the father stands on the other side of the door, waiting to be let in. Parenting for Finlay was just a concept, something you had to step into and make it fit. Something you had to stick with, however hard. But just to be present wasn't going to be enough. Finlay needed to be present and correct, to make up for the mistakes that others had made. He wanted to show me that fathers could be loyal and trustworthy and stable and that mothers loving their babies more than they have ever loved anything in the world would be enough. He wanted to show me that together we would do our best to be good parents.

So it really was no surprise that to avoid any baby eating prospects, he suggested we move Mabel's bed to the kitchen. It was a small step toward sensible, responsible parenting but one that took a while to be fully signed off. After an extremely feeble attempt at keeping her out of the bedroom on day one, for the last three years she had made her home on our bed, often under the covers or curled up tightly on a pillow. Her basket, chosen with a level of care and consideration suitable for a much larger purchase, could have been sold as brand new on eBay with a completely clear conscience. She had sat in it once, possibly twice, before rejecting it as "too dog." She chose the sofa, or the bed, depending on the time of the day. But despite the snoring and the yipping noises that multiple night-time dreams produced, we had gotten used to her being there. It was as much her bed as it was ours and to move her now felt mean and unnecessary to me.

Except that it was necessary. There wasn't really enough room and deep down I knew I had to set some boundaries — for Mabel if nothing else. By the time I got the basket out of the cupboard and dusted it down, I was past my due date and had run out of excuses. It was placed in the kitchen, a nice little corner spot, and, as I closed the door on the first night, I lobbed the contents of a whole packet of Schmackos in there to help soften the blow.

"She's quiet," Finlay whispered as I crept in next to him in bed. "I told you it would be OK. We should have done this ages ago."

In case you were wondering, it takes precisely two and a half minutes for a Jack Russell to eat a packet of chicken Schmackos. That was before Mabel started scratching and whining at the door and she didn't stop until after I heard the first plane to land at Heathrow go over at five o'clock in the morning. I put a pillow over my head and sobbed as the baby repeatedly kicked me in the stomach. She was already on Mabel's side.

"I hate your dog," Finlay groaned as the alarm went off an hour later. We'd had no sleep.

"*Our* dog," I mumbled sleepily. "You hate *our* dog."

He rolled over slowly and smiled. "I hate our dog."

As the days waddled on and the baby stubbornly stayed put, Mabel's nighttime protests got shorter and shorter, till one night they suddenly stopped.

"That's it," I said to Finlay. "The baby can come now. Brace yourself, Mabel."

She was born in a rush and panic just as the sun came up at ten to eight on December 6 at six pounds, six ounces. She had waited and waited, sat it out until the last feasible moment, before a rushed, emergency arrival to the largest possible audience of doctors and midwives. It was an hour or two at the most of the most transformative, euphoric, screaming pain. She was placed on my chest and melted into my body as she bellowed out those first vital cries and, despite the urgency and noise and lights, the room slowed and narrowed so that for a long time it was just me and her trying to make sense of each other in the eye of a storm. We'd already been together for nine months, entwined in blood and tissue, and yet we were complete strangers. I wondered if she really was mine. We spent the first few days just staring at each other under the hot hospital strip lights, sore, bewildered, and crying, but so full of love that I worried that I might never sleep again. She was tiny and beautiful. We called her Belle.

"You've got a little 'un there," said the taxi driver cheerfully as we sat bleary-eyed in the back, clutching onto the car seat on our way home. We had been in for four days and had almost forgotten London was outside. "A new one, is she?"

"She's freshly popped," said Finlay. "Like a beautiful pea."

Finlay went to collect Mabel from a neighbor's. She raced into the flat to find me, bounding down the corridor and to the sofa where I was sitting. Belle was sleeping quietly on my chest, legs tucked up as if she was still inside, black hair slicked down and pink skin trembling slightly. Mabel stopped abruptly, head cocked to one side as she sniffed the air. Something was different. Everything was different.

"Come and say hello," I said, aware that I was suddenly quite nervous.

She carefully jumped up and started to sniff Belle's head, delicately at first and then more urgently as she tried to get her nose in under the baby blanket. She was taking in every bit of her, inhaling every fragment of her smell. She wanted to know everything she could about her, who she was and what she meant.

"Mabel, steady," said Finlay, hovering protectively.

"It's OK," I replied. "Let her take her time."

Perhaps she thought Belle was a temporary visitor, or perhaps she knew about her all along. Either way, it didn't take her long to settle down on the sofa next to me and start to snore.

"Well that went all right, didn't it?" Finlay said. His relief was palpable. "No baby munching today. Shall I call and tell your mum? I love it when she's wrong."

STANLEY, PART FIVE

Stanley was slowing down now. Stiller in his quiet moments, heavier when he moved. Hot days were difficult and the cold ones of winter meant that joints ached and bones creaked as dotage set in like freezing fog. The vet had said how well he was doing for his age, which, although still something of a mystery, had almost certainly entered the arena of the Old. He went to Battersea Park less, preferring local walks around his neighborhood and the occasional visit to Tom's youth center. Eating was still top of the agenda but he couldn't jump up anymore so Steph had come to the rather melancholic realization that she could leave food out on the kitchen surfaces and be confident it would still be there later. It was a more sedate life but almost a happier one, shrunk down to the basics, to the things that really mattered.

Nevertheless, when Tom took a trip to the

south coast to see his grandmother, he took Stanley with him — not as a hostage but as a friend. There was a coastal path he wanted to explore and he thought Stanley might like to keep him company while he helped to pack up his grandmother's house. She was moving into a care home after being diagnosed with dementia. Plus, Stanley had never seen the sea.

"This is OK, isn't it?" Steph asked me on the phone. "Tom taking Stanley. It's not . . . *weird* is it? I know it's a little unusual, but you don't think we are making a mistake do you?"

"No, not at all," I replied. "I think it will be really good for him, all that sea air and blowing away the cobwebs."

"Good for who?" she asked.

I paused for a moment.

"Stanley!" And Tom. It would be very good for Tom.

Tom was undoubtedly happiest in the company of dogs, Stanley in particular. I understood it more now that he had worked for me for so long. Or rather I had learned not to understand it but to just take Tom as he was and not to question it. I trusted him, not just because he had walked dogs for longer than anyone else but because his love of the job meant that he would always put the dog first. He would always turn up, maybe not bang on time and maybe looking like an inventor or a Roman centurion or even just like a slightly lost, scruffy thirty-something, but he would always be there, whatever else was going on. That was the most important thing you could give a dog.

They left just after Christmas and were due to return in early January. Steph and family were having a few days with relatives in Yorkshire over the New Year and had planned to do a lot of brisk dale walking so Stanley's quiet sojourn by the sea was timed perfectly. They got the train down, Stanley curled up under Tom's feet, snoring peacefully.

I almost forgot about the pair of them, the oddest of couples holidaying together in the middle of winter, but then Tom called at dawn one chilly morning. He was on the beach with Stanley.

"Kate? Kate? I'm sorry it's so early. Are you awake? I'm at the beach, Kate. With Stanley. He's loving it. He's in the sea! He's swimming in the actual sea! The Channel I think. Is this the Channel? Go on, Stanley, go on, you go, boy! I wish you could see him Kate, he's so happy. He's just so happy!"

A seagull squawked in the background, a

wave crunched onto the shingle and as I started to wake up I heard a dog barking. It was Stanley, except that he sounded different. Lighter.

"Tom? It's very early. Is everything OK?"

"Everything is great. It's all so bloody great. I just wanted to share this with you. And to say thank you. For letting me walk the dogs. For letting me walk Stanley. I think it will be a good year, this one. I can feel it in these old bones of mine. Well, I'll let you go now. Cheers Kate. Take care!"

It was the most unexpected but perfect start to the day.

I didn't have maternity leave as such. There was Christmas, a sleep-deprived, lactating blur punctuated by cheese and chocolate and unwelcome visitors, but everyone else was on holiday then and by the time the nation was preparing to kick off another working year, the phone had started to ring again. I hadn't really made a plan for exactly how I would run a business while caring for a newborn and hoped that my tried and tested wing-it approach might just work. It hadn't let me down yet, after all.

And it did, for a while. Babies sleep an awful lot — not always at the times you want them to but usually long enough for you to get a few emails done or chuckle along with some of the more needy customers. Sod the fact that you have just had a baby, Mrs. Heathcote-Jones must tell you in great detail about the adorable Christmas sweater her pug got from Santa and how he just couldn't take it off *all day long,* even when they went to their awful neighbor's house for carols and mince pies and how jealous they must have been because their cat had only been given a festive bow tie. Listening was always one of the most important parts of the job. I just wondered whether it should have really been someone else's ear.

I had planned to scale things back a bit, not take on any new clients and try to just keep it all ticking over until Belle was a little older. The other mums from prenatal class were all eating cake and waving rattles in museum tea shops while I was arranging a Weimaraner's holiday to the Lake District and coordinating the return of an anxious Akita's teddy bear left at the groomer's. The stupefying effects of broken sleep and days blurring into nights would often lead to strange, drowsy delusions about multiple lost dogs running wild all over London, catching cabs and drinking in pubs while their furious owners tried to get the government involved in shutting us down. We had over eighty dogs and forty dog walkers and that was more than enough. If I thought about it too much, I would feel sickeningly overwhelmed.

But then I had a call from Camilla. I didn't catch her last name as she talked very fast and very persuasively and before I knew it I was agreeing to something that I didn't fully understand or even really want. She worked for a concierge company, one of those places that organizes tickets and drugs and helicopters for the very rich with five minutes' notice because they'd only decided they needed tickets and drugs and helicopters five minutes ago and they naturally need them right now. I soon learned that being horribly rich means you can confidently make those sorts of impromptu decisions without anyone saying no or telling you how much of a knob you are. Camilla was in the market for a dog-walking company to service some of her clients, and she had "heard" we were the ones to use.

Remarkable, really, that you never actually get positive feedback from the customers themselves, only via some third party. Then again, she probably just googled us and saw we had been around for a while, which, in a roundabout way, is almost the same as a recommendation. It means that you haven't done anything *so* awful that you have had to be completely erased from the internet.

"There is a potential first client," Camilla said. "The Principal. He's in LA at the moment but due to come over soon while they spend some time in London. He needs a walker twice a day, sometimes more. Would that be OK?"

"Yes, I am sure it would be," I replied. "Is 'the Principal' the, um, the dog's name?" It wasn't a totally ridiculous question. We'd had dogs named Mr. Legend, Sir Waffleton Chops, and Henry the Avenger before.

"No," Camilla snipped. "The Principal is the client! That is how we shall refer to him at all times and you will have to sign a confidentially agreement, of course."

"Oh. Right. No problem." "The Principal" must then be a stage name I thought, perhaps a rapper like Jay Z or P Diddy, or maybe even a wrestler, and to refer to him by whatever real, civilian name he had would be seen as extremely uncouth and disrespectful.

"And there may be others," she continued. "I can't confirm at the moment but what I need to establish now is whether or not you have the availability. And the staff, of course. We need very good staff. These are

HNWIs. UHNW clients. Top tier. Page one. We need people who can rise to that challenge. Do you think you can manage it?"

I decided I could probably manage it after googling what on earth she was talking about. "Ultra high net worth individuals," apparently, who wouldn't put up with a substandard service. Perhaps it was the peppering of unknown but impressive-sounding acronyms or the frisson of fame and wealth that piqued my interest. There was certainly an element of flattery at being recognized, of being seen as "good enough," the best even, however likely it was that we had just been around longer than anyone else.

There was also the fact that I still found it virtually impossible to say no to anyone, despite my resolution not to take on anything too stressful and to just absorb being a mother for a while. I knew the moment that Camilla spoke her first clipped word that it was all going to be far more trouble than it was worth and yet even with a tiny one-month-old baby tucked into my arms and more luck and good fortune than most ever see, I still felt the compulsion to push on, to achieve, to impress. Busyness. It's an almost impossible habit to break.

Camilla emailed over a ten-page confidentiality agreement with a multitude of complicated clauses in it, most of which didn't make very much sense. The general gist of it all was that "the Principal" was ultra famous and if you decided to leak any information about him, his house, his dog, or anything else, you would be in all sorts of grown-up trouble and any cash deal you may have brokered with the tabloids wouldn't even touch the sides of the enormous legal bill coming your way.

He was not a rapper, it turned out. Or a wrestler. Everyone of his ilk is referred to in this way to show people like me how very important they are. And his dog was called Dolly.

To balance out the arrival of the Principal and all the glossiness that was sure to bring, I also took on a dog who wasn't glossy at all. His name was Buster and he was both deaf and partially blind but had the sort of look about him that said he wouldn't let something as minor as that stand in his way. He was a mixed terrier breed, a classic mongrel, with tufty, salt-and-pepper hair and white-socked paws, which he liked to bounce up and down on as though he was doing a jig. He was a rescue dog, he lived near Clapham, and he was perfect for Tom.

Tom was the main reason I wanted to take

on Buster. I thought the challenge might be good for him, especially now that Stanley was less keen on adventuring. The task at hand wasn't easy and they needed someone with patience and kindness. Someone who perhaps understood vulnerabilities themselves. Buster had only been with his new owners a few short weeks but they had started working on teaching him a couple of basic visual commands. He was confused and nervous at times, but he was determined too. The infinite patchwork of sights and sounds that make up a dog's environment — the neighbor's cat, the postman's whistle, the ball being thrown, the squirrel, the bike, the car — was all lost on Buster. But he had smell, he had touch and taste, and he had life in his bones and that was enough.

Dogs don't really dwell on their physical ailments like humans do. They don't feel sorry for themselves or try to apportion blame. They take what they have in the moment and just get on with it, eking out every last bit of enjoyment and taking every new day as it comes. Stanley with his aches and pains, the body that didn't work as well as it did; Buster's sight and sound not working at all. This was their lot and they were going to make the most of it, because time spent dwelling on problems was time not spent living it up.

Tom worked every day with Buster, always spending longer than he needed to, slowly, patiently building up trust. Buster was smart, a fast learner, and physically fit but above all of that, he just wanted to be a dog like any other, to explore and run and to sniff as much of London as he could. You might not have chosen to be diminished in those two particular senses out of your list of five but when it came to smell, Buster certainly made up for everything else that he was lacking.

London is an eager nose's paradise, an unlimited bouquet of aromas. All of the City can be found within its scent — its people and its energy, the history and the landscape, and its glorious multiculturalism. From the brackish breeze that lifts off the Thames to the sweet verdant aroma of fruit in their bowls at the market; the grass as it's just been cut in the royal parks and the warm, rubbery engine fumes that seep out from the underground. Greasy spoons, fish and chips, spices and melted ghee, chicken shops, flower shops, stale beer, stale smoke and burning exhaust pipes, urinals, over-flowing bins and the musty upholstery smell on the top of a hot double-decker bus.

Smell was everything to Buster. He knew how his front door smelled — the lacquered wood and the chipped concrete step below it, his owner's shoes and whether they were in or they were out. Their front gate and the first lamppost on the right were different day by day, their scent changed by dogs, a cat, or a fox. The walk to the end of the street, past the cherry tree and down to the bus stop, might feature dropped lettuce from a kebab, a cigarette butt, or a man wearing oud fragrance. There could be a chicken bone or a new pair of shoes and the smell of a dog he hadn't met before. It all had to be gathered and processed so he might know his way home again.

It wasn't long before Tom and Buster were able to go a little farther afield, to walk down new streets and explore new smells, each day getting a little bit farther. Although the progress was hugely encouraging, the park was still a fair distance away and Tom wondered if they would ever get there. We talked about taking the bus, getting him in a basket at the front of the bike, or even borrowing a car but in the end, Tom had a much better idea. He took Stanley along.

Buster was unsure at first. Another dog in his space, on his street, was all too over-whelming. Stanley wondered why he was being asked to make new friends, particularly at this late stage in his life. The first few walks were a disaster as Buster refused to move off his top step and Stanley lay prostrate on the pavement. Adversity and age had made them stubborn and resolute and neither of them were happy about having to share Tom.

This would be the point at which most would give up and accept defeat in the face of such an enormous obstacle. Getting just one of these dogs to the park was an achievement, let alone two. But Tom was patient. He sat with them, quietly, calmly, until there was familiarity, until they began to sense the weaknesses within the other.

Stanley, his bones slow and tired, and Buster, without his eyes and ears, were a match, a perfect dysfunctional pairing, one complementing the other with what they were lacking. What Stanley missed in energy, Buster made up for with his vim and vigor, and what Buster lacked in sight and sound, Stanley provided with his constancy and his wisdom. Stanley was the elder statesman, a dog fazed only by his mood on any given day, infinitely trustworthy to younger, nervous dogs and Buster was happy to go in under his large, woolly wing. When he was walking next to Stanley, the older dog's heavy, lethargic plod took away some of Buster's fear of the unknown.

Stanley had always had a knack for spotting the vulnerable. He spotted it in Tom, the two of them leaning on each other day in and day out, and he knew when it was within his own four walls — when someone was anxious or sad and he would do his best to help. But it wasn't so easy when he needed support. He was proud and self-reliant, and if it hadn't been for Buster's own impairments, he would have almost certainly rebuffed any assistance. When he was slowing down, when he felt tired or gloomy, Buster would help to chivvy him along, encourage him to walk down the next street, until one day they made it all the way to the park.

It was all Tom of course. The perseverance and the intuition. He had not only managed to get the dogs to trust him but also to trust each other. He hadn't just gotten these two dogs to the park, an enormous feat in itself, he had managed to bring out the best in each one; in helping the other, they had also helped themselves. You have to have absolute faith in the dogs to get them this far out of their comfort zones. When all is said and done, dogs mainly just want to sleep and eat ham and have someone scratch them so adeptly that their back leg starts to jiggle. Compliance, even for something routine or favorable, is not always a given.

It was times like this that I thought, even just for a moment or two, that I might have the best job in the world, that what I did had a real purpose to it and that in some modest way, my team had made a difference to someone's life. It wasn't always easy to stop and savor those small triumphs before they were swallowed up into the tedious and thankless void of customer service. Even though our hard work and favorable reputation meant that we were now attracting a more discerning customer, one who had often come to us because of our reputation, I was rarely allowed to forget that, as the service provider, I was something of a second-class citizen and was to be treated accordingly, regardless of how happy BooBoo was when he trotted in through the door.

So those good moments, the ones that made me feel proud and fearless, had to be knotted together, one by one, till they wrapped all the way around, like an armor.

DOLLY, PART ONE

SILKY TERRIER, ONE, NOTTING HILL
JUNE 2012
NUMBER OF DOGS WALKED: 88

In advance of even meeting her, my first Dolly-related task was to find her a trainer. The monthlong, pre-London boot camp she had been dispatched to in Santa Barbara hadn't turned out as well as the Principal's staff had hoped and she was still using kitchen surfaces as her preferred toilet. Having spent most of her first year at various Hollywood day care centers she could confidently join a dog yoga class or sit still while she had a shiatsu massage but she wasn't so good at not biting people or going outside for a poo.

I had to immediately discount Elephant Dave, as his tough love approach would be a little *too* tough, and Monty Shears would be booked up of course, so it was a case of calling one or two and seeing if they sounded "Principal friendly." The problem was that the Principal wouldn't actually be there. Dolly was arriving a few weeks early on a private jet and needed to be trained, groomed, and refined before being handed back obedient and presentable like a Victorian child.

"I've worked with many, *many* celebrities," said one trainer in a deep, plummy voice. "Shan't name names *obviously,* but there have been some very top people come my way over the years. The main issue we have with these types of people, and the royals of course, is that they like to outsource everything and expect someone else to do the dirty work. They want a ready-trained dog, you see, and it simply doesn't work that way. The dog needs a master. A leader. I don't spend my time teaching flunkies I am afraid." So that was out.

I suggested the Italian trainer that Meredith had used for Fabio in Rome (the best in Europe, supposedly, and well used to Principal-level clients) but in the end they flew someone in from New York, a young guy called Manny who had no issues with training Dolly in loco parentis, particularly as he had been flown in first class and put up in a swanky hotel for a week. He preferred a "multidisciplined zen approach" and requested that we all attend the first training session at the house.

We went one early evening in late June.

London was at its most golden and beautiful, dressed up in all its summer finery and feeling quite pleased with itself, what with the Olympics coming up and everyone saying what a wonderful, vibrant city it was. It's easy to forget to look up and out when you have your head down all the time. Work and baby, tasks and chores, emails and texts, everything looking down or looking inward. We forget to notice all the lovely little things. But this was the summer to breathe it all in.

The Principal's house was enormous, at least five floors of it, and it seemed to rise out of the pavement and into the sky like a great red-and-white chicken, with proud pointed gables, glossy red bricks, white stuccoed windows, and immaculately coiffed foliage in the front garden. It was on a quiet, tree-lined street, quite unassuming really, and I wondered if the other residents — bankers and media types — knew who they lived next door to and whether or not they really cared. There wasn't really any indication, from the outside at least, except perhaps for the front door, which had two cameras pointing at it and was so black and shiny that it seemed to be melting into the steps below it. If you looked very closely at the window to the right, you would also see a stout Filipino lady jabbing her finger at you to go around to the back entrance. Only Principals used the front door, like a velvet rope at a private members club.

I was met there by a large, sweaty man in a black suit and thin sunglasses who led me silently to a basement entrance in the garden. From there, we went through a small security room packed with TV screens, a gym, a utility room, and finally to the kitchen, which was not only vast but utterly spotless and entirely monochrome. A Troika of Filipino ladies resided here, the one from the window and another pair, all of whom muttered things to each other under their breath while they wiped surfaces and folded tea towels. There was also a security detail, a rotation of four huge blokes, and a butler — although he was always with the Principal.

Despite the large numbers of staff, the house still felt empty and rather cold, like a very expensive furniture showroom. It was the sort of place where you automatically whispered in case you might be disturbing someone who was doing something very important and didn't dare touch anything in case you got told off.

The joys of cleanliness and of silence are lost in a house this size. Family homes need

313

a bit of messiness, a bit of tattiness, a lot of noise. Like Steph and Stanley's home, and all the ones I envied when I was a child. Stuff lying around, piles of random papers, things stuck to the fridge, an unwiped surface. Matter and clutter, telling the story of the family and the people who live there. It shows that there are ideas and interests and arguments going in here that are too much fun to stop and tidy every last envelope. It tells you that there's love. You could have doubled the Principal's staff and added a football team and it would have still felt like a mausoleum as everyone was so on edge, on guard, on duty. Nobody wanted to put a foot, or a cup, out of line.

Perhaps the sense of barrenness was because the Principal was still in the States and had been for some time, although his image, in framed black-and-white photos posing with other Principals, covered many a wall. There was one large painted portrait at the end of a hallway of the Principal draped casually on a sage green armchair in front of a library, whiskey glass tilted casually in hand and looking contentedly into the distance as if he might be watching someone make him a roast dinner.

Fortunately, I had taken my walker Jan with me, a cheerful, tomato-haired personal trainer who couldn't have cared less whose house it was and just wanted to meet Dolly and then leave. Jan knew everything about dogs but wasn't fussy or showy about it. Her parents bred spaniels and ran a boarding kennel and she wasn't the sort to get het up about training schedules and dietary requirements. I knew she would be perfect.

We were presented to Dolly in her playroom, another enormous basement room that appeared to have been kitted out just for the dog, with mountains of chew toys, tennis balls, and what looked like a mini obstacle course. Dolly sat in the center of the room, panting. She was petite and delicate, far smaller than I had imagined, with twinkly black eyes, sharp triangular ears, and long silver-and-bronze hair that she center-parted and wore down the side of her face like Meryl Streep in *Kramer vs. Kramer.*

Manny was lounging on the floor, headphones on, bopping.

"Whatsup," he said as he hopped up and sauntered over. "You ladies the doggie walkers?"

"I am, yes," said Jan holding out her hand for a shake. He fist bumped it and said, "Whack." I have never in my life, before or since, felt so awkward or so British. He was in his forties but looked around twelve on account of his outfit, which was mostly formed of white trainers and a huge cap with a bit of yellow tracksuit in between.

"I ain't got too much to say, ladies. She's a good doggie. Bit crazy. Bit out the loop. She gotta few issues here and there but nothin' you can get rock solid straight off the bat, man."

The "issues," aside from the confusion on where to defecate, seemed to center around biting people's fingers and humping soft furnishings, as well as the more pedestrian yapping and jumping up. Nothing too surprising considering she didn't know what country she lived in or who she was owned by, and the cushions scattered around the playroom did look pleasingly textured with lithe, gold tigers on them. I could see why she might be drawn to them in the absence of a father figure.

Manny's training approach, which he launched into straightaway, was hardly revelatory and seemed to revolve around a reward chart and "Italian pepperoni." For every finger or cushion or kitchen surface she abstained from, she got a gold star and a piece of pepperoni, except that nobody could find any Italian pepperoni and so we had to use Pepperami instead, much to

Manny's displeasure. For every ten stars she got a whole Pepperami and, at the insistence of the troika, a special trip to the groomer. Dog hair was the bane of their life and while they happily cut up her meat sticks and mopped up her urine, remnants of her fur was not tolerated.

"All right man, good luck. Any issues, you just gimme a call on the cell and I'll be right on over." He fist bumped Dolly's head as he finished speaking and she looked up at him, completely bewildered. It could have been the jet lag but I could sense she thought he was an idiot. We were at least on the same page with this one.

Neither Jan nor I spoke of it but I suspected we were both thinking exactly the same thing — that dog walking was clearly a massive waste of time and dog training for the rich and famous was the only sensible way forward. How Manny had wangled his way across the Atlantic to the leafy streets of Notting Hill on the Principal's dollar was a bit of a mystery but it was certainly not off the back of being a good trainer, or even a trainer at all. He must have something on the Principal, I thought, something from his past. A favor owed.

Perhaps it was his "zen" approach but for the week he was there, we never saw him touch Dolly or even interact with her at all, preferring to guide Jan and I through the rest of the training from the comfort of his hotel suite. He got her name and breed wrong on numerous occasions and he even asked Jan at one point how many legs she had, a mix-up apparently with a beloved canine client back in Brooklyn. Some people just have a way of convincing people of their talents, of drawing people in with their words. Or perhaps they googled him, as they did with us, and just saw that he'd been around for a while.

Thanks to the Olympics, for the first time in a long while, everyone in London seemed happy. Properly happy, even in the mornings. The woes of the recession had very gradually, page by page, become a previous chapter in history, one that we would all look back on from time to time and have a little moan about, but not one we were going to dwell on today. Not that summer, not that August, when everyone just wanted to be jolly and tipsy and to feel pride in who they were and where they lived. It was time to start a whole new chapter in a whole new book. This was London starting afresh.

As a small business, we'd been told for months to "get ready," to prepare for the impending chaos that planeloads of athletes and press and visitors would create, the overexcitement of Londoners as they got to play the bride instead of the bridesmaid and the strain on the already stuffed transport system. But in the end, all of our clients seemed to pull a two-week-long sickie so they could stay at home and watch the telly, clutching their dogs during all the exciting bits. The dogs, already confused as to why their owners were home *all the time* and hanging out with them on the sofa for eight hours straight, developed very specific, short-term neuroses around people jumping up unexpectedly, the words "Come on, Britain" yelled very loudly, and the repeated sound of starting guns. Mabel developed a temporary aversion to Clare Balding but it fortunately passed quite quickly.

London had never felt so vibrant and exciting, a city giddy with attention and glory, and yet, even at its very best, I knew that I wanted to leave. It wasn't an idea that just tapped me on the shoulder one day but one that had grown over weeks and months, years even, until it was impossible to ignore. I had started to feel uncomfortable, in an itchy sweater sort of way, about where we lived. Not the flat, although that was rapidly shrinking with the huge amount of baby paraphernalia that seemed to magically double week by week, but the City. I desperately craved big, open, green spaces. Now that my role in the business was primarily managerial, I reasoned that it could almost be done from anywhere.

"Go and sit in the park," Finlay said (in a much nicer way than it looks written down). He thought that some fresh urban air and a sprawl on some Wandsworth grass would be a quick, quietening tonic. And it was some of the time, particularly a walk down to Barnes along the river or a ramble up on Wimbledon Common with Belle in a baby carrier and Mabel chasing through the undergrowth. Sometimes we drove out of London at the weekend, to Surrey or Sussex, and we'd all watch Mabel racing through the fields, her senses all fully alive. I would be mollified for a while, a day or two if the weather was good, but then the itchiness would return and I'd find myself tempted to take out a subscription to *Country Life* or watch YouTube videos of sheep dog trials.

I had broached the subject of us leaving London once or twice but it was always met with a "What?" or a "Why?" and never a "When?" or a "Where?" Like me, Finlay was raised in the countryside but in a bit more

of a suburban way, among small town cul-
de-sacs and large busy villages. He could
always walk to a shop, a bank, a library,
whereas I grew up in a field of one sort or
another, surrounded by more fields, folded
into the hills and forests. I had the remnants
of a farming rhythm somewhere within.
March was lambing, long hours, and early
starts, and May the sunshine sprigs of
rapeseed. August was harvest and the low
drum of the combine through the night and
winter frosts meant worrying about the
crops. I realized that London had never
really felt like home. Unless you're born
there, or in another city, you are always
aware of the calling back to the soil. Now
that I was a mother, the calling was harder
to ignore. History wanted to repeat itself.

"But this is where we live," Finlay would
say incredulously. "This is our home." The
logistics alone were enough to shut the
whole concept right down as far as he was
concerned. Since Belle had arrived, traveling anywhere, even within the same borough, was an organizational nightmare and
took depths of reserve and fortitude that
even the toughest of souls found hard to
summon. Moving to a whole other part of
the country was beyond the limits of sane
and rational thought.

"Isn't home wherever we are? Wherever the family is? You, me, Belle, Mabel? We could be happy anywhere, couldn't we?"

"Maybe not in Hemel Hempstead," he said.

"What's wrong with Hemel Hempstead?"

"I had a very bad curry there." And with that we closed the conversation until the next time, one suburban town out of thousands crossed off the hypothetical list.

By the time the Olympics came to an end and London returned to its standard, mildly irritated self, the Principal had arrived from the States and taken up residence in the giant chicken. Dolly's walks with Jan had been going well and she was very slowly showing signs of improvement. The Manny school of training had been replaced with a simple, common-sense approach that involved not letting her onto the kitchen surfaces and making sure she had regular exercise. The real, key change was that she finally had some consistency, a person she saw regularly, twice a day at least. And that was Jan.

The Principal clearly loved Dolly. She always had a new collar, a new diet, a freshly groomed coat, but he didn't really get involved in the walking, playing, *seeing* part of her care. He liked to delegate, often firmly, as I suppose you have to do when you are a Principal. As soon as he arrived in London, instructions on Dolly's care went from the general to the painfully specific, including how and when Jan was to enter the property, acceptable walking routes, cleanliness of fur, timekeeping, and general security. She was clocked in and out by a guard and asked for a summary of each walk.

"It was good," Jan would say, as if there was any other possible response. Walks were all good as they were a chance for Dolly to leave the house.

Jan would see him occasionally as she left for a walk, the Principal looking out of the window as they wandered down the street. She would turn around sometimes and wave and he would smile and wave back and she wondered whether he would also like to leave the house. What's the point of it all if you can't even walk your own dog?

Mabel, Part Four

Eventually, we compromised on moving to the countryside by letting somewhere bigger in the Victorian end of Wandsworth — a tiny terraced house with a garden the size of a pad of paper and an enormous monthly rent. The square footage might have just passed muster with a country gent looking to stable his horse, or a socialite remodeling her en-suite, but for a family home it was a little cozy. The upside was that it had stairs, stairs to take you up to bed or down to breakfast and a large under-the-stairs cupboard for shoving all the baby crap in. Nothing is more gratifyingly grown-up than stairs.

As with all our major life decisions, it was made on a bit of a whim. We weighed up the importance of space versus cash and, in that moment, space won. Having more of it seemed sensible with a dog and a nearly-one-year-old, as did having some sort of garden. This is what people do, we thought. They trade up, step by step, until they can't afford anything bigger or can't face moving again. Some of our friends had graduated to this next level, although they were paying a hefty price for it. Some had been fortunate enough to have grandparents die and leave them large deposits or parents who were savvy about the taxman and siphoned off some early inheritance. Everybody worked long hours and worried about money because we were all suddenly realizing that this wasn't a trial run anymore and that everything we were striving for — more space, more time, more options — cost a huge amount of money.

My mother helped us pack up the flat. She was simultaneously horrified about the increase in rent rather than a mortgage but thrilled that we were moving up in the world and could now have her to stay in the tiny spare room. She bought *Time Out* and started planning exhibitions and plays she might like to see while also tutting about how we were throwing all our money away to unscrupulous landlords.

"I've missed the Titian but I might get to see Munch at the Tate if I get my skates on. And maybe even *Singin' in the Rain* if it's a matinee. I'll need to stay two nights at least."

We now needed a van to move, a small one, but a van nonetheless. Most of its contents were pink and plastic or small and fluffy and belonged in Belle's room. We bought a new table in a junk shop, preloved pine and big enough to seat eight if you all squeezed in, which delighted my mother as it promised the use of at least two-thirds of the virgin dinner service. I wondered when we might have time or inclination to entertain six among the child-rearing and work but that was hardly the point as far as she was concerned. There was potential.

We moved on a Monday in heavy rain. Finlay did the heavy lifting while I sat with Belle and my mother in a nearby café, waiting for the signal to start the unpacking. Tenants were moving into our old flat and it was a tight schedule.

"Is this a 'delicatessen'?" my mother asked the waitress who delivered her latte.

"Um, I don't know. I'll have to ask my manager."

"Were there any delicatessens near the old place, Kate? I expect there are *boutiques* near here too."

But then the bill arrived and she physically recoiled away from it, telling Belle in a volume that was just over the acceptable about the very decent coffees you could buy in her hometown for a fraction of the price. What she had just been subjected to was nothing less than daylight robbery and how could you possibly live in a place that wanted to rob you so brazenly?

"I do wish you would just move up to my neck of the woods. Far less expensive and I could be around to help a bit more."

"With what?"

"Children. That sort of thing."

"Really? Like . . . *childcare*?"

"Well, no, not exactly. Popping in, going to the park, you know the sort of thing I mean."

"But you are always so busy, aren't you?"

"Well, yes. There is always an awful lot going on. I'm *exhausted* really."

She looked tired. Hers was a full and busy life of coffee mornings and garden openings and senior's tennis; the need to be permanently busy and keep occupied was clearly a familial trait. Moving closer to her might have interfered with all of that. I could see the appeal, on the surface of it, of having us closer. I would be drawn further into her orbit, back to the days when decisions were made for me and I could be molded closer to her image. She would worry less about me if I was nearby. I wouldn't be capable of making as many unpredictable decisions

327

and could be encouraged to entertain more, to roast some cows or play long, complicated card games with other women.

"But you wouldn't be able to come and see the shows and the exhibitions or queue for Wimbledon tickets if we moved. You would have to get a hotel."

She paused, just long enough that I caught the sound of her plans beginning to crumble.

"Well, you're fine where you are for the moment, aren't you? It's a lovely, *lovely* area."

We had forgotten the size of the house in the interim — the dream-filled period between being aggressively swayed by the estate agent and turning the key in the front door for the first time. That period where you buy things willy-nilly on eBay and then visualize where you will put them, blithely giving yourself a few meters and inches here and there. By the time moving day came around, I had conjured up a small palace.

"How much rent are we paying again?" Finlay asked as we started to squeeze the boxes in the door. Some of the furniture didn't fit down the corridor and had to be dismantled into smaller parts on the street.

"It's not about that," I lied, feeling slightly sick about the whole thing and wondering if

I could blame the recklessness on postpartum hormones. "It's about the light and the air. The quiet. The space. And the stairs, of course."

Finlay opened the door to the minuscule back garden. The house behind was in the middle of a loft extension and a builder was angrily hammering at the wall, raining clouds of brick dust down onto our tiny flower bed.

"Well, isn't this wonderful?" he said, as Belle put her hands over her ears to drown out the noise. "Just what we were looking for."

"But have you seen the stairs? They are really, *really* good stairs."

Mabel, Belle, and I hadn't spent that much time in Wandsworth Park in the run-up to the move. Weaning had meant Mabel was overweight again and so we tried to get up to Wimbledon Common to help burn off the bounty of dropped buttered soldiers and dollops of Petit Filous that she'd been enjoying. One of the tasks that Mabel had taken most seriously since Belle's arrival was keeping the area under her high chair scrupulously clean. It was a small recompense for having her world turned so utterly upside down.

But the day before the move, the weather was warm and sunny and I took Belle down to the park in the buggy. Mabel tagged along miserably. She had seen bags being packed and it had unsettled her. As Belle drifted off to sleep we sat on a bench, Mabel up next to me, and felt the warm autumn sunshine on our faces. It was only a few moments later that I heard steps approaching and turned to see Agnes coming along the path with Rabbit. He was off the lead and bounded forward as he recognized us, tail wagging excitedly. But before I even had a chance to say hello, Mabel had leaped down off the bench and had Rabbit pinned onto the tarmac, her teeth bared and the adrenaline coursing. Rabbit was still for a moment, shocked and winded, before yelping loudly as he tried to wriggle his way out from underneath her. But the more he wriggled, the more he tried to pull away, the more Mabel growled and snarled, forcing her weight on top of him so that he could barely move.

Agnes came hurrying over as I jumped up and started to shout Mabel's name, frantically searching for a treat in my coat pocket to try and entice her away.

"Oh god, I'm sorry, I'm sorry, I'm sorry," I repeated over and over to Agnes. She was trying to fish something from out of her fanny pack but was otherwise extremely calm. "I don't know what happened. She just sat there and then all of a sudden she jumped off and I don't know what she is doing. MABEL! MABEL!"

Agnes eventually retrieved a whistle, silver and very beautiful with the end shaped like a hound, and blew it so hard that both dogs sprang up in fright. Rabbit shook himself down, shrugged casually, and sauntered off down the path as if nothing had happened. Mabel turned to look at me briefly, seeing my astonishment, before slinking off into the bushes.

"I am so, so sorry, Agnes, I really don't know what just happened there. She has never, ever done anything like that before. Is Rabbit OK? Is he all right?"

"He is fine," she said. "Embarrassed probably. He wouldn't have liked that. He thinks he is a big dog really. The boss."

"Poor, poor Rabbit. What a horrible shock for him. And his old girlfriend too. I really don't know what came over her. She's such a softy normally. I mean, I have never even seen her growl before, let alone do anything like that."

"It is fine. She was just protecting the baby."

331

"The . . . ?"

"The baby. In the buggy. She was protecting your baby."

Of course she was. How could I not have instantly known? Brilliant, faithful, amazing Mabel.

"She saw Rabbit as a threat somehow and was just being protective. It is very natural."

"Yes, yes, absolutely. That makes sense."

"Congratulations by the way. A girl?"

"Yes, yes, a girl. She's growing up fast."

"Well, enjoy."

And with that, she turned to leave.

"Agnes, Agnes," I called after her. "Thank you." A thank you seemed right somehow, although we were both embarrassed by it.

I might have been forgiven for not fully appreciating Mabel's depth of commitment to Belle. There had been quite a bit going on and the thing was that she was just always there, right by our side, and you only ever appreciate these magical, obvious things if they are walloped in your face or taken away all together. Luckily for me, it was the former.

Mabel had found herself in a job that she had neither applied for nor could ever possibly leave, a full-time position, with no off days or coffee breaks, long tiring hours, and a noisy, hectic workplace. And while she may not have wanted the role, she was preternaturally suited to it and dedicated herself to the task as passionately and diligently as any vocational calling. It was her duty to look after Belle and, as such, we had both become mothers, in our own way.

Life became a little more serious than it used to be, the weight of responsibility always on those broad white shoulders. Walks in the park were no longer just about fun and games; they were about safety and surveillance. She stayed by our side, never once running away, not even when tempted by squirrels or ducks or the odd stray cat. Friends visiting the flat were no longer just another lap option but a potential deadly threat and must be sniffed extensively before being reluctantly approved. Every cry, every screech, every knock at the door or tumble on the grass, every dropped toy or lobbed breadstick, every unfamiliar sound, every change to routine, she was alert, on call, ready to muscle in.

There was a certain sadness too, a melancholy that sat by her side and rarely left. She looked at me differently, sometimes with large lachrymose eyes but often with a challenge, an unflinching stare that signaled she wanted answers. She wanted me to answer for what I'd done, for the monumental shift that bringing this baby into our home had caused in all of our lives. For her demotion to second place, for not giving her the time and attention that I once did. At times, the guilt felt overwhelming.

"Look, look at the way she is looking at me," I would say to Finlay, often tearfully. Tired and tearful was second nature now. "She feels betrayed. Let down. She's angry with me, I can see it."

Finlay would sigh patiently. He saw a dog, nothing more. A beloved dog, but a dog nonetheless.

"I'm not sure dogs can feel betrayal, can they? She's probably just hungry."

And, to prove his point, to make me feel better, he would give Mabel a biscuit from her treat box, which she would happily wolf down.

"There. See? Just hungry."

The new house brought its own fresh challenges for Mabel. She had only ever known the flat and the unfamiliar environment agitated her. She knew how to guard the family at the flat, she knew the sounds, the footsteps in the flat upstairs, the sound of the doorbell next door, the beeping of the lorries as they reversed in the street behind. She knew the way that the door opened and closed in the corridor and how the number of seconds between the two would indicate if it was Finlay coming home or just the neighbors across the hall.

The first week was an initial reconnaissance mission, a sweep of the area inside and out to ascertain any potential perils, followed by a period of general worry where she refused to leave Belle's side. She slept next to the cot, one eye open, before retiring to the sofa in the early hours of the morning.

As we unpacked the last of the bags and the boxes and finally settled in, Mabel's concerns with the new environment had narrowed down to just one: foxes. They had their own local army and took to the streets as the sun went down in large, rowdy gangs looking for food and sex. They were bold, startlingly so, which was what annoyed Mabel the most. All other creatures, domestic or otherwise, had run away from her, fled into undergrowth, into burrows, bushes, or down into holes. Squirrels belted up trees and cats leaped onto garden walls and the chase would be on. It was all about the chase. But the fox stood still, resolute and unafraid, the territory his, at least in the inky shadows when the streetlights glowed Lucozade orange.

A youth club of adolescent cubs met in

335

our garden on a nightly basis, shouting and pissing and rifling through the bins. They would chat and scrap and screech and gossip before rounding off the evening with some predawn heavy petting. One fox, a large strident male and head of this particular pack, liked to kick off his night on top of our tiny garden shed, calling for his friends in a throaty, smoker's bark, the king of his own urban jungle. It was the thump of his wide paws as they landed from fence to shed that would alert Mabel. She would take her position at the back door, nose pressed against the cold glass, squinting into the darkness as the strange agile shapes moved in and out of the gloom.

Then her barking would begin.

In an attempt to get some unbroken sleep, we moved her upstairs to our room, away from the back door, but what a dog lacks in sight, they will of course make up for in sound and smell. Even before the thump on the shed, she would always sense when he was nearby and would be up, out of her basket, alert, head cocked slightly to the side before jumping up on the bed and climbing onto one of our faces to try to get a better view out of the window.

"I think you are allowed to shoot them," Finlay said one night as Mabel, perched on top of his head, growled down into the darkness.

"Foxes?"

"Yes, foxes. Well, possibly dogs too in very exceptional circumstances. I think this might be an exceptional circumstance."

"Shoot them with what?"

"I don't know, a gun? A crossbow?"

"Well, who has a gun in the middle of London? That we know of, anyway?"

"Maybe we could hire a hitman."

"We can't afford a hitman. All our money goes on rent."

"A trainee hitman then, one who is just starting out. An apprentice. Or a retiree. They'd be cheaper."

We compromised on some "vulpine repellent spray," which the foxes laughed at and then rolled in, before Finlay took matters into his own hands. After some careful research in the deepest, darkest caverns of the internet, he concluded that the only way to see them off was to pee in the garden, preferably first thing in the morning, which can make things awkward with the neighbors. Fortunately for everyone the pee didn't work and, as we headed toward Christmas, there seemed to be more foxes than ever. We bought earplugs, moved Mabel's bed into the bathroom, and became very grumpy.

On Christmas Eve, stockings out and Santa's mince pie placed carefully by the blocked-up fireplace, Mabel went out into the garden for her usual sniff and a pee. Seconds later, there were the sounds of an almighty fight, a furious tooth-and-claw battle that echoed through the crisp night air. She was right in the corner, squeezed in between the shed and the fence, her head shoved down into the hole underneath where Mr. Fox and his family lived. She had cornered one, she'd threatened it, and it had retaliated, ripping part of her mouth open and tearing a large hole in the side of her face.

As Finlay hauled her back into the house, her blood pouring onto the kitchen tiles, adrenaline coursing, she made a desperate attempt to get back outside, thrashing wildly and biting at my hands while I tried to wrap her mouth in a tea towel. In that moment, in the post-skirmish rage, she was as wild and as feral as the fox outside and she would have fought with it until one of them had died. Gone were the fondness for a tummy rub, the crusts of toast she only liked buttered, the fear of wind, of rain, and her distaste for swear words. She was just a

338

basic animal, defending her home, her people.

The waiting room of the emergency vet in Wimbledon is not the place you want to be on Christmas Eve. It was far from festive. There was an old lady with a sad-looking cat in a crate, a couple huddled over a bloated, hiccupping spaniel, and a man, sitting alone, red-eyed and tapping his foot on the wipe clean floor.

The vet, a young Italian guy who had drawn the short Christmas straw, seemed unfazed by Mabel's injuries. He'd seen far worse, though not from foxes, who rarely attack unless provoked. She needed surgery, multiple stitches, and industrial-strength antibiotics and would be able to come home on Christmas Day, wrapped up in bandages like a very bad present.

She slept solidly for a few days, her head poking out from her cone, groggy from the anesthetic and painkillers. Perhaps she was just relieved that she'd finally been able to do her job, to tell whatever fox that lived under the shed that she lived there too and had a family to defend, just like they did.

Fortunately for us all, there appeared to be a truce of sorts in the days that followed, a period of reflection and recuperation where Mabel took a much-needed break from her nightly post and the foxes were mysteriously distant and quiet. We slept properly for the first time in months.

A couple of weeks later, Christmas long forgotten and the jagged scar now dark and craggy, we had snow. Beautifully thick, fat flakes that fell noiselessly over London, closing airports and schools and stopping dogs from being walked. Belle, Mabel, and I huddled up inside, our tiny garden as crisp and white as a brand-new notebook. As the light faded and the snow turned from white to bruised gray, a young fox appeared on the garden fence, burned-treacle orange with a jet-back tail. It stood still for a moment, gauging the risk, before hopping gingerly onto the quilt of snow.

Its legs sank deep into a drift and it immediately leaped up again, startled at the cold and the sudden disappearance of its paws. It started to prod at the surface with its long nose, investigating, sniffing and then tossing flurries up into the air as if they were confetti, batting them and catching them again with its mouth and its paws, skipping and tumbling and rolling on the floor until its back and head were almost completely covered in white.

"Gone," said Belle, as the fox became almost totally submerged. The three of us stood transfixed at the back door as this beautiful creature danced and melted into the snow.

The vulpine mating season started not long after, the vociferous screeching and wailing of the vixens shattering the stillness of the night, and the barking resumed once more.

DOLLY, PART TWO

SILKY TERRIER, TWO, NOTTING HILL
MARCH 2013
NUMBER OF DOGS WALKED: 92

While we were settling into our new home, the Principal had his own vulpine dilemmas. One had been spotted in his garden and, in what might be described as an overreaction, he'd had a giant spiky fence erected with high-tech motion detector lights and sprinklers, all linked up to the security hub in the basement.

To be fair to the Principal, Dolly wasn't the kind of dog who would venture out into the dark to confront an intruder, so he could be forgiven for wanting the extra help. Dolly would be far more likely to offer herself up as a whole meal, seasoned on a silver platter, as was her slightly pathetic nature. She had been coddled, like a very expensive egg, to the point where she refused to get her paws wet if it rained or eat her food unless it had been cut up into easily digestible chunks with a knife and fork.

It wasn't just about the foxes. A series of break-ins in the area had put the household on high alert. A car here and there, a few bicycles — standard fare for London — but then a diplomat a few doors down had his top-notch barbecue stolen in broad daylight. It wasn't the most shocking of crimes but a mystery all the same as it was an enormous outdoor grill complete with roasting spit and nobody could work out how on earth it had been pilfered without anyone noticing, or even why anyone would want it so badly in the first place. This was clearly a different breed of criminal, cunning and perverse, and as a result, security was stepped up on all fronts. This included a new decree from the Principal that Jan was to be accompanied by a bodyguard on all of Dolly's walks.

There were five of them now — an extra one had been drafted in — enormous, miserable blokes in black suits who lived in the basement, somewhere between the security room and the kitchen, where they continuously hassled the Filipino Troika for cups of tea and competed on who could raise a smile from them the quickest. If any of them managed to crack it before midday, they got to choose the biscuits for the week — high stakes in the world of security.

Their small and windowless room was

thick with testosterone and boredom, the memories of previous, often rewarding careers in the police or the army dangling in the acrid air like the strands of old cobwebs. While they liked Jan and her easygoing nature, they had little time for Dolly, a dog that clashed painfully with their image, but were stuck with nevertheless. They clomped along funereally behind Jan on the walks, huffing and puffing about when it might be time to go home again, like sulky children. If they were out with Jan and Dolly, it meant they were on the "home rota" (the "away rota" being the heavy accompaniment to the Principal on one of his engagements) and along with babysitting a small, neurotic terrier, they also had to deal with Sean.

Sean, a thin, small, black-haired braggart from Belfast, was the Principal's butler and an unpleasant human on all counts. In the absence of anything that might recommend him to others, including animals, he had focused all of his time and energy on his job, a role he saw as the very pinnacle of life's achievements. He'd been with the Principal for just over a year, traveling with him wherever he went, and was in charge of running the London house. His fortes were meticulous organization, fussing, attention to pointless detail, and an unwavering loyalty to the Principal. A loyalty that hovered around the realms of the unhealthy, driven by his boundless enthusiasm for money and power. Fame's noxious, intoxicating allure had utterly seduced Sean until he had slowly and quite willingly turned into a monster.

Before serving the Principal, Sean had had a short posting at Clarence House and one for another Principal in Monaco, assignments that gave him that first addictive taste of money and success. Fame and power and all their hangers-on gleamed and glistened like the reflected sun upon a yacht and Sean seemed mesmerized by them.

Unfortunately, his tenure in London coincided with the huge popularity of *Downton Abbey,* which, on its own, may not have been too pernicious but when combined with the frequency of American visitors to the house threw buckets of fuel onto an already ignited ego. The Americans — Anglophilic TV executives, film producers, and lawyers — were all too impressed by a man in a three-piece suit opening a door and saying, "Good morning, sir," in carefully perfected upper-class accent. "Gee, you're a regular Mr. Carson," they would say as they slapped him on the back and took photos of him on their iPhones, and it wasn't very long before Sean apparently decided he was probably the second most important person in London. After the Principal, of course.

Jan and I soon realized that all the rules, the schedules, and fussing that had arrived when the Principal took residence hadn't been instigated by him after all. It had all been Sean, a man who liked to change the status quo just for the sake of it, even if it meant upsetting everyone and making life far more difficult than it needed to be. It appeared that the more people he upset and the more difficult he made life, the better, for he was one of those people who enjoyed making others miserable, most likely due to being miserable himself, perhaps as a result of having been teased at school for liking Westlife or B*Witched or something. That unfortunately extended to Jan and also to me via his daily emails about Dolly's routine and quibbles about the invoices. Every morning I would receive at least one email along the lines of:

Jan returned five minutes early on the 15th. Please deduct accordingly.
Please explain the reasoning behind the higher price weekend walks????

He clearly didn't like Dolly or, I suspect,
any hairy animal as anything that could possibly leave a shred of itself on his suit was
wholly objectionable. And yet despite being
closely aligned to the Troika in this respect,
he made their lives a misery too, threatening them with claims that he knew people
in the Home Office who might be interested
in having a look at their visas. He was jealous of the Principal's affection for Dolly, of
the way he lit up when she was brought up
to see him, of how much time and effort
went into her care. He resented the fact that
Dolly didn't like him, despite the fact that
he disliked her, intensely, and would often
quietly hiss at her as they passed each other
in the corridors of the basement. He resented how much Dolly loved Jan, how
Dolly would wait at the back door for her,
how she recognized Jan's footsteps coming
through the garden and her tail would swish
excitedly across the polished marble floor.
He seemed to resent almost everything
about our presence in the house but he
could do very little about it because the
Principal wanted Dolly to be happy above
all else and we were the ones who helped to

347

make that happen.

It was hard not to get bogged down by the bad behavior, by just how disappointing humans could be. You had to try, if you could, to go behind the enemy lines and imagine what awful things had made them this way, what sadness, what tragedy, because being a horrible person, without any cause, just wasn't possible. But in this case it was proving difficult. Sean was not even the owner. He was a butler, an uppity, rude, pretentious butler, and my patience for his silliness had worn perilously thin.

Belle was not really a baby anymore. She yelled and laughed and threw and jumped and she only ever ran anywhere, so vital and so urgent and so all-consuming was her need to experience all of life in every moment. I had started to resent that work would follow us around, tagging along wherever we went — the shops, the park, the baby groups, and the play dates, a constant nagging beeping of the phone, the stacking up of the emails. I resented the irritation I would feel at my inability to cheerfully deal with both, the way I would snap, my patience worn down to the quick.

One of the most unexpected things about becoming a mother is that you care a whole lot less about most things than you did before. Spiders, for example — once utterly terrifying, now far more manageable. There simply isn't time to skip around the bathroom wailing pitifully while you wait for a man to appear when there's a toddler in the house with a bottle of your nail varnish. If you don't want to find the creature on your pillowcase at bedtime, you had better stick a glass over it and chuck it out the window before the toddler repaints the walls "Sexy Coral."

Nails are far less important too, as is most grooming, and you walk around with hair unbrushed and eyebrows woolly, although you will occasionally feel a strong and powerful urge to get shockingly dolled up and drink enormous neon cocktails in order to cast out the grotty feeling of weeks spent in the same pair of black leggings and to remedy the fact that your social life now resides at the bottom of the nappy bin. It's obvious really: you don't have the time you once did and you are not the most important person anymore. Your brain, once wonderfully clear and shipshape, is now a seething, boiling vat of tasks and tickets, forgotten birthdays and overdue bills, of bums that need wiping and food you haven't bought yet. So, in an attempt to pull back a tiny bit of control, a teensy bit of order, it simply ejects those things that you no longer need, like the concept of ironing, your inexplicable phobia of Tom Jones, or your insistence on locking the front door three times at bedtime.

The best thing about this little bit of cerebral housekeeping is that you aren't even aware of it taking place. It happens silently, in the half dark, like an office cleaner sweeping up the debris at the end of the day, until you suddenly find yourself confronted with a familiar neurosis, an old adversary, and you realize that you feel a little bit differently than you did before. You're no longer quite the same person — you're bigger and bolder and braver (though tireder) and you haven't even had to read a self-help book or sat on an NHS mental health waiting list to get there. Focusing yourself entirely on another human being means that there simply isn't space for the superfluous anymore. According to my brain, however, this also included work.

One day, I realized that I didn't care as much as I used to or feel the need to always please, to always say yes, to stretch myself too far, or to habitually apologize. I had boundaries, for the first time, and I hadn't even noticed building them. What was left was far more manageable, streamlined; something that could sit alongside family life, not on top of it. It was how I should have approached it all along — a simple service, a dog moving from A to B and back again, served up with some basic politeness.

Thank you for your email. We don't do walks earlier than 9 a.m. at the weekends.

Thanks for contacting us. I am afraid we do not provide bottled water on walks but I can certainly point you in the direction of a supermarket who might do.

Thank you for your email. I apologize that your walker was not able to attend today but as she broke her wrist, I am sure you can appreciate that her need to visit the hospital was slightly more important than walking Miranda.

Thank you for your email but if you want your Labrador to have a massage you will have to contact a masseuse.

Thank you for your inquiry but I am afraid we don't walk ferrets.

But with liberation from the more trivial concerns of the dog community, there were new worries, vivid and potent, all wrapped up in the gut-punching, breath-stealing love for your offspring. These were the ones that helped to sweep the work nonsense clean away and freed me from stress about butlers and lost keys and paw prints on the sofa. Motherhood leaves you like a half-open wound, vulnerable and exposed, your nerves eviscerated, your heart on the butcher's block. This was an open invitation for Panic to squeeze in. And it did, very occasionally, just to let me know that it could.

It was different this time, targeted; like a dose of a powerful drug, it coursed sharply, right to the very core, to the only things that really mattered anymore, my new family, my loved ones, and holding it all close. In the more fearful, lonely moments with Panic crouched upon my shoulder, when Belle had high temperatures or when she wasn't eating or even just on the days when I felt I had gotten parenting all wrong and the guilt would consume me whole, I would often think of my mother. Married, divorced, single, or trying to please a new partner, all while making sure her children ate and slept and smiled. When she went to bed, when the troubles of the day would settle alongside her. It wouldn't matter if she had someone there to support her or not as she would still be utterly alone, the parental worries only hers to bear. They couldn't be carved up and shared out like mine. Hers had to be consumed whole.

For a long time, I believed that she couldn't have loved me as much as I loved Belle. There wasn't any love bigger than mine; nobody could possibly do more or love more; there was no sacrifice I wouldn't have made to keep the family together. But when it all simmers down to the essence, when I was exhausted by the tantrums and the teething and the endless rounds of guilt, I realized we were just the same. We would do anything for our children; we wanted them to have the best of it all, and all the rest too. The traditions and the rules and the needing for things to be just so, that was just the safety net, what you fall back on when you are not sure what comes next. Mine was Finlay. How lucky I was.

On the day that I realized I cared a little less about the business, Camilla from the concierge company called. We had done *so* well and everyone was *so* happy with us and there were now more Principals with dogs, at least three, and a cat belonging to a movie star who needed stroking twice a day. On top of that, the Principal wanted me to accompany Dolly on his private jet to New York. He had work over there that had taken longer than expected and he was missing her. It would be a commercial flight home but I could book it whenever I liked and there would be a night at a hotel chucked in for free.

Finlay said I should go. Of course I should go, it was a once-in-a-lifetime type of thing and a symbol of just how far I had come. The reward for all the hard work. The prize. He would take some days off work and we would muddle through. But I just didn't want to go. I didn't want to do any of it — the jet, the cat, the new shiny dogs. I had finally reached the peak and I didn't even want to look at the view.

I didn't even tell my mother. It just didn't seem that relevant anymore.

Instead, Jan took Dolly to New York. Dolly had diarrhea on the flight and Jan spent most of the trip huddled in the tiny jet loo with a towel wrapped around the dog's bottom. There were issues at immigration and while Dolly was finally allowed through and chauffeured straight into Manhattan in a stretch limousine, Jan was not. She was packed straight back on a flight home the very same day.

As we turned into spring Sean was becoming intolerable. He endlessly flapped and fussed over the Principal, falling out with the entire household in the process. Believing himself to be the only person who could competently look after a "celebrity," a man he treated more like a rare exotic bird rather than just a normal human being, he tried to curtail his colleagues' responsibilities. The Troika were gradually discouraged from any Principal interaction; meals, drinks and messages all to be delivered by Sean himself; and he would shoo them out of the kitchen and in with the security guards if the Principal came downstairs.

Dolly, too, was being phased out. Sean moved her bed around at least three times, from her room to the kitchen to the gym and finally into the utility room where she was given a small space next to the washing machine. Room by room, he was trying to remove her from view so that she wouldn't be quite so important anymore. He was spectacularly petty.

But as a result, Dolly started misbehaving. Jan was trying her hardest, but the constant changes at home had started to affect her. She started peeing in the kitchen again and humping the legs of chairs and tables, a sight which Sean found deeply disturbing and would alert me to every time it happened. The emails just kept coming:

The dog is copulating with the furniture again. Please see to it urgently.

I have sent two <u>very</u> expensive chaise longues to the restorer today. This must stop!

The dog has <u>no</u> respect for the contents of this house. Urination AND fornication. I shall be speaking to the Principal about it and suggesting we make some VERY significant changes.

Not long after the New York trip, Jan did her last walk. It was the afternoon one and the Principal was at home. He had seen her come back into the house via the back gate and called down the stairs for her and Dolly to come and see him in the office. They'd had a nice chat, not for long, but long enough for Jan to tell him of her concerns for Dolly and for him to thank her for all of her hard work. The Principal had suggested that maybe he should get a second dog and Jan had agreed. A friend for Dolly would make sense, a calming, stable influence. Perhaps a rescue dog, an older one, a dog who Dolly could depend on, and a basket in the office would be nice. If the Principal could just spend a little more time with her, take her for a walk perhaps, throw a ball for her in the garden, Jan thought that everything would all be OK.

As Jan and Dolly came out of the office, Sean was standing down the hallway glaring at her, arms folded, his hands balled into fists.

"You!" he called. "Can you come here please."

"Yes?"

"What on earth do you think you are doing?" he asked curtly.

"What do you mean?"

"In *there,*" he said, jabbing his finger toward the office door.

"The Principal just wanted a quick chat. About Dolly."

"You never, *ever,* speak to the Principal. That is not your job. How dare you go in there."

"He asked me to come in! It would have been rude not to."

"I decide who goes in there. Not you!"

"What are you talking about? He asked me to go in there. HE ASKED ME! Who do you think you are anyway?"

"I AM THE BUTLER! I am in charge!"

he bellowed as he snatched Dolly's lead from Jan's hands, his face a fuming, blistering red. Dolly resisted and tried to pull back toward Jan but Sean yanked her and she yelped. "You are banished from the house, do you understand? You will wait outside from now on. On the street. You will never, ever, *ever* come inside again."

She told him to fuck off and a small, happy cheer could be heard from the security room downstairs where the guards had watched the row unfold on the screens. She then left the house through the front door, the black shiny one, the one only Principals can use, the velvet rope.

LILY AND LUCY

KING CHARLES SPANIELS, SIX,
KNIGHTSBRIDGE
SEPTEMBER 2013
NUMBER OF DOGS WALKED: 95

"It's a civilian," Camilla said on the phone. "A VIP civilian but definitely a civilian. She's a mother, like you, and there's no staff. No dramas. It's just her, Rebecca, and she works long hours so you'll hardly see her really. It won't be like last time. I promise."

"I'm not sure, Camilla," I replied. "We are already quite busy." I had already pictured her — brusque, rude, fussy, reminding me how busy she was every five minutes. They were always *far* busier than you.

"I really think this would be a good one. We've never had any problems with her. Why don't you meet her and see what you think?"

I took Jan. She had been a bit short on dogs since Dollygate and I thought with her family's spaniel connection, it might be the perfect client for her. Plus, the client had some work trips abroad coming up and needed someone to stay at her flat, a nice lucrative side earner. Jan had happened to mention she was feeling a bit broke.

"We'll meet her and see what we think," I said. "No pressure, Jan. If it doesn't seem right, then we can just say no and something better will come along. Only nice, normal people from now on."

"*Nice and normal?* You don't get many of those, do you?" Jan chuckled.

"We get quite a few," I replied, trying to count them up in my head. "And I guess it depends on what you mean by normal?"

It was a balmy, late-summer evening, the sun a warm, soft blonde and as we made our way to Rebecca's flat, on the ground floor of a mansion block tucked in behind Cadogan Square, I was feeling hopeful. Relaxed. We didn't *need* this client, or any other client. They would either like us or they wouldn't and there was very little I could do to change that, particularly as there was so much choice now. It was no longer a case of picking the first dog walker from Google or even getting a glowing recommendation from a trusted friend; it was a lengthy interview process where you were interrogated, dissected, and then graded against the next person. "We are meeting other people, of course," they would say as they twirled their pens around their fingers, mentally marking you out of ten. "We will be in touch."

Lily and Luna had already met three other walkers, sourced by Rebecca's PA, but all had been discounted. That's where Camilla had come in, to provide someone pre-approved. Yet Rebecca wasn't what I expected from an enormously powerful, well-respected CEO. She was scatty and giggly, wearing a silk dressing gown with a martini in her hand like a Noël Coward heroine. She had not long packed off her two preteen children to boarding school in Surrey and was drowning her sorrows.

"They've been begging to go for yonks. All that fresh air and countryside. They shan't miss me one little bit, not when there's all that fun to be had. But we'll miss them, won't we, my darlings?"

Rebecca's dogs, two sisters, were overweight and boggly eyed with small bulbous heads and chestnut and yellowy white fur that looked like an old, pee-stained bath mat.

"These are my darlings — Lily, the one with the weepy eyes, my poor little baby, and Lucy, the one with the face like an angel. Come here, my little angel face, you are so beautiful. Mummy loves you, yes she does!"

As far as I could tell, they both had weepy eyes — wet streaks like freshly inked commas that made them look like they were always crying. Though I was now slightly biased when it came to the aesthetics of a dog, as I couldn't imagine a dog more pleasing to the eye than Mabel, fox scar and all. But even to the casual passerby, Lily and Lucy were extremely unappealing. They were lumpen and plodding and showed little sense of joy or enthusiasm for the world, despite Jan making a Herculean effort to engage with them.

Rebecca's flat was tasteful, impeccably kitted out, not too big but with some showy art on the walls and a healthy selection of gadgets. There was a yoga mat rolled out onto the floor and a gloopy pink protein shake was congealing on the coffee table alongside the prerequisite art books and interiors magazines. There was very little sign of children though, aside from the odd photo.

"There is nothing I wouldn't do for these babies. Nothing. They've saved my life once or twice. Haven't you, girls? And you'll see me through to half term, won't you? Yes you will, you will!"

She then got down on the floor, onto the thick beige rug, and started to roll around with the dogs, making loud barking and yipping and squeaking noises as she wrestled and grappled with them, revving them up into a wheezing, panting frenzy as they clambered on top of her, pawing at her and humping her arms. Jan and I sat silently on the sofa. Aghast.

"I'm *so* sorry," I said to Jan as we left. "Not at all normal. We'll find you someone else, Jan, I promise. A nice vicar or a teacher, someone like that. They've got to be out there somewhere."

"It's totally fine," she replied, as cool and calm as ever. "Nothing I can't handle. She's a bit odd but that's just the way it is now. They are only getting nuttier."

She was right. It wasn't just that the competition was now rife and tenacious; the customers were so much more discerning. Shrewd. *Demanding.* They felt entitled to have the absolute best (but only if it was in the right price bracket) and if anything was slightly amiss, they also felt entitled to be rude. They were harder. They were richer, lived more centrally, more expensively, and were even more used to getting what they wanted. They were accustomed to people doing things for them, to issuing orders, to

363

always hearing "yes." The nice and normal families, the 2.4-ers, the ones who ate beans on toast in places like Hammersmith and Tooting, they seemed to have all disappeared. London was shifting.

"Are you *sure,* Jan? What about the whole rolling around thing?"

"I just presumed she was just drunk," said Jan, and I had to agree with her, as the alternative was far, far worse.

We decided to take the situation into our own hands by making our own "nice and normal" assessment. We would give it a week to start with, just to see *how* unusual Rebecca was. She would be at work in the City so Jan wouldn't actually have to see her and I would log her calls and emails to see how many absurd demands she made. A bit of background research told me she was a litigious sort, taking a couple of ex-husbands down as well as a Greek plastic surgeon for being a bit ham-fisted with the Botox, and her career seemed to have jumped around rather a lot. Surprisingly, she passed the week with flying colors — a busy workweek perhaps, or maybe she knew she was in her own mini probation period, as it wasn't long until the requests started to come in.

They started benignly. Could Jan pick up

some dog food on the way home? There was a shop en route and Rebecca had an account so it was an easy favor. Then she needed some dry cleaning collected, a pint of milk, a bottle of wine, and some letters posted. Jan didn't mind. Rebecca left cash and told her to keep the change. Jan was making more than she did from most clients, including the ones she did her personal training with, and, most importantly, she didn't have to see her. Not even once.

She'd warmed to the dogs too. Away from Rebecca they seemed different, less moody and more willing to give life a go. She bought them a ball and they would begrudgingly play catch in Hyde Park, waddling in and out of the trees, finally getting up to a gentle trot. They liked to bark at the swans on the Round Pond and then lie under the trees as the dappled light pattered on their chalky fur.

A tourist took a photo of them in Kensington Gardens, the palace in the background, the dogs sat either side of Jan like small round sentries.

"Are they, like, royal?" the tourist asked, snapping away.

"They're King Charles spaniels, Cavaliers," Jan replied officially.

"King Charles spaniels? Are you serious?

Wow, how awesome!" he exclaimed, and then took a dozen more photos.

By the time Rebecca's first work trip came around, the leaves were changing color and the spaniel sisters were a pound or two lighter. Jan moved into the flat for two weeks, the prospect of living on her own in such a central location a luxury rarely afforded to the outer-zone, multiple-flatmate generation. And Jan was willing to put up with a lot to get it — particularly as the pay was good and the work trips more and more frequent. Most importantly, Rebecca wasn't there. Not in person anyway. But then, one week in . . .

"Jan, hello, coooeeee, Jan!" The voice in the room, but sounded distant, tinny, like it was coming from a radio. "Jan? I'm over here, on the mantelpiece."

Jan walked over to see a small cylindrical camera placed next to a photo frame. There was a light on it that was flashing green and a microphone at the bottom. A pet cam, high-tech, with which Rebecca had been watching Jan for the whole first week.

"You can't see me but I can see you-hoo! And the girls of course. Hello, babies, are you missing Mummy?" She then barked loudly into the microphone, causing the camera to vibrate. The dogs looked around, confused.

"Hi, Rebecca," Jan said, calmly, far calmer than I would have been. "How is the trip?"

"It's fine. Just missing my girls. Everything OK?"

"Everything is fine."

"Of course it is, I've been watching you!"

Jan sighed and looked blankly into the camera.

"Well, I just wanted to see that you were all OK!"

"Everything is *fine*!"

"So, I need you to do me a favor. I need a dress picked up from Harvey Nicks. It's been paid for. The receipt is over there, on the side table. Can you see it?"

"I'll need to check with Kate first."

"Why would you need to do that?"

"Because it's not my job to pick up dresses. I'm here to look after the dogs."

"Right. Well maybe you could check and let me know. Or I'll just keep an eye on that receipt over there, shall I, and see when it gets picked up?"

People had been watching their nannies on camera for a while but now they could watch their dogs too. And their dog walker, of course. It helped to alleviate some of the guilt of leaving them all day while they are at work. Watching them feeling lonely and bored, followed by watching them feeling confused as you yell their name into the microphone from the comfort of your desk, is apparently exactly what the dog wants and needs. Some cameras even dispense treats, so if your guilt ratchets up a notch, you can easily quell it by firing gravy bones directly at the dog's head.

I answered Jan's text message detailing all this in a rush. Belle was prostrate in the cheese aisle in Sainsbury's and shoppers were having to step over her tantrum to get to their Edam. I should have read it more carefully and considered the consequences a little longer, because as soon as you say yes, as soon as you agree to one small thing, answer one phone call out of office hours, one email on a Sunday, grant one tiny favor, the gates of request hell are flung wide open and it is then virtually impossible to close them again.

Once the dress was collected, there were calls for medication, obscure foods from Harrods, thin blue cigarettes and bottles of champagne to be picked up. There were utility bills that must be wrong and needed looking into, letters that had to be posted and dry cleaning that wasn't good enough. An electrician was coming over to collect a hundred pounds. By the end of the second week, as her trip was coming to an end, Rebecca's requests became more incoherent, more irate, and often slurred. They were accompanied by bouts of loud barking, often in the middle of the night, followed by the shouting of various, random swear words like "fucker," "shitting bastard," and "cunt face John," which is a lot to deal with at two in the morning when you only signed up to look after a couple of dogs.

Jan waited until the day Rebecca was due home, walking the dogs as usual before packing up her things and putting the pet cam in the bin.

Besides approving Rebecca's first request for Jan to collect the dress, I had made a few other bad decisions while in a hurry or distracted. There was the walker I hired on two hours sleep who told me he had a serious stomach issue and would likely need to stop for the loo at least twice an hour. I paid the wrong walkers or I forgot to pay them at all, I forgot the names of the dogs and names of their owners, I sent people to the wrong addresses and lost people's keys. Worst of all, I lost the urgency and commitment that the job needed. Caring less was liberating. I felt lighter, looser, and far more content, but if the business was to continue, if it was to remain successful and buoyant and capable of managing the many whims of the humans and the dogs, then it needed someone with far more energy than I was currently able to muster.

I had been thinking about hiring someone for a while but had somehow always dismissed it. At first, it seemed like an admonishment for not being able to manage it all myself, for not organizing frequent, reliable childcare, for not getting up earlier or working later. Then there was the foolish, misguided notion that nobody else could possibly do the job. I was the only one who could understand the endless intricacies: the way to speak to a client on a Monday morning versus a Friday afternoon; the difference between a long-haired and a short-haired dachshund, not just in looks but in personality too; how to know when a walker is lying about dead relatives and which clients are bad at paying. These, I thought, were the myriad rules and tips and pointless bits of information that, stitched together, made it all work.

Sitting down to explain to someone the ins and outs of your business is like trying to show someone how to make that old family recipe where you just chuck in a whole load of ingredients and somehow it works out. You should be giving them exact measurements, timings, and temperatures, because that's what they want and what they need, but as you have always just muddled through, providing specific instructions is surprisingly hard. Doing it all has just become part of who you are, something you don't even think about anymore.

There was also fear. The fear of handing over the stress and the worry, the whining and the tantrums, the walkers that let you down and the clients who yell at you. Could you possibly explain how difficult it could be? How every day was so completely different to the day before? How challenging it still was, how unusual, how utterly bonkers? Or even should you? I had created something to be proud of, a profitable, smooth-running business that genuinely helped people, but it was also unruly and fickle and prone to misbehavior and I was fearful of being told that it was simply too unmanageable.

"I'm writing the advert," I said to Finlay, cursor hovering over the page for the twentieth or so time.

"About time," he said, as he had all other nineteen times, usually followed by, "You don't have to hire anyone. Just see what sort of response you get."

"I'm not sure if I am ready," I said. "And I don't even know what I am looking for."

"Neither do they," he said.

It *was* just a job after all. For all my fears and misgivings, there wasn't really anything so unusual about it, was there? Not really. People are all the same, once you get down to the nitty-gritty. That's what all jobs have in common — people — and a series of small triumphs and disasters hung together by emails and paychecks and a little bit of hope.

In the end, I wrote:

Help Needed.
Small Business.
Part-Time Role.
Flexible hours.
Dealing with employers and employees.
Can work from home.

I posted the advert in the usual places — Gumtree, local papers, Facebook — but it was in the mum forums where I got the biggest response. There were so many brilliant, talented, clever, and miserably unemployed women, desperate to work, to contribute to their family's finances, use their brains, to just get out of the house and take a break from making sandwiches and watching

CBeebies. Most wanted to return to their previous jobs after having babies but hadn't been able to due to a combination of inflexibility from their employer and/or impossible childcare requirements. One had been a top lawyer at the BBC, another a financial analyst; there was a former hedge funder, a writer, and an accountant at Shell. All far too qualified to be running a dog-walking company, not that that seemed to bother them in the slightest. They were simply looking for a way to balance work and family in a way that didn't kill them or involve bending the laws of time and space.

It was hard to narrow it down. Some fell by the wayside when I explained what the business was all about, some became more enthused, and some questioned whether the job was even real. Was someone really going to be paying them to organize the lives of London's most privileged dogs from the comfort of their own home?

"Dogs? Wow! I love dogs," they would say, before giving me a full rundown of their family pets, the dogs they had growing up, their long-lost ambitions to be a vet, a zookeeper, a dog trainer, or a cat psychologist. "How are you with *people*?" I would ask in return, because that was really what it was all about. The dogs were just the accessory, the garnish on a huge, messy plate of human stew.

I decided on someone eventually. She was a mum of three in Wimbledon and wanted a job she could fit in around her kids and her border terrier, Minnie. It came down to one test email in the end, one I had recently received from a wealthy American client who asked if someone could come into her house morning and afternoon to pick up her dog's poo off the carpet. No walks, just the poo. My new employee was the only one who told her no.

Rebecca had been on the wagon, the one that parks up at The Priory, and everything had been a lot quieter. Jan kept her head down and got on with walking the dogs and when Rebecca returned, she politely declined any further dog sitting.

It was a Sunday afternoon, mid-November, and we were pushing Belle on the swings on Wandsworth Common when my phone rang. A number I didn't recognize, central London.

"Kate? Is that Kate? Oh my god! I can't believe I got through to you. I have been calling and calling and just didn't know what to do. Do you know where Jan is? I can't get hold of her, Kate. I just can't get hold of her."

"Jan? She works as a personal trainer on a Sunday. She won't be answering her phone. Is everything OK, Rebecca? What's wrong?" She was sobbing, blubbering, drunk.

"It's all just terrible. I don't even know where to start. There's been an emergency. An awful, terrible accident. The dogs are in danger. I'm in danger. We are scared and we don't know what to do. Do you know how hard it is to be on your own in a crisis? Do you know? I literally don't know who to turn to. I am tearing my hair out here and there is nobody to help me. Nobody at all. Do you know what that is like? DO YOU?"

"No, no I don't."

"We are alone here. We are alone and we are scared. Very, very scared."

"I'll come over and help," I said. "I'll come over now."

I left Finlay with Belle and Mabel and jumped into a taxi, my heart racing as awful, terrible scenarios raced through my head. But as we got closer to the flat, the adrenaline dropping, I realized I had made an awful, terrible mistake.

Rebecca was standing in the doorway as I arrived, dressing gown on, drink in hand. There were mascara streaks down her face and she had a spaniel clutched under each armpit.

"In here," she sniveled, and led me to the kitchen where she pointed to a puddle of water on the floor, just under the washing machine.

"Can you see it? *Down there?*" she whispered. "It's been there for a while now. I don't know how long exactly but it's been at least an hour or two."

"The water?"

"The water, the water, yes, and the machine! The machine was making these awful, terrifying noises. A sort of grinding and screaming, a hideous grating noise and the dogs just got so scared. They were crying and then I was crying and I just didn't know what to do!"

"You mean . . . *the washing machine?*"

"The machine! The machine! Yes! Can you see it? Can you see what it has done? It's everywhere. And the noise. The awful, hideous noise."

"Is that . . . is that the problem?"

She stared back at me, the dogs still firmly pinned under her arms, wheezing. She looked vulnerable, scared, confused. She looked lonely.

"There wasn't anybody else," she said, quietly. "I didn't have anybody else to call."

"How about a plumber?"

"Yes, yes, I should have called a plumber. I'm very sorry."

"That's what plumbers do. They do washing machines. I am not a plumber."

She put the dogs down and turned away to dab her eyes with some kitchen roll.

"Would you like me to call one for you? I think I have the number for one."

"No, no, absolutely not. I can do it. It's fine. I mustn't take up any more of your time. I really am very sorry."

"It's fine. I can call one. I don't mind."

"You have children, don't you?"

"I have one. A girl."

"I have a girl too. And a boy."

"Are they away at school?"

"Yes, well, they were supposed to be here today, weekend leave, but their father never picked them up."

"Oh, I'm so sorry." My heart lurched as I remembered all the times I was never picked up, the crushing, asphyxiating disappointment, followed by the many excuses you would then concoct for him — the traffic, the weather, a terrible accident. Anything but just *not* turning up. The pain of that would have to be shared, the mother taking the larger portion, carrying it around with her until she could find a way to make it go away.

"I could have gone of course but I'd already had a drink by then. Silly me, drunk as usual. So they're stuck there, miserable, and I'm stuck here, miserable. Just me and the dogs. And a broken washing machine."

"They'll be OK," I said. "They'll be fine, in the long run."

"The dogs?" People only expected me to talk about dogs.

"Well, I meant your children but the dogs will be fine too. They'll all be fine, and the kids will have friends and hobbies and lots of things they want to do. They'll be busy, and happy and full of ideas and they will go out into the world and get jobs and then have their own family, one day. I am sure you are a wonderful mother. You love them. That's all there is to it, really."

She sniffed and then smiled weakly. We all have the same worries, the same knots.

"You have been very kind but I better get on and call the plumber. You wouldn't mind just wiping that water up before you go, would you?"

I got the bus home, top deck, and watched as London rumbled along beneath me. The light was fading and there was a chill in the air. Winter was almost here and people were drawing closer together, keeping warm. The streets were just as full of dogs as they always were: the chocolate Labrador bouncing alongside a young couple on Kings Road; the ratty brown terrier running next to a woman jogging in neon near World's End; a Staffie with two friends walking in the dusk on Eel Brook Common; and, over Putney Bridge, as the dark dropped in, a man on a street corner, sat sullenly with his German shepherd, cap in hand. Everything was just the same as it always was, the changing of the seasons, the walking of the dogs happening just as it always did — London's own familiar rhythms.

But I didn't feel in sync with it anymore. My pace was off, my timing different. London was the same, its shifts and turns in its people and in its fortunes not enough to change the core. It was me that was different. I was tireder, busier, more chaotic than I had ever been but I was also stronger, prouder, able to say no, and far more sure of who I was. I wanted to move on to a new chapter now.

When I got home, Belle was finishing her tea, fish fingers, and baked beans, and *Peppa Pig* was on the telly.

"What happened?" Finlay asked. "Is everything OK?"

"Everything is fine," I said. "But I think I might be ready to hand some of the work over for a while. It's probably about time that I stepped back a bit and let someone else do it. Spend a bit more time with Belle."

"Good idea," he said, smiling.

I took Belle upstairs for her bath, lighter and calmer than I had felt for a while.

STANLEY, PART SIX

The funny thing about Stanley was that he just suited being old. It was hard to imagine him as a puppy, sleepy eyed and soft of fur, bounding clumsily across the grass, tumbling over his large paws. I couldn't picture him ever being small, fitting in your arms, falling asleep on your lap, the heavy warm breaths.

Stanley was a dog who was always just big and old, a large lumbering presence, the tail that bashed your legs, the gray-and-white muzzle, the mass of scruffy fur, the head that was always bowed a little too low. He would have no time for youth and its capriciousness, its need to try new things, new parks, or meet new dogs, the fickleness of its affections.

Since the moment he was taken in, hesitant and insecure, his loyalties had been absolute, his purpose clear. Here was a family who had decided to have him in their

381

fold, the most precious of all honors, and one he felt he could never fully repay. And so he would love those who loved him with everything he had.

But Stanley was tired now, crumbling slowly, the body giving way bit by bit. He didn't want to walk anymore, he barely wanted to eat. And that's the point at which you have to take their life in your hands, repay all that they have given you. But it's never that straightforward. There's always a doubt, the fear that you might be making a mistake, that he'll be all right once the weather changes, when you find a better medicine, if you just will him to go on a little longer. You can convince yourself all too easily that he wants to stay, that his spirit is stronger than his body, and that he's not really in pain because saying goodbye is so impossibly hard.

My mother was good at unsentimentality. She was raised on it by parents who had married just after the war. A dog's life had a beginning, a middle, and an end and there was never any blurring of the lines or dampening of the eyes. The dog had a good life and that was more than enough. If a sufficient number of faculties had worn away, then the decision to have it put down was clear. They would be buried in a field, a wood, or if they were very lucky, in the garden, and they would be happy with that. There would be no tears shed for Labradors or Jack Russells in public. If necessary, dogs could be grieved for in private, away from us, just like everything else.

Stanley's heart was packing up. The vet thought it would not be long until it went into cardiac arrest. He had suggested expediting the end.

"I know what I need to do," Steph said on the phone, her voice wobbling. "I just can't do it. I can't make that decision. I look at him lying there and he looks so sad, so helpless, and I can't bring myself to do the right thing. He's given us all so, so much and I am not able to give him the one thing he needs from me. It's so selfish, isn't it? It's so terribly selfish."

"No, no, it's not selfish. It's just an impossible, awful situation."

"And the stupid thing is that I work in a hospital, with very sick people, and I see suffering and pain every day. Every day, I see people dying; I see them bereaved, the awfulness of it all, and yet I can't do this one simple thing. Even when I can help him, really help him, I can't do it. I can't not have him here, in his basket, here when I come home. It's just not possible."

Stanley died a few days later. He was at home, surrounded by his family, exactly the way he would have wanted it. Except for the tears. He would have hated the tears.

Steph asked if I could let Tom know. She couldn't face calling him, but then she couldn't quite face calling me either. The phone rang for a second and cut out. Then came the email.

Kate, we have had a distraught weekend. Stanley died on Saturday night. We had taken him for a little potter around the garden and when we returned his breathing get very labored. We called the vet who suggested we get him some oxygen but we didn't have time in the end. We all sat with him until he died, stroking him and talking to him and we gave him a great send off and burial in the garden (where he used to dig up my plants — exactly where he would have chosen!). The good thing is that he didn't suffer too much toward the end. It all came very quickly and I think he was ready to go. He seemed peaceful somehow. I don't think we will get another dog. We can't replace Stanley. Although I was around a lot more when we first got him, when the children were all at home and

I could walk him myself, I think he really enjoyed the years with you guys. Thank you to all of you who walked him and cared for him. You allowed me to go back to work without feeling too bad about leaving him, which was everything really. Would you let Tom know? I don't know if I can. Steph.

As soon as I called Tom, he knew what it was about.

"He's dead, isn't he?"

"Yes," I said, not even really believing it myself. Stanley had been there right from the start. In fact, he'd been there all the way through.

"I knew it had happened. I could feel it. I looked up and I knew he was gone."

"He had a good life, Tom," I said, exactly how my mother would have said it, because there really is nothing else you can say. "You gave him a good life. A lot of it was down to what you did. He was so lucky to have you."

"Well, I did my job. I can be proud of that."

The grief hit him later, a few weeks on, when he realized he had lost his best friend, not just a dog he walked. Tom had gotten used to him being by his side, planning his day around him, coming up with day trips or new streets they could investigate with Buster. He had gotten used to seeing London through Stanley's eyes, how simple and joyful it could be if you just looked, the delight to be taken from an old tree or a shard of sunlight on the grass, the shelter of a doorway when the heavens open, the weekly fish and chips. There was so much that could be gleaned from so little. . . .

Dogs sneak up on you like that, burying parts of themselves deep within you, bits that are only revealed later, once they are long gone. In full daylight, when you are doing something quite ordinary, one of these parts will be dug up again, quite by accident, and it will stop you in your tracks. Sometimes the memories will appear at night, in the dark, when they're harder to get away from and it feels as if you might be smothered by the sadness of it all. It's a complicated grief when the dog is not even yours. You wonder if you are even allowed to mourn them. You wonder if you got too close, took a step too far.

I felt more responsible for Tom than I probably should have. There was enough to worry about within our own four walls but I thought about him a lot in the weeks after Stanley died and I looked for projects that might take his mind off it all. There was a

rescue dog in Brixton with a fear of motor-
bikes and a very hungry Labrador in Waterloo who kept pulling nice, timid female
walkers into oncoming traffic to retrieve
crisp packets or banana skins. Standard fare
for Tom, who knew dogs and their many
idiosyncrasies better than anyone else. I
apologized for it not being Stanley, as if
there was anything I could do about that,
but I knew it wouldn't quite be the same
again. At least not for a while.

If only they could have all been like
Stanley — the challenge, the uncertainty,
and then the eventual triumph. A life improved, a beginning, a middle, and then an
end. When I started the business, I had
naively hoped that all the families would be
like Stanley's — the bustling kitchen, the
kicked-off shoes, the noise and the laughter,
and the all-enveloping love. Some of them
were, in their own way. There was always
something to be taken from each home,
even if it was just knowing that there was a
dog at the heart of it.

Tom sent me an email a month or so later.
It started with "I'm sorry."

I'm sorry, Kate, but I am going to have
to go my own way now. I've been thinking a lot about it recently and I haven't

really known how to tell you. I've missed Stanley so much, more than I have ever missed anything really. I never had a friend like him before. Bit sad really. He was such a good dog and we just sort of got each other, you know? I don't think another dog is going to be able to replace him really, which is fine. I don't think they are all meant to be replaced. But it got me thinking about what I was going to do to make it all better and I think I might have figured it out. I'm going to do the dog walking on my own for a bit. Give it a go myself, like you. And maybe some training if anyone needs it. I think I might be quite good at that. I'm not going to tread on your toes, Kate, I promise that, because I wouldn't be here without any of these old dogs. Without Stan. Let me know it's OK when you get a chance. I'd really like that.

"It's a wonderful idea," I replied. "Do it all and don't look back. You will be great."

Mabel, Part Five

If you turn left out of the cottage and walk to the end of the road, you can cut through a little gap in the hedge that leads to an alleyway. It's a bit overgrown in places, the nettles often skimming your knees, but if you stick with it and go all the way to the other end, you will find yourself in a huge open field, the grass as green as Emerald City, and at the bottom a tiny tinkling stream and a bridge where you can play pooh sticks. There is a wood at the other end, dark and thick with branches of lime, ash, and oak, and beyond that a meadow with sheep and cows and hundreds of rabbits and a small, muddy pony called Fudge. Bronze pheasants trot across the horizon and red kites circle in the sky above. Mabel was the happiest dog in the whole of Oxfordshire.

The village is small enough for everyone to know who you are but big enough for a mini co-op. There are stone cottages and smoking chimneys, rusty swings and Saturday football, and a pub that backs onto a large medieval church. There's a history club, a thriving Women's Institute, a farmers' market on Thursdays, and "Stitch and Bitch" on a Friday. Every autumn, the village celebrates the apple harvest by getting very drunk on cider and in summer they throw sticks at a dummy in a game called Aunt Sally. Maybe you live somewhere similar, with people who have lived there all of their lives and people like us, arriving from London like the circus coming into town without a clue on how any of it worked.

You must quickly tell everyone that although you have arrived from London, you are not *from* London or you will be seen as suspicious or haughty or crude. They get to know you of course, on walks around the village, at the playgroups or in the queue for a pint, and they realize that you are just like them really, except for the fact that you don't know much about roses or badgers and you rely a bit too heavily on delivery food. But you do have a dog, a Jack Russell, and that counts for something.

We moved in a lorry this time — a small

one but a lorry nonetheless. We were grown-ups by then, I suppose, in our own way. We had furniture now, old sofas and chests of drawers and the table that could squeeze in eight. We had a toddler bed and a cot and a huge pink pig that oinked when you pulled its tail. We had an iron and an ironing board and a second-hand vacuum cleaner; we had three plants, five pans and a block of knives and at least two chopping boards, a wok and a teapot and a good selection of un-chipped mugs, a cheese grater that you turn a handle on, and a large iron pot to make casseroles in. We had roasting trays and wooden spoons and a turquoise colander with a handle missing and bedding that matched and new towels (including ones for guests) and welly boots and coats that actually kept out the rain and the cold. I had a hat and a scarf and some sheepskin gloves and more than three pairs of shoes. I had my own proper, noisy, exhausting fam-ily. I had a business too, although I had finally managed to leave a lot of that behind now that it was run so efficiently by some-one else.

There were five of us when we moved. Our new baby boy had been born in late summer, finally prompting us to take out a road map and stick a pin somewhere beyond the M25. We were sleep deprived and overwhelmed but we knew what we needed to do and nobody made a fuss about it. Belle worried about country foxes and Finlay worried about the commute but there was never a moment of regret, not even when the lorry pulled away and I cried on the street at the thought of never walking in the parks again, on Putney Common and Hampstead Heath and all that is in between. I would see the City again, the people, my friends, but I doubted I would see the parks. That was where I had really grown up.

We had left it all to the very last minute — the decision, the location, the packing — but that was the way we had always done things — chaotically, spontaneously — and there comes a point when you can't fight that anymore. The plan to move had always been there, hovering just over our heads; we just needed it to drop down into our laps. Plus everything is so much easier when you don't really have a choice. It takes out all that boring middle bit when you write sensible lists headed "pros" and others headed "cons" and then you panic when you realize that you feel differently about them every single day.

When you start to overspill in a house you can't afford, the options are narrowed right down to one. We had to move and it had to be farther than the home counties because we couldn't afford those but close enough that Finlay could still commute. If we wanted to factor in the occasional parental visit (primarily as a base from which they can still go to London), then it had to be the M40 corridor. So, North Oxfordshire, second star on the right and straight on till morning.

We knew nobody, which was just as well as I couldn't drive and was knee-deep in children. I would open the door some days after a solid four-hour stint of feeding and wiping and shushing and cooking and be genuinely surprised not to see London there, our old street and the busyness of the world going by. At its most hectic, there might be a random cat, a stern farmer, or a postman who was a bit lost and I would stand for a moment, trying to take it all in, retracing all those thousands of steps that brought us back to the countryside, to waterproofs and wellies, to lambs in the field and eggs left on the doorstep and a sky so clear and so studded with stars that it looked like a pot of glitter had been lobbed into the air. We had only been there a week when it started to feel like home.

My mother proudly brought down the

twelve-piece dinner service in the car. I had told her repeatedly that the table was the same one as before and could only fit eight, not to mention the fact that the number of people we knew in the county was precisely zero.

"One day, darling, one day," she said breezily as she poked around the cupboards and drawers. I was tired and hormonal and I got a bit angry. I saw the dinner service following us around forever, unused, sad, waiting for the day it would eventually be carted off to a charity shop.

"But it's OK if I don't do that, isn't it? It's OK not to use these hideous plates, if I'm not like you with *everything*? I know it's about tradition and being proper and what everyone used to do but I don't need to have twelve people over and cook them beef or be a bloody secretary. It's OK *not* to do that and still be all right with you and whoever else cares about these things, isn't it? It's OK to just be *me*?"

"Well, you have always done what you wanted to, darling, haven't you?"

"What does that mean?"

"Exactly what it sounds like. You have done your own thing."

"Aren't you meant to do that?"

"Do you have a meat thermometer yet?"

"A *what*?"

"A meat thermometer. You put it in the joint to see when it's cooked."

"NO! I don't have a meat thermometer. I don't want a bloody meat thermometer."

"I might have an old one you can have."

"But I don't want one. Can I just *not* have one?"

She was kneeling down, her head in a cupboard sniffing for damp, but she got up and before she had even brushed herself down she put her hand on my arm and said, "That's fine, darling. But you do need a gravy boat."

When I was a child, when I thought about that family that I wanted, the noisy house and all its many residents, there was only one thing that I definitely didn't want. The building would often change its color or its location and how many secret passageways it had, and sometimes we had one dog and at other times there would be ten. I could plot and place the supporting characters as if it was all a giant dolls' house in my head. The kitchen, the room I worried about the most, was far more precise. The kitchen had to be exactly right.

It was big and bright and painted deep sea blue with a sofa at one end that we would all sprawl over and a huge wooden table covered in books and board games and old scribbles. There were doors that led out to the garden and a little corner where you could read books and there were always crumpets and cake and mountains of biscuits. But there was to be no cooking — no baking or boiling or frying. The food would just be there or was brought in somehow, as there was no cooker and no hob. That was the only rule and it was a rigid one because my mother would always cry over a cooker, usually when stirring gravy. Gravy, in my dream kitchen, was banned. The gravy always seemed to set her off, the back and forth of the spoon, the simmering and the reducing dislodging some old sadness.

But still she made the gravy regardless. It was there with our small family roast on a Sunday and the Christmas dinner for three and it was trying to pretend that everything was normal and just as it should be. Gravy was the effort made for children you had wanted more for; it was the preserving of family traditions against all the odds, holding your head high, summoning the grit and the guts. Gravy was not letting the father who had failed to turn up again ruin a perfectly good weekend. It was making the absolute best out of things, of not wanting the actions of one man to change the course of two other lives. It was finding the strength and resilience and energy, day after day. Gravy, and the boat it sailed in, was everything.

"I'll get a gravy boat," I said quietly, and she smiled and took my hand. It was the passing of a baton, the moment when she could finally step back.

"You choose one. It's best that you pick something that's just right for you."

"OK," I replied.

"You've made me very proud," she said. I think she was talking about the gravy boat, although she just might not have been. "How about a walk? Mabel looks keen."

We took the path through the gap in the hedge and down the alleyway toward the field and the wood, the baby in the carrier and Mabel racing ahead. The grass was crunchy under our feet, dusted with silver frost, and the ice-blue sky rose like a huge glass dome above our heads.

"Countryside foxes are nice foxes, aren't they, Granny?" inquired Belle, as the two of them trundled along together.

"They are, darling," Granny replied. "They are very nice and very polite and they all wear these lovely little velvet jackets, made by the fairies, I think."

They went off in search of country animals

while Mabel and I carried on walking to the woods. She stayed close to me, close to the baby, but as we approached the trees, she surged ahead, nose to the ground, tail high, on a scent. We reached the edge of the wood and she stopped abruptly, paw raised, head tilted to the wind. Something was there. We stood motionless, blinking into the thicket as our breath puffed into little white clouds around our faces and there, right in front of us and only a few meters away, was a small deer with pale dappled fur, a white bobbed tail, and large pinky ears. She stared straight back at us as we stood in silent awe at being so close to something so wild and so beautiful.

The deer flinched suddenly and sprang off into the trees, twigs, and sticks crackling under her feet as she was enveloped into the darkness of the wood. Mabel, quivering with excitement, took a quick look up at me before darting off into the trees after her.

AFTERWORD

Finlay and I still live in a small village in Oxfordshire with Belle and Mabel. Joining the family are Milo, Jesse, and a petulant sausage dog, called Henry.

The dog-walking company still operates today and is managed by the same mum of three with her border terrier, Minnie.

Tom is a successful dog walker and trainer.

The Principal now has two dogs and is looking into getting a third.

Sean works for a Principal in Switzerland. He has no pets.

The diplomat's barbecue had not been stolen. It had simply been sent out for cleaning.

Felicity — who had been the downfall of the Team in Islington — turned up on a reality television show. She was the first to be evicted.

Huxley recently placed third at a local dog show. He has failed his Pets as Therapy test three times.

Meet and Bone was never resurrected, although dating with your dog is now widely accepted.

Rupert is now a private detective and has a Labrador called Jason.

All the fathers from the prenatal class had girls. None of them play rugby.

Agnes still walks dogs in southwest London, although nobody ever found out why she didn't like dachshunds.

ABOUT THE AUTHOR

Kate MacDougall is a writer and journalist who now lives in rural Oxfordshire with her family. She writes features for publications including *Country Life,* the *Telegraph, Horse & Hound,* and *Homes & Antiques* while also wrangling three small children and two disobedient dogs.